The X in Mexico

by the same author

FIREFLY IN THE NIGHT:
A Study of Ancient Mexican Poetry and Symbolism

The X in Mexico

GROWTH WITHIN TRADITION

Irene Nicholson

1966

Doubleday & Company, Inc., Garden City, New York

Library of Congress Catalog Card Number 65–19944

Printed in the United States of America
First Edition in the United States of America

To
my Mexican colleagues
on
Radio Universidad de México
and on the
Boletín Bibliográfico de Hacienda y Crédito Público
with whom I have worked since 1958

Acknowledgments

Thanks are due to the following sources for permission to use material from published works:

Universidad Nacional Autónoma de México for the words from the Maya religious book, *Chilam Balam of Chumayel* in the translation into Spanish by Antonio Médiz Bolio from their edition of 1941; Grove Press Inc. New York, for passages from *The Labyrinth of Solitude: Life and Thought in Mexico* by Octavio Paz, translated by Lysander Kemp, on pages 54, 55, 102, and 104; University of Texas Press, Austin, Texas, for the extract from *Profile of Man and Culture in Mexico* by Samuel Ramos, translated by Peter G. Earle, on pages 61–62; Random House Inc., Alfred A. Knopf Inc., and Martin Secker and Warburg Limited for extracts from *The Children of Sánchez* by Oscar Lewis on page 81; José Hernández Delgado for the figures from *La Confianza como Factor Decisivo en el Progreso Económico y Social de México* on pages 132 *et seq.*; Antonio J. Bermúdez for the extracts from *The Mexican National Petroleum Industry: a Case Study in Nationalization* on pages 135 and 141; Dr. González Rojo for the poem by Enrique González Martínez which is to be found in most Mexican anthologies and which appears in the original Spanish and in translation by the author on page 189; Martín Luís Guzmán for the representative passage from his novel *El Aguila y la Serpiente* (as recorded by him in the gramophone record series *Voz Viva de México* with which the original Spanish text is supplied), which appears on pages 191–92; *Fondo de Cultura Económica* for the extract from *La Visión de Anáhuac* by Alfonso Reyes (spoken by him on a *Voz Viva de México* record which goes with accompanying text) on pages 192–93; University of California Press for the quotation from *Churches of Mexico* by J. Armstrong Baird on page 205; Reinhold

Book Division, New York, and Colin Faber, for the extract from the latter's book, *Candela: the Shell Builder,* on pages 209–10. Full bibliographical details of the publications here mentioned appear on the relevant pages.

Contents

List of Illustrations

The X in Mexico

Prologue

Myth and Mexico: they blend imperceptibly. For Mexico is a land in which men have survived against heavy odds, like a cactus in the desert or a golden dome built far from civilization. It is a country that seems to have been created to show man where he stands in the cosmic scheme. A godmother has bestowed talents generously, but there are ogres too, macabre transformations of flowers into skulls, queer shapes like those thorny organ cacti that can be explained only as one of nature's jokes or as a symbol of life's resilience in the midst of drought.

The abrupt contours of mountain and canyon, the dry corn, the misty yet spiky cacti, the great wheel hats above Oriental faces: the very harshness of the material shapes leads the mind on to metaphysical speculation. Every opposite is true in a land that is arrogant and poor; delicate and tough; cynical and tender; hot and cold; high and low; garrulous and silent; passionate and indifferent; courteous and crude; hospitable and introspective; kind and stern. If we look at the outer skin alone we can make nothing of it. Mexico is more hidden, more Oriental, than any other country in the Western Hemisphere, and yet it is a leader in the Spanish-speaking West. It was the first country in Latin America to achieve a modern social revolution and a take-off into industrialization. But it is not a forward-looking country. It is forever turning back to its past, to its myths.

At each crossroads in history it has reaffirmed a principle enunciated long before. Even the Aztecs, arriving late on the high plateau, adopted the gods and the speech of their predecessors. The Spanish friars studied the ancient religions (even while they were destroying them in fear) in order to base their new Christian faith firmly in the minds of a tradition-loving people. The seventeenth-century nun, Sor Juana Inés de la Cruz, linked Christianity with the symbolism of blood sacrifice.

Much later Benito Juárez undertook a reform backward to the principles enunciated by the priest José María Morelos at the beginning of the independence struggle. The 1910 revolution returned a second time to the same principles. Revolution has never meant for this country a blind jump into the future but literally re-volution—return to the best of its past in an attempt to correct the errors of each historical cycle. We see the name Mexico on a printed page and the X jumps to the eye because it is an anachronism. It ought not to be there. Modern Spanish would turn it into a J. But paradoxically it is this old-fashioned spelling that has come to stand for modern Mexican liberalism. The outmoded X has become a symbol of revolt—revolt against Spain, against corruption in the Mexican hierarchies, back to Indianness and national identity.

It has become a point of honor to keep a letter that runs with a characteristic rustle through so much Mexican geography and history, like those fierce winds that whip up out of the dust of the high plateau, only to die away through the corn stalks as suddenly as they came: Xochipilli, god of flowers, Xochimilco, village of the floating gardens; Ixtaccíhuatl, the sleeping princess, Taxco with silver-tinkling hammers; Xalapa, Tuxpan, Xolotl. . . .

In his novel, *Where the Air Is Clear,*[1] Carlos Fuentes makes oratory out of Mexican historical names which seem to tell all that is essential about the country's origins, so very far from being entirely indigenous and so tangled with Europe for good or ill: ". . . Justo Sierra, Amado Nervo, Zumárraga, Xicoténcatl, Bazaine, Axayácatl, Malinche, Zapata, O'Donojú. . . ."

Our concern in this book will be with modern Mexico, compounded of the Spanish, the French, the Irish, the American, and a good bit else besides the indigenous Indian. But in order to understand this amalgam we shall have to look back to the remote past that has stamped on Mexico that typographically assertive X; and also to the long struggle between the forces of diehard reaction

[1] Fuentes, Carlos. *Where the Air Is Clear*. Ivan Obolensky, New York, 1960. Published first in Spanish as *La Región más Transparente* by the *Fondo de Cultura Económica,* Mexico, 1958.

and the liberal idealism that has in a defiant gesture kept the X intact. We shall then be in a position to assess the role that Mexico must play today—together with Brazil, Chile, and the other non-dictatorial Latin countries—in the struggle to establish a place for this area in the liberal-democratic tradition of the West while yet conserving the Spanish-Moorish-Indian which prints a unique shape upon it.

Latin America stands at a crossroads. Either it must overcome the niggling, petty jealousies of centuries, or go under. This is what the economists are saying: men like Raúl Prebisch, the Argentine creator of the Economic Commission for Latin America; and Felipe Herrera, the Chilean heading the Interamerican Development Bank. Such men are no longer thinking in terms of individual countries but are planning for the whole area.

Because of political unrest, military coups, and economic depressions in many countries, Mexico has almost involuntarily jumped into the lead. Ever since independence, and in slightly different terms back to the conquest and before, Mexican idealists have upheld policies of self-determination and non-intervention. They have resented any attempt by foreigners to order them about. They have included in their condemnation the Church in Rome and the international financiers. Their stubborn (some people would say intransigent) Mexicanism is one of the first things the foreigner notices when he comes new to the country. These idealists have been both heroic and quixotic. Their ends have been achieved sometimes at such cost that the clock has been put back half a century. All the same, without them Mexico would long ago have become a hopeless dictatorship and a toady to the richer countries of the world.

Ever since the conquest the idealists have been opposed by a totally different type of Mexican—thugs who have seemed to believe that laws were made for their own convenience, to be wriggled out of whenever too great a respect for justice might obstruct the amassing of fortunes. Yet there is no sharp line—such as the left would like to draw—between exploiter and exploited. Out of the ranks of the diehard right have come men with a sense of responsibility toward their professions, and these have built the solid basis of Mexico. They have taken a generous slice of material reward, but have felt justified in doing so.

The people, with their gentleness and artistic talents; with their religious sense which has very little to do with what priests may or may not tell them; with their apparently callous disregard for life; and with their ability in whatever circumstances to extract fun from trivial things: these have for the most part shrugged their shoulders and continued to till the soil with the inadequate means at their disposal. Now and then they have weighed in on one side or the other according to their special notions of what life is about. Their day-to-day common sense has restrained the idealists, but when their patience with the exploiters has become exhausted there has been bloody revolution. Their sense of humor—macabre at times but unembittered by rancor—has allowed them to bear a good many things that might have become intolerable, including their meager staple diet of beans and corn pancakes. They are long-suffering, but not for ever.

Their *tierra,* the little, circumscribed world of their village or ranchland, has been in the past the extent of their horizon. Today the government is trying to extend their vision. Those in power believe it is the anonymous peasants and small townspeople who will in the long run be able by practical testing to discover what works and what is only treacherous theory in this complex country: Mexico, in many ways so modern but stubbornly retaining the ancient X.

1 Today's Variety

On the forty-first floor of a skyscraper you may dine off lobster and white wine. From here you look over the lights in the valley, the lights climbing the far hills, marking the presence of nearly five million city dwellers.[1] From a building across the way a sky-sign, brazen and cocksure, announces, "There's a Ford in Your Future."

It is an effort to remember the saddle-sore donkeys; the peasant families living on corn, beans, and chocolate gruel; the remote Indians such as the Huicholes with their traditional *peyote* ceremonies and their coolie-like dress; Indians to whom a city Mexican is as odd a bird as any foreigner.

The names of Mexican wines and rum, Mexican gasoline, Mexican office furniture flash off and on in neon signs. If it is Christmas, wire-and-bulb Magi will be prancing in the wind among the treetops. Little Mexicans in silver-buttoned trousers will sweep their *sombreros* in jerky, neon salutations.

The twang of American tourist voices sounds in the restaurant, the feline tread of waiters in the discreet half dark of this expensive observatory high in the sky. Outside a motto keeps vying with the stars: "There's a Ford in Your Future."

You are at the hub of a vast republic whose essence is contrast, in the Latin American Tower at the center of the Federal District which, like Washington, D.C., keeps the capital on neutral ground, outside the twenty-nine States and two Territories,[2] each with its own character and in some sense its independence, but knit into a single republic. Mexico's 760,375 square miles make it the largest Latin American country after Brazil and Argentina; and its 34.6 million people (at the 1960 census) with a growth rate of over

[1] 4,870,876 at the 1960 census.
[2] See Appendix I.

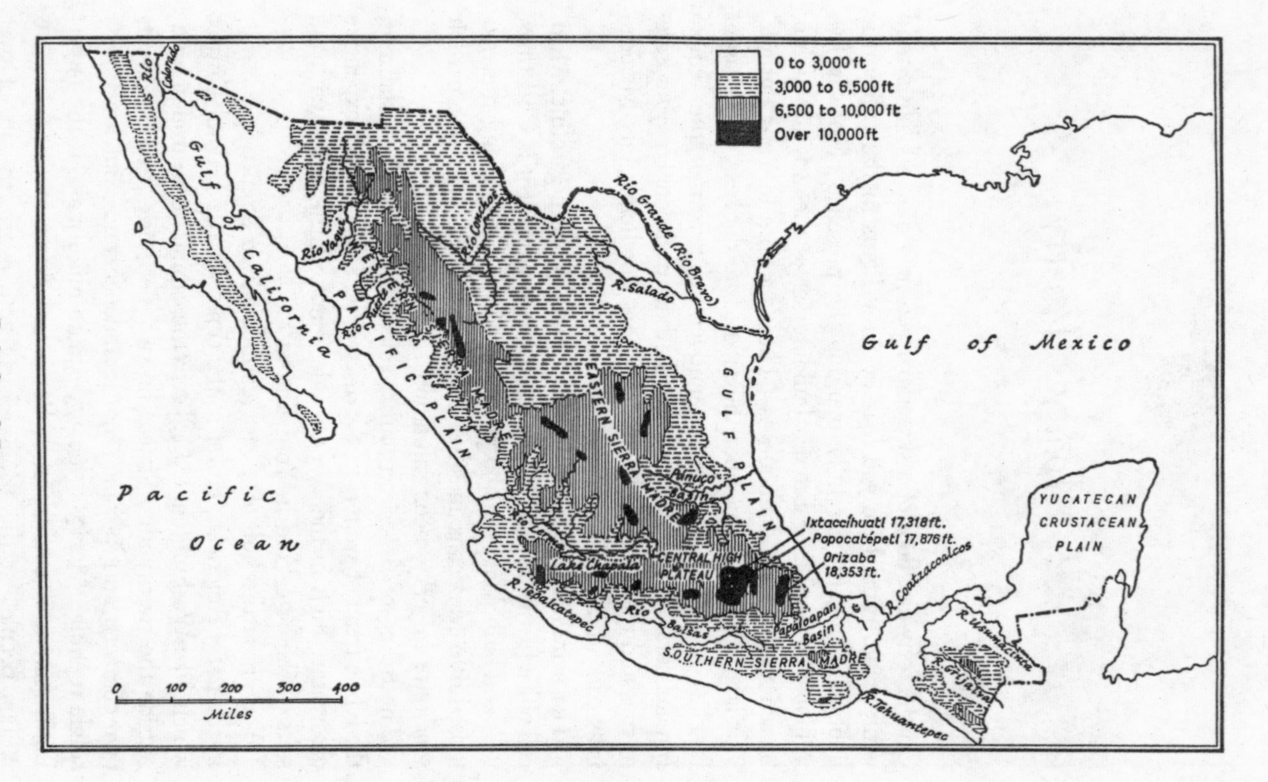

1. Relief and Rivers

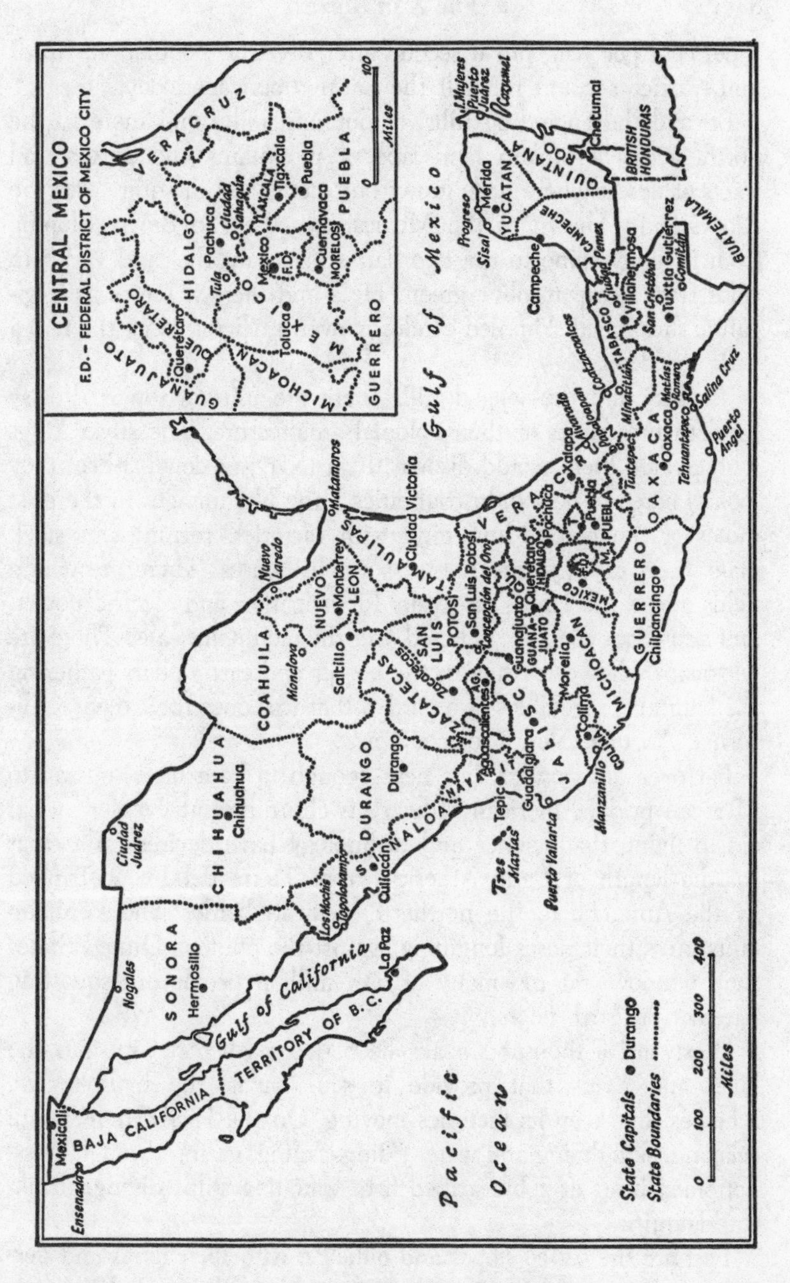

2. States and Territory Divisions

3 per cent per year, put it second after Brazil in population. Brazil and Mexico account for half the Latin Americans today.

Beyond the encircling hills, a thousand miles and more to the north, across a broken landscape of mountains and gorges and tracts of desert where little grows but cactus and mesquite, lies the Río Grande, known to the Mexicans as the Río Bravo. Sloping from its bony spine to the two flanks of ocean, the land varies in color from hemp to olive green. Here and there it seems as if gigantic shears had skimmed carelessly over it, slicing away the nap a little too deep.

Tucked into the jagged hills there are mining towns drowsy beneath the domes of their colonial architecture. The silver kings who created them would disown them today, so down-at-heel they look. There are new industrial cities hung like mirages in the dust motes of the plains, humming with factories, turning out steel, glass, beer, railway trucks, transportable houses. There are cotton fields and cattle lands, reservoirs for irrigation and electric power, and new roads cockily cambered over the mountain walls. There are Mexicans who yearn to cross the border and earn dollars gathering the fruit and vegetables of a garden that was once their own: California, Arizona, New Mexico, Texas.

Far over the frontier, but near enough to be a little souring to Mexican pride, American industry is churning out every material aid to living that science and technology have devised. Alas that for the length of Latin America, from Tierra del Fuego fringed by the Antarctic to the northern Mexican border whose inhabitants press their noses longingly against the opulent United States shop window, far too many of 210 million people are squatting barefoot on earth floors.

Westward a thousand peaks lie between Mexico City and the lakes and rivers that provide it with water, the hydroelectric schemes that keep its factories moving. On the Pacific tourists are relaxing, skin-diving and water skiing, sailing, gazing through glass-bottomed boats at zebra-striped fish, watching stunt diving, drinking daiquiris.

East are the coffee slopes and oilfields, with their flares and derricks rising out of banana and orange and vanilla, and their ports where young cadets, innocent in crumpled starch with swords and gloves, parade round the plaza with girls in lace and taffeta, while hawk-eyed matrons sit chaperoning. Southeast are sugar *usines*, and more coffee, and the rural gentleness of Oaxaca and the Tehuantepec Isthmus, and more oil; and then the highlands of Chiapas where villagers still speaking their susurrating native tongues, trot with their burdens of charcoal and firewood.

Two balancing peninsular arms—Baja California and Yucatán —lie northwest and directly eastward across the Mexican Gulf. Baja California contains a State and a Territory. The former, bounding the United States, is so Americanized that pesos and Mexican newspapers are sniffed at, and nothing will do but dollars and the Los Angeles dailies. The neglected southern Territory is one of the most primitive and depopulated parts of the republic. Here Indians live literally from hand to mouth, ignorant of the first elements of husbandry.

Yucatán, on the contrary, is a little kingdom on its own, proudly separatist as—let us say—Wales from England or Catalonia from Spain, and from its aloof distance regarding Mexicans as foreigners. The profiles of its small, birdlike people are exactly those on ancient carvings. The women, clean even in poverty, wear a traditional embroidered sackline and bright satin ribbons in their black hair. This is the land of *henequén* sisal and Maya ruins—the one blue-green as a mist but spiky and hard of pith, the other outlasting the decay of the old priesthood and the jungle's entwining roots.

Mexico. So much of its palpable materiality ready at any moment to vanish in cloud or sunlight. A country that seems at times to be created as a symbol for another, inner world. Symbols everywhere if you have a mind to see them: geraniums in discarded gasoline tins hanging from adobe walls; cupolas like marigolds against brown corn; ecclesiastical purple and red of the bougainvillaea, the poinsettia, the dahlia; strident bands in villages where people speak with muted reticence; children playing hopscotch in the dirt with Coca-Cola tops; shoeshine boys with *"Justicia Social"* embroidered on their uniforms; revolutionary mosaics in the university and huddled shanties just beyond on the lava rock.

At any season of the year, here and there over the land, villagers will be exploding a year's savings in fireworks. Catherine wheels will be lighting faces to tawny beauty; children will wear bull-masks with firecrackers exploding out of the horns; the banner of the brown Virgin, Guadalupe, will be poised above a castle of fire; and physical near-starvation will be temporarily forgotten in a prayer that is no more pagan, when all is said, than plum pudding or Druid mistletoe.

Though in many areas time seems not to have moved since long before Cortés came with his horses and gunpowder, Mexico is being propelled today at vertiginous speed in a direction determined by principles formulated during the last century and a half, or even before. A psychology that mingles indigenous Indian with Spanish is still sufficiently pliable to make this a profitable time for the country's leaders to indulge in some fundamental questioning.

At this moment in history Mexicans see several object lessons before their eyes. There is the United States, champion of democracy but with its promised Utopia slipping bewilderingly out of grasp, with too many people attending psychological clinics and with a drug addiction problem that it accuses the northern border Mexicans of fostering. There are totalitarian states announcing goals that sound sufficiently similar to those of the West to make Latin Americans wonder whether the cold war has not turned into a kind of ideological fratricide; and there are new nations finding self-government a painful process, democracy an expensive luxury that has to be paid for, they tardily discover, with the bloodshed of civil war.

Mexico in this context looks monolithic, single in aim if ragged in its execution; full of vitality but holding aloof; noncommitted but not neutral; aware, it is true, that some avowed principles have eluded her and brooding introspectively on her problems, but young and exuberant in an aging world.

In the total Latin scene Mexico has not done badly. There has long been a stable government run by a technocracy known as the Partido Revolucionario Institucional (PRI). The seven then living ex-presidents, the most senior of whom served his term in 1915, were given posts in the López Mateos régime (1958–64), which is proof of a continuity that no other Latin American country can boast. After three great movements in their history—independence, reform, and revolution—Mexicans feel that they are in reach of the fruits these movements were supposed to bring. In reach, but not quite within grasp. The fabled gold of Mexico may once again prove illusory, and this time (so it is believed) through no fault of the country's own.

The pride and sadness of Mexicans begins to harden. It seems to them that the so-called democracies are taking for granted a great many canons of behavior that are due for drastic revision. One cannot be sure that the up-and-coming countries—Mexico, Brazil, India, the new African republics—are going to accept those canons as the only right and sensible ones. New friendships are shaping in the club of the developing countries, with Mexico paying fruitful calls on India, Indonesia, the West Indies, and former British Africa. At the Geneva Conference on world trade, and at the Tokyo meeting of the International Monetary Fund and the World Bank in September 1964, there were signs that the developing countries have found new political strength through unity, and that policies can no longer be dictated by the great powers with quite the same godlike ease.

Of course the have-not areas of the world are eager to be lifted out of their marginal existences. Mexico, together with the rest of them, is making an effort to pull out of the lethargy of centuries. But in the Mexican nature there are deep and hidden desires that have very little to do with hungry mouths and shivering bodies. One new arrival to Mexico describes a scene through a Pullman window as the train crossed the northern desert. A hummocky mountain with a single cactus thrown into relief by the moon, and, riding from nowhere into nowhere (there was not even a trail in sight), a man on a donkey carrying a cello. It was a vignette outrageously foreign to the total context. Bewildered by the moonlike unreality of the landscape and the petty officials expecting (if not actually demanding) bribes, the newcomer glimpsed in that scene the other, super-logical Mexico upon which materialism sits so uncomfortably.

Amid the preoccupations of economic progress, such an impression can easily be forgotten. Mexicans know how much they need the bulldozers and pneumatic drills, the power plants and Penstocks, the anti-malarial drugs and the synthetic fibers of the new technology. No country where so large a percentage of the population lives in conditions that chickens would not tolerate can afford to sneer at the business tycoons and the economists planning its future. But neither can a country whose kings were once poets and seers afford to forget that material well-being is only—if importantly—the infrastructure of human life.

There is one sense in which, among developing countries, Mexico is unfortunate. India—a similarly noncommitted nation trying to industrialize—still has her ancient religions alive today, studied and respected in the West. British rule did not cut off her traditions. Mexico's equivalent cultures—or what was left of them after the last, decadent, indigenous priest-kings had twisted holy symbols for the purposes of empire-building—were drastically severed by the Spanish conquerors.

A thread of these old cultures did persist through colonial times, although the Spanish census-takers, with a foretaste of apartheid, thought it unnecessary to take count of the "nations of aborigines." Even in such circumstances, the indigenous tradition flowered here and there, in stone or bright gesso. Every now and then an Indian craftsman tucked an ancient symbol among the cherubs.

But in spite of lingering manifestations of the old, the conquest of Mexico was the first big break, the first embittering moment of destruction in the country's history as we know it. Mexico has now to find her past as well as her future; and this will not be done without integrating into the pattern of the modern industrial world a good many concepts from the ancient philosophies and languages (which are now being restudied) and from the days of Spanish rule as well.

Spain, Roman Catholic as she was, nevertheless brought to Mexico a Moorish (Muslim-Arabic) psychology and artistic-religious flavor which found in many ways a sympathetic soil. Whether the Indians of the Western Hemisphere will be proved to have come from the Orient or not, they show characteristics which Europeans attribute to the East. These include physical features such as slanting eyes and sparse body-hair, but also languages that depend on tone value, and a certain psychological inward-turning.

The Spaniards arrived in the New World from a homeland that stood at that time at the hub of world trade routes and had close contact with the Ottoman Empire's Arab dependencies. The Spaniards cannot have failed to recognize in Mexican indigenous psychology traces of those same cultural traits that had reached them from the Middle East, that had given a Moorish flavor to peninsular versions of Gothic, and a Levantine rhythm (itself influenced from farther east) to folk music such as *cante jondo*. In the conquest of the New World, cultural patterns seemed to come almost full circle, so that later the strongly Muslim-influenced baroque of Spain was grafted naturally onto the tradition that had created the elaborate and flowing friezes of Teotihuacán and the mosaics of Mitla.

But even in this union there was conflict; though curiously Mexican antagonism against Spain was fostered as much by the Creoles —born and bred in the New World—as by the Indians. It was a Creole-Spanish clergy that led the fight for Mexico's independence, just as it had been the Spanish friars who had earlier been true friends of the Indians. As soon as independence was achieved, there followed the long struggle for liberation from Mexico's own tyrants and usurpers, from wolves and coyotes and *rateros* (as the exploiters and racketeers are called). The 1910 revolution was only a phase of this struggle, which technically might be said to have begun with Benito Juárez (1806–72) who said, "Respect for another's rights is peace" (*El respeto al derecho ajeno es la paz*). But its formulations, its first principles, went even further back, to the moment of the first uprising against European domination.

Because Mexico's post-conquest history is one continuous struggle for the establishment of a set of principles that have not changed, the whole of it is very close to Mexico still. The principles were broadly these: national sovereignty; freedom from monopolies including those of government and of Church; sovereignty residing in the people, who should freely choose their representatives; tolerance toward foreigners provided always that they are useful to the national effort; no slavery or caste distinction; rule by law; the sacred nature of personal property; no judicial torture.

These principles ran from independence, through reform, to revolution; and the irrefutable proof that the revolution was not Marxist is that they were formulated by the priest José María Morelos at the Congress of Chilpancingo in 1813, five years before Marx was born.

Traces of the struggle to give these principles practical shape are everywhere to be seen in Mexico today: sometimes noble, sometimes sad monuments to the frustrations and deviations suffered by a country determined to learn through direct experience without foreign intrusion.

On the high plateau, for example, you may come upon a village where the view from the half-ruined tower of the old church stretches across dusty fields to the pyramid of the sun. Close to the village stands the shell of an *hacienda* that must have been the commercial and social center of the region. The owners of these massive buildings had provided a livelihood for many hundreds of peasants. The land was green with crops where today there are only a few skinny sheep. Now on a distant hillside, the remnant of some past election campaign is both hope and warning: the single word *Promesa* picked out in white stone.

After the mysticism of Teotihuacán, after the upper-class splendor of Spanish rule and the ruthlessness of revolution, that promise is still unrealized. It is drawing closer perhaps, for Mexico and for other Latin American countries too. Their potential, be it of intellect, culture, or material wealth, has never been even approximately realized. Today the vitality cooped up in them for centuries, first under foreign rule and later through some chronic inability to close the gap between achievement and aspiration, is erupting into somewhat undisciplined activity, at once creative and dangerous. Throughout the area the sheer need to survive, the need to think ahead to a total population of perhaps 333 million in 1980, is forcing a desperate effort.[3] The new promise can be sensed in extraordinary bursts of energy totally at variance with the traditional picture of Latin Americans as shiftless dreamers spending their days in *siestas* and their nights in serenades. The area is shaken with *inquietudes,* a word that means rather more than mere disquiet. It includes a searching for answers to social and philosophical problems; and if you are young and do not possess an *inquietud* you may almost be suspected of being immoral.

Although Brazil, Argentina, and Chile are better placed geographically to take the lead, Mexico has greater political stability and a richer past on which to draw. She is in some ways a special

[3] The latest calculations suggest that there will be 600 million by the year 2000.

case. She is, for instance, closer to the temptation of accepting, or of having thrust upon her, the "American way of life." Mexicans who most admire American qualities are the first to deplore the so-called *pocho* Mexican, who apes the American until he becomes a man without a country. With the rise of the middle classes this tendency is becoming more prevalent, and there is some danger that Mexico's special qualities may become submerged. The very poor have their traditions, and the very rich have time to cultivate the xenophobic abstraction known as *Mexicanismo*. But the culturally voiceless middle classes live on an increasingly more Americanized diet of pep drinks, Hollywood movies, soap opera larded with advertising, drugstores, and predigested magazine articles.

The Indigenous Institute, which is responsible for educating and guiding the remote Indian tribes that have not yet become assimilated into modern civilization, is afraid that this cosmopolitanization—Americanization in effect—will seep down to the poor and remote villages. "The very ignorance of the unassimilated Indians is their protection from all kinds of modern contaminations," said one of the Institute's anthropologists, "but the present stage won't last. Today it may be possible to take precautions to preserve dignity. Tomorrow it will be too late."

It was not that he had any intrinsic objection to American ways. He was distressed by the hybrid. Mexicans are not at home either with the austere faith of the pilgrim fathers or with naïve material optimism. When the American way of life is exported southward it tends to assume an air of cynical self-seeking. The Americanized Mexican is a double-talking clown. He seems to regard even his financial successes—when they come his way—tongue in cheek. Often he gives the impression of seeking material well-being for no better reason than to thumb his nose at the Americans, to show that he can do better than any international tycoon if and when he chooses to put his mind to the job. But there are songs to be sung, and death around the corner, as no Mexican ever quite fails to remember.

Mexico is an original country with a unique past. It will not easily assent to become another nation's appendage. For all its erratic course, the revolution was a Mexican movement, with Mexican causes, carried out regardless of foreign reproof so strong that it amounted at times to ostracism. There is little wonder that, having suffered boycotts and international censure, Mexico has adopted self-determination and non-intervention as the twin banners of her foreign policy.

To people more politically sophisticated these doctrines may sound naïve. "Dog-eared" a correspondent of *The Times* of London called those pages of the Organization of American States Charter that embody them. But for Mexicans they are fundamental and in upholding them they are not afraid to seem commonplace.[4] Self-determination does not mean merely the right to turn up at the polls from time to time. It means the right to spend money on *fiestas* when you cannot afford it for meat. It penetrates to "that domain reserved for man as man," as the Foreign Minister, Manuel Tello, said at Punta del Este, Uruguay, in 1962. It means being atheist if you choose, yet believing in Guadalupe. It means marching on national days but without a hint of militarism, breaking rank to borrow a cigarette from a friend and marching on with it hanging from your lip in urchin-like defiance of authority. It means criticizing Mexico and wishing her rulers to perdition; but hotly contradicting any foreigner who dares to do the same. Transferred across the Atlantic to a Nahua-Spanish-Mestizo environment, it is a close cousin to European nationalist thinking born in the Renaissance out of rich differences in styles of architecture, art, literature, and living.

In Latin America today this process is already beginning to go into reverse, with twenty nations realizing at last that it may be suicide not to join a commonwealth with a common culture. The wife of a Mexican under-secretary, who on a picnic chose to eat *tortillas* and black beans like the peasants, was expressing the kind of area nationalism which every Latin American can understand and which no country in the world need fear. South of the United States, from the Río Grande to Cape Horn, there is a set of values

[4] These lines were written before the Dominican crisis. Mexico's attitude to U.S. action in the island and to the formation of an O.A.S. force makes it all the more evident that she will on no account abandon her principle of non-intervention. It will require more than vague accusations of Communist activity in the hemisphere to convince her that foreign action—either unilateral or under the name of the O.A.S.—is justified.

that perplexes Americans, though it lures many of them by its illogical charm. Mexico belongs to that other culture, and it is both short-sighted and futile to hope to inveigle her, against all her history and her blood, into becoming some kind of artificially grafted fifty-first state. Mexico is in no serious mind to be unfriendly to the West, but if the West proves either uncomprehending, or coercive, or simply arrogant toward the ebullient non-English-speaking mass of the new hemisphere, her ultimate loyalty must be with Latin America.

2 *Gods and Ruins*

Dislodge a clod of earth in Mexico; and up will come, as likely as not, an obsidian knife, a diminutive clay head, a blackened corn cob: clues to a history that is still largely speculation.

The country is an archaeologist's paradise; which does not mean that the pre-Hispanic heritage is all moldering ruins. The Indian heritage exercises a strong influence over the present, both because the Indian himself is rooted in tradition and because the anti-Spanish sentiments engendered during the struggle for independence have been kept alive by the extreme nationalists. Such sentiments seem somewhat unrealistic considering that modern Mexico stands on a foundation of Spanish language and literature, Spanish customs, Spanish architecture, and Spanish blood. Except for a more or less harmless baiting of the *Gachupín,* as the Spaniard with his alien-sounding "lisp" is called, it does not extend to individuals. Mexico was generous in receiving Spanish-republican refugees and has benefited from them. However, in the eyes of a few pro-Indian, anti-European propagandists, the Spanish conquest rankles still, colonial times are looked upon as a slur, and Cortés was a syphilitic. The name of the conqueror's mistress and interpreter, Marina or Malinche, is commonly used as a synonym for Quisling.

Many Mexicans still speak their ancient tongues, and not so very remote from the highways there are villages where ancient rites are practiced. In caves in the mountains about the town of Puebla there are Indians who worship preconquest stone idols. In the southernmost State of Chiapas, secret rituals unfold behind the locked doors of Christian churches. In Nayarit the lives of the Huicholes revolve round their *peyote* ceremonies; and in Papantla, in the tropical vanilla country of the Gulf, the mast-high ancient maypole dance known as the *Voladores* has been grafted on to the Christian feast of Corpus Christi.

Hundreds more examples of ancient survivals could be cited, some of them so embedded in Mexican psychology that they pass almost unnoticed. For example, at meetings of village elders, or *caciques,* in any remote district, one finds deeply rooted a respect for protocol, for a strict step-by-step hierarchy through which every youth must pass before he can presume to command. Entering the antechambers of government officials in Mexico City one notices the same respect for title, the same formidable wall surrounding the great man guarded by private secretaries, porters, and locked doors.

The revolution brought Indian thought and heroes into fashion. General Cárdenas named his son Cuauhtémoc after the last Aztec emperor to make a stand against the Spaniards. A champion swimmer, Tonatiuh Gutiérrez, is called after the old sun god. Fashionable tables are graced with pre-Hispanic dishes and above all with the corn *tortilla,* or pancake, once considered fit only for the poor. *Sarapes* are made in new styles suitable for elegant town wear. It is chic to decorate houses with old sculptures, and pseudo-Aztec carvings adorn modern buildings. Children, if they are asked to name Mexico's rulers, begin not with the first president of the republic, Guadalupe Victoria; still less with Cortés, but with the old names—Tenoch, Ilancueitl, Acamapichtli. . . .

There is a reason for this effort to put the clock back. The West has lived a large part of its history in close union or contact with the ancient cultures of Greece and the Orient, but there was a time when the Upanishads, for example, were scarcely heard of, a time further back when even Plato had to be rediscovered by Renaissance scholars. Mexico wants recognition for her cultures too, and the deep-rooted but quite wrong notion that all was blood sacrifice takes a lot of living down.

THE RIDDLE OF THE ANCIENTS The most credited theory about the origin of the Indians on the American continent is that a mass exodus across the Bering Straits sent Oriental peoples exploring east and then south; although there is also the reverse theory (the Kon-Tiki hypothesis) of a movement westward from the Pacific coast of South America to Polynesia. "Why," as Mexicans say, "did we have to come from anywhere? Why were we not simply here?"

Fossils of the so-called Tepexpan man, discovered in 1949 by Helmut de Terra on the edge of the old Texcoco lake bed, suggest that there were human beings in the Americas at least 6000 years before Christ. In 1952, Mexican workers found in a nearby site the skeleton of a mammoth together with flints, a scraper knife, and other signs that the animal had been slaughtered by humans. Still another mammoth, similarly buried with human artefacts, was found in 1954; and charcoal unearthed with a third has been dated at approximately 7710 B.C.

Some very small wild corn cobs have been brought to light in caves near Tehuacán, Puebla, and these are thought by some authorities to date back to about 8000 B.C. They became progressively larger as the corn became cultivated, perhaps around 5000 B.C. or earlier. Corn may have existed on the continent from the beginning, along with man. Its forebears seem to have been tripsacum which, crossed with another primitive ancestor called Manisuris, gave a plant known in Mexico as Teocintle—a food fit for gods. This, crossed once more with Manisuris, gave modern corn with its good resistance to the climate of the Mexican tableland.[1]

Without doubt there were civilizations possessed of artistic techniques at least as early as 1500 B.C. This date may yet be proved a conservative estimate, but it corresponds to the earliest discoveries made so far in Mexico of any complex with pretensions to be called a human settlement: those at Chiapa de Corzo in the Grijalva basin.

Archaeologists are timid about linking the diverse cultures on the continent; yet many of the myths are so similar in their general structure, and even in their precise symbolism, that it is not too extravagant to suppose a single central revelation from which they all sprang. The settlement at Tlatilco in the Valley of Mexico, which has been dated around 800 B.C., has been likened to sites thousands of miles south, in Peru.[2] The similarity suggests early contact, for the cultures did not reach maturity for another thousand years and more, somewhere between A.D. 200 and 800. Tlatilco

[1] The chief worker on this subject in Mexico is Dr. Czeslawa L. Prywer, working at the government agricultural college in Chapingo.

[2] Coe, Michael D., *Mexico,* Thames and Hudson, London, 1962, p. 77.

seems also to have been in some way connected with the mysterious Olmec culture, to which we shall return later. The Olmecs seem to have been the source of all ancient Mexico's greatness, though unorthodox workers disagree, and some would place the origins of Mesoamerican civilization in Teotihuacán or even in the Maya lands, whence culture could have spread north.

The Olmec center at La Venta was inaccessibly situated and would therefore have been an ideal center for a priestly caste which guarded its secrets jealously. It was destroyed deliberately and for no known reason between 400 and 300 B.C., leaving Tres Zapotes, northwest of it, to continue whatever culture the former had represented. This was during the formative period, extending for several centuries on either side of the birth of Christ and typified by the earliest Tres Zapotes finds and by the rudimentary pyramid at Cuicuilco on the lava bed just south of Mexico City. By this time there was already the beginning of a culture at Monte Albán outside Oaxaca, but not yet at Teotihuacán on the high plateau —which flourished on either side of A.D. 300 according to the most recent datings. From Monte Albán the Zapotec culture spread to Mitla nearby, and from Teotihuacán to Tula almost due north of Mexico City. Tula is generally supposed to have been the capital of the Toltec empire, but there are workers who dispute this and would put the center of the great artistic Toltec culture in Teotihuacán.

The Aztecs did not appear on the scene until the fourteenth century, and until their time there is no sign of degeneracy in architecture or art. Nevertheless the extreme degeneration to which the cultures had fallen by the time of the Spanish conquest strongly suggests a longer history than has yet been admitted. It is difficult to imagine how else such lofty concepts as the need to create a deified heart, or a face that shall be truly man, or the idea of the poet as seer with access to the word of the gods, could end in mass human sacrifices. One Mexican authority, Professor Eulalia Guzmán, asserts that there never were human sacrifices. These, she says, were an invention of the Spaniards to cast a slur on the natives. Perhaps. But the unlikely theory that Hernán Cortés was a deformed syphilitic also emanates from Professor Guzmán. If such a theory were taken seriously it would hardly reflect favorably on the peoples he defeated. If we erase from history the firsthand accounts of human sacrifice and other signs of decaying cultural standards, we find it a little difficult to account for the ease with which a small band of Spanish adventurers could overthrow a great empire. It better fits Indian dignity to suppose that the sacrifices were a late perversion of an older and deeply spiritual religion; and this view tallies with known facts.

One internal proof of the extreme age of the cultures on the American continent is the extraordinary knowledge of the heavens, which suggests that the indigenous peoples were aware of the true heliocentric structure of the universe when Europeans were still trusting the evidence of their senses.[3] The Mayas gave names to time periods up to 3 million years, which suggests a very long history. Yet they used the true arch hardly at all. Pre-Columbian peo-

[3] Whereas our calendar measures only the passage of the Earth about the Sun and the Moon about the Earth, the Maya and Aztec calendars took note also of the movements of the other planets in the Solar System, and possibly even of the Solar System within the Galaxy. This breadth of measurement was achieved by various sliding scales. By adjustments of scale against scale, the Mayas achieved a calendar of which the average year was 365 days 5 hours 48 minutes 28.8 seconds, which gives an error of 3 days in 10,000 years.

The Mexican calendar wheel, similar to the Maya, had cycles of 13, 18, 20, 73, and 260 days. The 13-day cycle (called Companions of the Day) when multiplied by that of 20 days, made a 260-day cycle known as Tonalpohualli; 73 × 260 made 52 years. There were also lesser 9-day cycles known as Companions of the Night. The 20-day measure combined, in turn, with that of the 18 days to make 360 days. The extra 5 days in the year were "outside the calendar" because they did not fit into the sequence of 20-day periods. They were observed as fast days in which people performed no creative work until a festival ushered in the New Year. At the end of the 52-day cycles an extra intercalary period alternatively of 12 and 13 days brought the calendar into line with the position of the Sun among the stars.

The reasons for the choice of these complicated time periods are being studied. Cottie Burland in England and Raúl Noriega in Mexico have found interesting data relating to eclipses of the Moon. Noriega also points out that in 5 periods of 260 days, that is in 1300 days, the Moon circles the Earth 44 times. Mercury's cycle is 116 days, or about 9 × 13. The cycle of Venus is 584 days, or 8 × 73, or 2.25 × 260. One cycle of Mars is 780 days, or exactly 3 × 260. Jupiter's cycle is 399 days, roughly 22 × 18. Saturn's cycle is 378 days, or 360 plus 18. Thus the cycles of all these planets could be calculated more or less accurately by the various time measurements contained in the sliding scale.

The Mayas measured larger units not in centuries, but (starting from an 18-day period) in multiples of 20. Thus 20 × 18 made 360 days, making (with the 5 days outside the calendar) 1 year. This was a *tun*. A *katún* was 20 × 360 days, or 7200 days (roughly 20 years and exactly 12⅓ cycles of Venus). A *baktún* was composed of 20 *katunes*, or 144,000 days (approximately 400 years). A *pictún* was 20 *baktunes* or 2,880,000 days (about 8000 years). A *calabtún* was 20 *pictunes*, or 57,600,000 days (about 158,000 years). A *kinchiltún* was 20 *calabtunes*, or 1,152,000,000 days (about 3 million years).

ples made toys with wheels, yet the wheel was put to no practical use. It is intriguing to wonder whether their attitude toward this obviously useful invention could have foreshadowed a science fiction tale by John Wyndham, in which a child who discovers that a wheel will save him from burden-carrying is persecuted as a sorcerer. (The wheel, with all its evils, had been banished from the frightened civilization in which the child lived.) But perhaps the ancient Americans were quite simply uninterested in fast propulsion, like the Chinese peasant who, seeing a newly imported steamboat chugging up the Yangtze, is said to have turned his back saying, "Long ago we thought of that; it wasn't worth while."

THE RELIGIOUS BASIS The motives of the ancients are hidden. Only fragments of the great ritual centers are left: Teotihuacán and Tula in the central highlands together with Xochicalco (about A.D. 800) and the Aztec center of Malinalco with its eagles and ocelots carved into the rock; Tajín (about A.D. 600), La Venta, and Tres Zapotes in the Olmec-Totonac area of the Mexican Gulf; Monte Albán and Mitla in Oaxaca; Chichén Itzá, Uxmal, Palenque, and Bonampak in the Maya area (whose classical period according to most authorities extended from the fourth to the tenth centuries A.D. with a second period of influence from the Toltec-Aztecs from about the eleventh century to the conquest); and innumerable other sites being uncovered bit by bit as money allows.

There are also the codices with their elaborate ritual drawings and their suggestions of philosophical, economic, social, and legal systems. Among these should be counted the picture-book wall paintings such as those at Bonampak or the more recently discovered frescoes of Zacuala near Teotihuacán, where the embryonic god is enclosed first in an egg-shaped cocoon, from which he unfolds through pain to full maturity and bliss. The transcendent concept here recorded in paint suggests a profounder thought than could have existed in Aztec times, at least in the more popular aspects of the cults of Huitzilopochtli (their sun god) and human sacrifice.

Polytheism can usually be taken as a late and degenerate religious manifestation. It was noted by the Spanish conquerors, who were horrified by the multitude of gods and the proliferation of cults and sacrificial feast days, but it is evident that the true religion of the indigenous peoples originated much further back in the worship of a single, all-powerful god. The monotheism of the anonymous author of the Maya bible, the *Chilam Balam of Chumayel,* is as unequivocal as *Genesis:*

Where there was neither heaven nor earth sounded the first Word of God. And he unloosed himself from his Stone, and descended into the second time, and declared his divinity. And all the vastness of eternity shuddered. And his Word was a measure of grace, and he broke and pierced the backbone of the mountains. Who was it that was born when he descended? Thou knowest, O Father. His First Principle came into being, and pierced the backbone of the mountains.[4]

Here is no decadence or superstition, but the same faith in the unity of creation that is to be found in all great religious teachings. The word *Mayab* (the noun from which Maya and Mayan are derived) is itself significant for it means "The Land of the Not Many." Over this kingdom ruled Kukul-cán, and lesser deities such as the rain god, Chac. Monotheism existed in the one supreme being whose servants were the lesser gods representing created elements on a level somewhere below.

One can hardly believe that the builders of Chichén, Uxmal, and Palenque, with their classical serenity, had lost the sublime sense of the dignity of creation expressed in the *Chilam Balam;* one can hardly believe that these were nothing more than centers of blood sacrifice, and that the climax of the ball game was the beheading of the captain of the losing team. Recent explorations in the sacred well at Chichén, where a pure maiden is supposed to have been sacrificed each year, have brought to light hundreds of small wooden figures covered with latex. Some Mexican archaeologists think that these were dolls sacrificed symbolically in place of flesh-and-blood maidens. The original explorer of this underwater treasure trove, Edward Herbert Thompson, wove a stirring story of the horrors that took place there, based on the account of the Spanish Bishop Diego de Landa. De Landa, however, wrote in

[4] Mediz Bolio, Antonio. *Libro de Chilam Balam de Chumayel.* National University Mexico, 1941, p. 79.

1566, at a time when the Spaniards were naturally determined to see only the most distasteful aspects of the indigenous cultures. His technicolor version of pre-Columbian history does not fit the mood of the sculptured friezes, or of the jeweled dog (or ocelot, or jaguar) in his dark niche at the center of the great pyramid, which—in its suggestion of a glowing treasure to be found in the depths of solid matter—recalls that strange line in the *Chilam Balam:* "There Wisdom is formed, beating the stone in darkness."[5]

It is logical to suppose that, if these Maya temples had been places originally or primarily of human sacrifice, something less than the dignity of the ball court at Chichén or the Governor's House at Uxmal or the words of the anonymous Maya bible would have sufficed.

As one wanders at dusk and alone, after the garrulous guides have gone, through the tangled grass and scrub surrounding the ruins of Chichén with the clock-birds flying low or perching always, oddly, on the corners of moldings (so that they give the impression of being part of the fretted carvings), one's mind is cleared of the day's occupations and one seems to see these buildings free of the incrustations of centuries of incomprehension. Their lines and proportions are peaceful, attracting calm. A mood of serenity seems natural to people who live constantly among them: to the Indian boy, for instance, who takes tourists, even if the sky is emptying a tropical deluge, through squelching bog at Uxmal and who speaks of the "Governor's palace" or the "House of Turtles" as if they were lived in still.

Yet there is a Mexican archaeologist who replied to anyone talking in such terms, "I don't believe in ghosts . . ." Very well, the stones are dead, and what the builders expressed is lost in time. It is a point of view, but it wipes all meaning out of art. That same archaeologist would be the last to deny religious meaning to the Maya temples whose builders—it is the view of Laurette Séjourné who was one of the early explorers in Palenque—must have overcome hate and fear.

A similar sense of joy can be captured in the Zapotec temples of Monte Albán and Mitla. It is an emotion that fills the Maya-

[5] *Ibid.*, p. 76.

Quiché myth of creation, in which the gods make a man of clay, but he crumbles in water and—what is much worse—has no mind. Their next essay is a man of wood, who turns out to have no soul, to be forgetful of his creator, and to be incapable of walking except on all fours. He is transformed into a monkey, and the persistent gods then forge a man of gold. But the gold man's heart is like a stone, hard and dry. At last the humblest of the gods cuts off the fingers of his left hand with a machete; and from these fingers are created a man of flesh, who is so full of loving kindness that he is able to melt even the hard heart of the man of gold. And the man of flesh is pleasing to the gods.

This creation myth from the *Popol Vuh* is matched in beauty by the Nahua-Toltec story of Quetzalcóatl, the god incarnate. Quetzalcóatl is himself partly Mayan, for the quetzal bird is native to the highlands of Chiapas and Guatemala. *Coatl* means snake; and a modern Mayan, Domingo Martínez Paredez, splits this word into *co,* generic name for serpent or snake in the Maya language; and *atl,* the Nahua word for water.[6]

Quetzalcóatl incarnate was a lawgiver and civilizer, a compassionate king who, like the Buddha, could not bear to hurt any living creature. It is one of the most tantalizing gaps in human history that we do not know just who he was. He becomes fair game for every romancer, from D. H. Lawrence with his back-to-instinct philosophy, to those who would suggest that he came from the Celtic lands or from lost Atlantis or the Mediterranean Bible country. Most of the so-called "proofs" of his origin depend upon comparisons of Mediterranean, Celtic, Oriental, and Mexican low-relief designs; which show nothing more than that these people happened upon universal truths and put them into universal symbols.

There was more than one historical Quetzalcóatl, for in ancient Mexico the name was given to any priest who was supposed to have attained enlightenment. Laurette Séjourné[7] believes that the original Quetzalcóatl was a king living about the time of Christ. If it was he who discovered that corn was a good staple diet for humans,

[6] Martínez Paredez, Domingo. *Un Continente y una Cultura.* Editorial Poesía de América, Mexico, 1960, p. 18.

[7] Séjourné, Laurette. *Burning Water: Thought and Religion in Ancient Mexico,* Thames and Hudson, London, 1957.

as legend has it, then he must certainly have existed much earlier.

The high priests of the ancient religion were supposed to be "perfect in all customs, exercises, and doctrines" (as Sahagún says), "living in chastity, virtuous, humble, peace-loving, considerate, prudent, not frivolous but grave and austere, loving and merciful and compassionate, friendly to all, devout and god-fearing."[8] These models of virtue were, at the time when Sahagún and the first Franciscans arrived in Mexico, the high Aztec pontiffs; but the Aztecs were, as we have already noted, relative newcomers on the scene. They arrived at Lake Texcoco in 1325 and took over the older cultures—gods, language, and all. Whether or not earlier Quetzalcóatls lived up to the high ideals of human conduct laid down for them, it is fairly certain that after 1325 there was a sharp change for the worse.

The question "who was Quetzalcóatl?" becomes irrelevant when we turn to the myth itself, whose very existence proves that a great religious innovator did at some time establish his doctrine in Mexico. In his symbolic representation he was water, earth (in the crawling snake), and bird. Add to this that he was described as being the color of jade or of some precious stone; that he was the wind god and the god's messenger and road-sweeper; that he discovered corn which allowed man in his fullness to come into being; that his heart was consumed by the flames of a funeral pyre which he himself built, whence it rose to become the planet Venus; and that he has also been identified with the later Aztec sun-god Huitzilopochtli: and we have in this composite symbol a description of the basic materials of creation. Quetzalcóatl is a kind of ladder, extending downward from man into animal, water, and mineral; and upward to the planets, the star at their center, and the god creators. This is a ladder which, in its fairy-tale way, is similar to the steps leading from crystals to life as described by the modern paleontologist Pierre Teilhard de Chardin. It might be equated with the seven powers of nature described in ancient Oriental texts, and it echoes Picco della Mirandola's description of ideal man, "the intermediary between creatures . . . intimate with the gods above, as he is lord of the beings below."

[8] Sahagún, Bernardino de. *Historia General de las Cosas de Nueva España,* Editorial Nueva España, Mexico, 1946, Vol. I, p. 330.

According to the myth, man was not created until the gods had first found and bestowed on Quetzalcóatl the special human food. Quetzalcóatl became a black ant in order to steal the tiny grain that could transform the whole life of humanity. Corn became the symbol of "man made man"—in the phrase of a Nahua poet. Man, to be truly man, must be nourished on some special substance which is here symbolized by corn.

This idea connects with another early Mexican concept: *quallotl in yecyotl*. *Quallotl* is derived from *qua*, to eat, and implies edibility, or the capacity to be assimilated. The good is that which can be eaten or assimilated, whatever can nourish the true heart, the true face, the true inner character of man, which the Nahua peoples believed had to be created by a special and deliberate process. *Yecyotl* means what is right. Corn, the highest food, symbolized rightness, holiness, goodness; and Quetzalcóatl was the agent through which this food became available to man.

In Zacuala, Teotihuacán, Laurette Séjourné[9] has unearthed the foundations and lower walls of what she believes to have been a palace, with fragments of wall frieze showing scenes from the life of Quetzalcóatl. Here is the raft spilling over with flowers which, according to one version of the myth, took him to the land of the sun. Here too is his serpent body, and the blood that runs in its veins seems to have crystallized into flowers and shells, symbols of song and life-giving breath.

It was principally around this symbolism—together with that of Tláloc, god of rain, Xochipilli, Lord of Flowers, and Tezcatlipoca (Lord of the Smoking Mirror, god of the noumenal world)—that the great schools of sculpture and architecture of the high plateau revolved. The apparent cruelty of this art is the result of a realistic, totally unsentimental cosmic view of the universe. In the statue of the goddess Coatlicue death and life are interwoven as creature eats creature; and the heavenly bodies, terrifyingly remote, seem to infuse the snakes and warriors of the high plateau with something of their compelling power. In the Maya lands, too, we are not allowed to forget the all-pervading power of death, for the copyist of the *Chilam Balam* scribbled into his manuscript a manikin

[9] Séjourné, Laurette. *Un Palacio en la Ciudad de los Dioses*, Instituto Nacional de Antropología e Historia, Mexico City, 1959.

holding crossed swords or staves above his head, to show that death rules over all.

Trading among the Mayas, Toltecs, and other peoples of Mexico went peddlers known as *pochtecas,* who must have been to a great extent responsible for the otherwise unexplained interlocking of cultures that were in some respects separate. The wandering merchants, however, cannot account for the presence in the Gulf Coast region of the colossal heads with their Negroid features now in the museum in Xalapa. Their presence in Mexico has led to speculation whether the early Olmecs had some contact with Africa, and whether the Africans actually arrived in the New World long before Columbus. There is, for instance, a low relief which is stylistically reminiscent of early Egyptian carvings and which is dated by its finder, Dr. Medellín Zenil, as anywhere between the fifteenth century B.C. and the first of our era. Most workers will not dare to push dates so far back, however. Even Coe,[10] who favors an earlier dating than United States archaeologists like to admit, will not put the earliest La Venta finds before 800 B.C. He places the major developments of the Olmec culture within the middle formative period, but says that there is not the slightest doubt that all later civilizations in Mesoamerica, whether Mexican or Maya, rest ultimately on an Olmec base.

One of the puzzles of the cultures of the Gulf Coast is the unexplained variety of its artistic output. There are laughing heads almost Japanese in form, completely different from the austere sculpture of the high plateau. For anything like them in Mexico we have to go west to Colima and Nayarit, where sculptures of women with child, men laden with market wares, musicians, thinkers, all burst with quiet laughter. In their plump anatomies their makers have planted the seeds of universal comedy.

In the widely divergent styles of ancient Mexican art there is such plastic power and inventiveness that through clay and stone we seem almost to be able to communicate with the ancient people as they pursue their daily lives. We wonder again as we look at them how it was that degeneration came upon these virile Indians, how it was that the rule of poet-kings gave way, in spite of the

[10] Coe, Michael D. *Op. cit.,* p. 84.

abortive revival of the psalmist Nezahualcoyotl, to a philosophy of "chosen people" and the practice of human sacrifice.

No one knows the explanation of the mysterious rise and fall of the ancient civilizations, proceeding from the Olmecs via the Toltecs to the Aztec empire builders, and in the south from the pure Maya (almost Egyptian in some characteristics) to the confounding of its culture with the influences from the north. What is certain is that decay had set in long before the Spanish conquest delivered the final blow. Political atrophy and the growth of a police state were merely the results of deeper causes. Thought had grown rigid; philosophy and religion had degenerated into superstition; and it is by no means impossible that the indiscriminate use of narcotic mushrooms and cacti had killed all sense of responsibility in the priesthood and given it power untempered by compassion. It is well enough known that psychological changes can be artificially induced in man by the use of *peyote, mezcalin,* and the mushrooms *Psilocybe cubensis* and *Stopharia.* Mexican peasants still use mushrooms and *peyote* to encourage dream states in which they believe they can communicate with their gods. It is evident from modern studies that, unless they are carefully controlled, such induced states hold dangers; and serious workers deprecate the use of hallucinogenic drugs except on carefully selected subjects who are aware of the peril of attributing objective results to subjective and purely fanciful states.

In the ancient world there was something heroically but perhaps unhealthily one-pointed in the dominance of religion over all other activities; and one can suppose that, if to this dominance were added a drug addiction uncurbed by a sense of responsibility, the results could quickly have been disastrous. In the old cultures, even economics and sport were god-inspired. Chemistry served psychology; and psychology could be juggled for the sublime purpose of reaching closer to the gods. It is easy to imagine that under an unscrupulous ruler such manipulations could have been exploited for diabolical ends.

Intimacy with the heavens, too, seems finally to have degenerated into fatalism. It was gross superstition, and not cowardice, that was responsible for the defeat both of Moctezuma in the north and of the Mayas in the Yucatán peninsula.

THE CONQUEST By the early sixteenth century, the body-politic was rotten, the priests were augurs of the most superstitious kind, and the Aztec empire was ripe for conquest. The achievement of Hernán Cortés was none the less remarkable. To have plucked up the courage to march over the sheer rock bastion that separated Veracruz from the Aztec capital; to have held together a tiny band of Spaniards often quarreling among themselves; and to have been so astute a diplomat that he could play off Tlaxcaltecans against Aztecs: all required not only an iron nerve but a quick wit and shrewd knowledge of men.

In 1519 the governor of Cuba, Diego Velázquez, appointed Cortés to command a fleet fitted out for trade and exploration in Mexico, which had been discovered by Francisco Hernández de Córdoba two years earlier. From the island of Cozumel off the northeast tip of the Yucatán peninsula, Cortés coasted Tabasco, defeated the Mayas there, and reached a point north of the present town of Veracruz.

The expedition was fully documented by Bernal Díaz del Castillo, who provides many details suggesting that Cortés was far from being the uncultured soldier legend has sometimes made him. We have on the contrary the testimony of Doña Marina, la Malinche, herself a person of consequence who was obeyed by her Indian vassals without question and who said:[11]

> . . . that God had been very gracious to her in freeing her from the worship of idols and making her a Christian, and allowing her to bear a son to her lord and master Cortés, and in marrying her to a gentleman such as Juan Jaramillo, who was now her husband; that she would rather serve her husband and Cortés than any else in the world, and would not exchange her lot to become leader of all the provinces of New Spain.

Malinche knew the languages both of the Mexican Gulf region and of the Yucatán peninsula. Cortés therefore availed himself of her services and those of Jerónimo de Aguilar, a Spaniard who in 1511 had tried to navigate from Darien back to the Island of Santo Domingo but had been wrecked off the Yucatán coast and had been

[11] Díaz del Castillo, Bernal. *Historia Verdadera de la Conquista de Nueva España*, various editions. Book II, part 1, section 23.

enslaved by the Indians. (Another wrecked Spaniard, Gonzalo Guerrero, who had settled happily among the Mayans and married a native wife, refused to abandon his adopted people in favor of Cortés.)

Aguilar and Malinche were able to translate for the invaders as they marched inland through an alien and hostile territory. Cortés had come to plant the true cross, and he was serious in his task. "How can we ever accomplish anything worth doing," he asked, "if for the honor of God we do not first abolish these sacrifices made to idols?" In order that no cowards in his ranks should prevent him from fighting for Christ and his church, he took the extreme precaution of burning his ships. By this move he also strengthened himself against any reprisal from Velázquez who, in spite of having given Cortés command of the Mexican expedition, was by no means certain of the latter's loyalty.

It is believed that two ships may have been left afloat, one to take dispatches to Spain, the other as a dupe to the cowardly. Any who wished to return to Cuba in it might do so, it was announced (or so the story runs). The turncoats stepped forward, their names were taken; but far from being allowed to go, they were made to march with the rest and were spied on from that moment in case they should show further signs of dissension against Cortés.

The march from Veracruz to Tenochtitlán is one of the heroic episodes in history. Taking the pass between the 13,000-foot peak of Perote and the volcano of Orizaba, snowcapped at 18,700 feet, the Spaniards climbed ever upward, ignorant of what lay ahead and with hostile Indians on all sides. On more than one occasion they were ambushed, tricked, and forced to give battle. But, just as Cortés had been lucky in finding willing interpreters, so now the superstitious emperor of the Aztecs gave him a heaven-sent chance of victory. He badly needed this good fortune, for when he set out from Veracruz he had with him only 600 men, a few light cannon, thirteen muskets, and sixteen horses—and some of these last were soon killed in battle.

In spite of the poor equipment of the Spaniards, Moctezuma became convinced that the god Quetzalcóatl had returned according to the soothsayers' predictions. Gifts were at once dispatched to mollify the advancing Cortés. They included a mask of Quetzalcóatl with twists of the snake's body forming the eyebrows, and a mask of pyrite eyes representing the god Tezcatlipoca, both of which are now in the British Museum.[12]

Cortés crossed the 14,000-foot pass between the volcanoes of Popocatépetl and Ixtaccíhuatl, and was at last rewarded by the sight of the Mexican capital, Tenochtitlán; a glittering island city with a causeway spanning a lake crowded with canoes. The little band of 400 Spaniards suffered conflicting emotions of awe, greed, and fear. They remembered how they had been warned by the people of Huexotzingo and Tlaxcala that if they ventured into Tenochtitlán they would be massacred.

With the friendship of Moctezuma apparently secured, Cortés felt no need to hesitate, however. He entered Tenochtitlán in peaceful triumph, but was obliged a little later to return to the coast to stave off the envoy of Velázquez, Pánfilo de Narváez, who had been sent to seize him and to substitute Pedro de Alvarado as head of the Mexican expedition. Cortés defeated Narváez in Zampoala just north of Veracruz, reinforced his own small army with the men newly come from Cuba, and returned to Tenochtitlán. There he met trouble. The hot-headed Alvarado had ordered a massacre of Aztec nobles. The population, under Moctezuma's son-in-law, Cuauhtémoc, had become incensed and had besieged the Palace of Axayácatl where the Spaniards were lodged. When Cortés asked Moctezuma to calm his people by addressing them from the palace roof, the Aztec emperor was stoned to death. Cortés attempted to withdraw across the causeway. In a crushing defeat known as the *Noche Triste* he lost two-thirds of his men by drowning, all his artillery, and most of his horses.

A year later, reinforced by his allies from Tlaxcala and Texcoco, he returned to besiege Tenochtitlán. Although the city was bravely defended by the young Cuauhtémoc, last emperor of the Aztecs, it fell on August 13, 1521. Cuauhtémoc was captured and tortured in the hope that he might reveal the whereabouts of the fabled Aztec treasure. Throughout his trial he behaved with a dignity

[12] For a full list of the gifts made by Moctezuma to Cortés, and for a technical description of the mosaic work for which the Aztecs were famous, see Saville, Marshall H., *Turquois Mosaic Art in Ancient Mexico,* Museum of the American Indian, New York, 1922.

that Cortés was compelled to admire. In compensation the conqueror allowed Cuauhtémoc to accompany him on an expedition to Honduras, but, suspecting him of conspiracy, hanged him on the march in 1525.

In 1949 Dr. Eulalia Guzmán announced that she had discovered his bones hidden beneath the altar of the Roman Catholic church in the mountain village of Ichcateopan, in the State of Guerrero. A local legend, handed down by word of mouth from generation to generation of Indians, told how the friar Toribio Benavente known as Motolinía, had entered into a conspiracy with the Indians to rescue their emperor's bones and hide them. One peasant had even a written document which, though it turned out to be later in date than the sixteenth century, was believed to be a copy of a lost original. Now, in the twentieth century, the story grew that Motolinía had been farsighted enough to believe that centuries after his death the bones might serve as a symbol reconciling the Catholic and the Indian cultures. In the church at Ichcateopan, excavations were undertaken beneath the Catholic altar and the bones were discovered, together with a plaque engraved *Rey e S. Coatemo* (King and Saint Cuauhtémoc). The colonial retable was moved to one side, and local Indians mounted guard about the little whitewashed church to insure that nobody should disrespect their emperor. The tribute was touching, the story romantic enough to catch the imagination. Indeed, on the night of the finding of the bones the church bells were rung and thousands of peasants crowded into the village almost as if they had been expecting a miracle.

Since then a commission has decided that the bones (suspect from the first as being too small, probably not from one body, and even perhaps including those of a woman or a child) are not those of Cuauhtémoc. Undaunted, Dr. Guzmán attended a ceremony of homage to her emperor which was held in Ichcateopan in September 1963. With evident emotion she heard the president of the local congress invoke the gods Quetzalcóatl, Tláloc, and Tezcatlipoca before exalting the memory of Cuauhtémoc whose alleged remains rested in a crystal urn surrounded by floral tributes. Except perhaps to historians it scarcely seems to matter whether the bones are genuine or not. Cuauhtémoc remains a great national hero and a symbol—larger than mere literal truth in its message.

It is difficult to understand, however, why hero-worshiping of Cuauhtémoc should entail denigration of his great adversary. The anti-Cortés movement that has grown to such proportions in this century seems not to have existed in the conqueror's lifetime—or not among the Indians at least. Bitterness against him came rather from his own countrymen, and he was forced to return to Spain in 1529 to plead his cause before Charles V, who, though he rewarded the conqueror with the title of Marquis of the Valley of Oaxaca, refused to name him governor of New Spain.

Returning to the New World, the conqueror was received warmly by Indians and Spaniards. He put aside his battle dress and revealed his versatile talents by promoting architecture, shipping, and agriculture. He set up the first sugar usines on the continent and planted the first mulberry trees for silk. He wished to expiate sins that weighed heavily on him, and one of his most humanitarian acts was to order the building of a hospital for a doctor-friar named Bartolomé Olmedo, who had been treating the sick in the open streets. This hospital, founded about 1524 and finally called the Hospital of Jesus of Nazareth, exists today and as late as 1917 was still administered by an Italian descendant of the conqueror, Don José Pignatelli Aragón Cortés. Pope Clement VII had given the family perpetual charge over it, with permission to use a portion of the church alms for its upkeep.

Disappointed by the Spanish Crown's somewhat grudging recognition of his exploits, Cortés returned to Spain in 1539 and died in his native land in comparative obscurity in 1547. In memory of his own greatness he had bequeathed his remains to Mexico, and they were buried in the church of San Francisco de Texcoco in 1562. In the eighteenth century they were transferred to the Jesus Hospital. When feeling rose against Cortés during the independence struggle, Spanish well-wishers concealed them in the hospital wall, where they were discovered in 1946. In spite of protests from the Mexican left wing they were reburied in the hospital chapel, where they now rest.

Cruel Cortés undoubtedly was, but probably no more so than was customary among soldiers of his time. Once the conquest was over he behaved with an uprightness equalled only by the two conquerors of Yucatán, the Montejos father and son. Mexico was indeed lucky in not being subjected to the kind of treatment meted out to the Incas by the brothers Pizarro.

Francisco Montejo had taken part in early expeditions under Juan de Grijalva and Hernán Cortés himself. In 1527, six years after the fall of Tenochtitlán, he attempted to conquer the north of the peninsula, but the Mayas were hardy fighters and by 1535 they had driven every Spaniard from their territory. It was not until 1540 that Montejo's son, also Francisco, returned to the attack and was able to found the modern city of Mérida on a site occupied by a Maya township, T-Ho. He went on to conquer the valley of the Grijalva River, the present States of Chiapas and Tabasco, and a part of Honduras.

Like Cortés, the Montejos were fierce opponents, but like Cortés they had come, as sincerely as they knew how, to Christianize. It was not as a rule the soldiers, but the loophole-minded lawyers, the schemers and political climbers, who turned out in the end—as we shall see—to be the worst enemies of the Indians of the New World.

3 *Causes in the Modern World*

Below Chapultepec Castle, which is now a museum of colonial relics, and on the heights from which the child heroes threw themselves rather than capitulate to the United States forces in 1846, there is a museum designed to teach Mexican schoolchildren their country's history.

It is a small, snail-shell gallery, winding gently downward in a ramp like Frank Lloyd Wright's Guggenheim in New York, but without the aesthetic precocity of the latter. It is not built for tourists. There is not a single descriptive sign in English, and the United States' annexation of half Mexico's territory under the treaty of Guadalupe Hidalgo is dramatized in maps and over a loudspeaker. If American visitors are indiscreet enough to stray into this sanctuary of Mexican patriotism, that—the museum authorities seem to think—is just too bad.

The museum is a domestic affair. Parents and children recognize their ancestors with the same everlasting features: anonymous burdened peasants in the cathedral square, Indians in loincloths, sansculotte fighters for the revolution and their women, the sinewy *soldaderas*.

Bronze doors, technical gymnastics by José Chávez Morado, show on one panel the indigenous peoples and their cultures, on the other the conquering Spanish soldiers and the friars. Within the museum the exhibition begins at a moment when Spanish rule had already been established, and breaks off gracefully in 1916, thus avoiding recent and thorny controversies.

Here are the simple elements of the Mexican story, the kind of thing the authors of that much-beloved parody of English history *1066 and All That* would have labeled "memorable": the equivalents of "thin red lines" and gunpowder plots, burnt cakes and "Kiss me, Hardy."

As we enter and leave we read the arrogant statement by a Spanish Viceroy, the Marquis de Croix, made in 1767 when he was expelling the Jesuits from his domain and the common people were threatening to rebel: "Once and for all the subjects of the Great Monarch who occupies the Spanish Throne must understand that they were born to be silent and obey, and not to discourse nor to hold opinions upon high matters of government."

The first tableau is an idyllic glimpse of the central square of Mexico City as it was in colonial times. Peasants are shading their wares by kite-like awnings as they do in villages still. Only the clothes of fashionable Spaniards, and the whipping post, remind us that times have changed.

Throughout the exhibits the Spaniards, like the Americans, are presented just a bit blacker than they were; but the social and evangelizing work of the friars, and the technical help given to Mexico by miners and bankers, are acknowledged. It is a good tale, creating that kind of interlocking of myth and fact that is always a little truer and a little richer than the stark dates of textbooks.

SOLDIERS, FRIARS, AND JURISTS If we turn back to the early days of Spanish colonization, the point where the museum sets the children moving on their journey through history, we shall see that church and state, autocrats and liberals were in conflict from the beginning, both among themselves and in their policies toward the Indians.

Tenochtitlán had fallen in 1521. Hernán Cortés had established Spanish supremacy in New Spain. He held sway over a territory stretching from Coyoacán (now a suburb of Mexico City) to the coastlands of Veracruz and the Tehuantepec Isthmus: an area of about 25,000 square miles. In Coyoacán his captains were building themselves homes that still stand as testimony to their flamboyant New World ambitions. Undoubtedly many of the soldiers were avaricious. The Spanish Crown thought so at least, and appointed to watch over them the first *Audiencia* headed by Beltrán Nuño de Guzmán, who loathed Cortés and was much fiercer. Nuño, who in post-conquest native codices crouches glowering in his saddle, the very personification of vice, became virtual dictator of New Spain. He did his worst for the Indians, and it was he rather than the original *conquistadores* who sowed the seeds of several centuries of bitterness. His invasion of the great western tract, Nueva Galicia (now Michoacán, Jalisco, Nayarit, and Sinaloa), brought reprisals against the Spaniards in the rebellion known as the Mixtón war. He seized for his personal enrichment the tributes exacted from the Indians, which were strictly speaking payable to the Spanish Crown. His shameless immorality combined with his elevated legal status to give him absolute power; so that with his entry upon the Mexican scene jurisprudence began to shape itself as an instrument of despotism. Even after a second and more upright *Audiencia* had been appointed, the struggle between the *conquistadores* and the presumed representatives of law continued. It was not easy for Spain, several sailing months away, to keep in close touch with policy.

It was particularly difficult to assess such legal concepts as the *encomienda*, an institution whereby a *conquistador* was given power to collect tribute due from the Indians in return for acting toward them as instructor in the ways of the new civilization. The *encomiendas* fell into disrepute after Nuño had begun arbitrarily granting them to his friends, and the second *Audiencia* was obliged to hand over the job to public officials called *corregidores*. But the modern habit of the *mordida* (bite, or bribe) had already begun to influence Mexican life. At first it was the rich who exacted tithes from the poor and failed to hand them to the Crown. Later the poor got into the habit of expecting largesse as a right, and the *mordida* was reinforced from below. The habit of expecting something for nothing—and illegally at that—started with Nuño.

Into the post-conquest mêlée of legal and power politics came the friars with their task of converting the apparently barbarous indigenous peoples to the one true faith. Three (of whom the most active was Pedro de Gante) arrived in Tlaxcala in 1522, and these were followed two years later by twelve more under Martín de Valencia. They traveled on foot from Veracruz to Mexico City, from the coast to the 8000-foot-high plateau, through an alien landscape and an unknown people, yet without the protection of arms or escort. It was evident that the friars, unshod, roughly clad, and without baggage, had not come for greed or conquest.

And yet in another sense it was precisely to conquer they had come. It was their cross and their culture, and not the gunpowder and horses of Cortés, that made Mexico—and makes the country still—at least half Spanish in pattern. It was the Franciscans who understood that in spite of idols and human sacrifices there were aspects of the ancient civilization that ought to be preserved. In order to help in this task they often contravened orders from the Church in Spain. Franciscans and Dominicans brought to Mexico the arts of Spanish baroque and made the most remote districts flower with golden cupolas. Teaching the crafts still practiced by Mexican peasants, they made contact with Indians exactly in those activities where Indian ability most evidently lay. Their austere but kindly and aristocratic Spanish faces (Gante, or Peter of Ghent, is said to have been an illegitimate half-brother of Charles V) are preserved in portraits that hang in monasteries now turned into museums, to remind us that idealists entered Mexico very close on the heels of the gold-seekers and with at least equal courage. The friars did not know the natives or what their temper would be; and even while they were winning strange new friends, whose languages they were learning, they were having to contend with reactionary elements among their own countrymen. Sometimes their reforms were directly opposed, sometimes they became political weapons in the hands of the Council of the Indies, which used them to curb the power of the overambitious *conquistadores.*

The New Laws of the Indies for the good treatment and preservation of the Indians, formulated by the Dominicans in 1542 for strictly humanitarian reasons, were used by Spain for this second purpose and would otherwise have been unlikely to reach the statute books. The laws were inspired from Salamanca, where in 1532 an expert in international law, Father Francisco de Vitoria, had delivered two lectures under the title: *De Indis et de Jure Belli Relectiones.* There was only one justification for poaching on Indian preserves, the learned priest had argued: the spreading of the Christian faith. The "free vassals of the Crown," as he called the Indians, needed to be looked after until such time as they became mature within the western Christian culture. Caring for the Indians did not mean exacting taxes from them, enslaving them, and using them for forced labor.

In the despotic conditions of the new society, the friars found themselves obliged to trespass into realms that were more Caesar's than God's. When social standards are below a minimum of human decency the division between the two worlds is not easy to define, and only an immoral church could at that time have attended to the inner man and have disregarded plain human pity. The friars were doing the very thing for which the Jesuits were to be expelled from Mexico, as from Paraguay, two centuries and more later. They were earning the affection of the Indians (and gaining power in consequence) by upholding civil rights, working to improve living standards, and providing the indigenous people with an education fitting the new era.

Bartolomé de las Casas, the Dominican after whom the beautiful mountain city of San Cristóbal Las Casas (in Chiapas) is named, pleaded the Indian case in Spain and was personally responsible for lenient laws promulgated in 1553. His reforms were strongly opposed by Juan Ginés de Sepúlveda, an earlier upholder of the doctrine of the Marquis de Croix; and also by one of the first professors of Mexico's University, Bartolomé Frías de Albornoz, though he himself was in trouble with the Inquisition for a treaty on the conversion of the Indians.

Somewhat less preoccupied with material reforms, Pedro de Gante established a school of music in Texcoco and wrote *The Christian Doctrine in the Mexican Language.* But he too, like Bartolomé de las Casas, was forced into protesting against the enslavement of the Indians and the exacting tributes demanded of them. Perhaps it was blood relationship with the Emperor that emboldened him to address two letters on the subject to Charles V.

The work of the friars was supported by the more enlightened among the bishops. There was Vasco de Quiroga, for example, who founded in Michoacán what he called a "City of God," where he taught the Indians trades and Christian virtues. There was Archbishop Zumárraga who, together with the Viceroy of the time, Antonio de Mendoza, steered a middle course between the just demands of the friars and the greed of the now well-established local philistine aristocracy. Laws were enacted, cut to a pattern that would avoid a head-on clash between the two factions. Mendoza could have done nothing more sensible than walk a tightrope, avoiding bloodshed and appeasing hatreds. He was a benevolent and popular but nevertheless surprisingly efficient governor in a territory that included, besides the former Aztec Empire, Nueva Galicia, Central America, and the West Indian and Philippine Islands.

There seems to be no clear historical evidence for the story that Zumárraga destroyed the great Aztec library at Texcoco. It is not an act that is easily reconciled with his other policies. He set up courts for meting out justice to the Indians, and complained that his fellow-countrymen used the natives as beasts of burden, driving them to death. But the burning of the books, dramatized until it rivals the great fire of Alexandria and painted into Mexican history by Diego Rivera in his National Palace frescoes, is just the kind of popular myth most eagerly seized on in post-revolution Mexico to explain the paucity of pre-conquest written documents and to throw a little extra mud at the Spaniards. If it is proved true, it will be evidence of the profound struggle within the consciences of the early evangelizers, between hatred of idolatry, incomprehension of this exotic and often (in practice and before their eyes) cruel politico-religion, and their love for the Indians as human beings. Bernardino de Sahagún, who did more than any single man to preserve a knowledge of the native cultures, believed that the ancient songs were the work of the devil; but sixteenth-century Spanish churchmen could hardly have been expected to look upon Nahua rites with the eyes of a modern student in comparative religion.

By and large, Zumárraga seems to have been remarkably broad-minded, and it would be interesting to know whether he acted deliberately in encouraging—perhaps he even initiated—the myth of the apparition of the brown Virgin of Guadalupe to the peasant Juan Diego.

At the foot of the hill of Tepeyac there had once been an Aztec temple dedicated to Tonantzín, mother of the gods. As legend has it, on the morning of December 9, 1531, the brown Virgin, Guadalupe, appeared to Juan Diego (who was about some common chore) and ordered him to tell the Archbishop that a temple to herself must be built on that spot. Juan Diego did as he was bidden, but rather naturally the Archbishop was incredulous and demanded proof. Back went Juan Diego to the Virgin, who told him to climb the hill and gather the roses he would find growing there although it was winter.

A still more impressive miracle than the roses picked in December clinched the peasant's story. When Juan Diego spread the flowers before the Archbishop, there was the Virgin's image on the napkin in which they had been folded. She stood on a crescent moon, supported by an angel and dressed in a star-spangled robe surrounded by a nimbus. Zumárraga was impressed. He ordered a hermitage to be erected, but it was left to a future archbishop to build the first true temple on the site of the apparition.

Through the power of racial suggestion, through long faith in the holiness of the site, the old mother goddess was transmuted into a unifying symbol presiding over a land divided. The traditional image of Guadalupe, supposed to be the original napkin, hangs above the altar of the Virgin's basilica today, and cheap reproductions adorn huts and middle-class homes, public vehicles and factories. Beneath the Virgin's glance, thieves are supposed to stay their hands (which is not true, alas!). The basilica painting is so frequently reproduced that one ceases to find it sentimental. But there is an anonymous wood-carved version of Guadalupe that has the strength almost of a face on Chartres. Sturdy she has proved, for she led the insurgents into battle against the Spanish overlords, and she draws the unassimilated Indians and the peasants and middle classes together in common worship. Her image may degenerate until it is printed on cards advertising a bottled drink, or given away with razors. There is more power in her than in the posters of petroleum derricks with their subsoil-for-the-Mexicans slogan: "Not one step back!"

Guadalupe was not the only example of fusion of faith. Native sculptors of the baroque churches frequently slipped an ancient image among the cherubs, and there is a strongly pagan flavor in the details of Dominican churches in Oaxaca and Puebla.

Much the same happened with the legal structure of villages, where the Spaniards found it useful to retain the ancient *caciques* or chiefs. The conquerors interfered as little as possible with native customs, provided these could be dovetailed into the Christian code and did not threaten to cut off the supply of organized labor. Christianity often clashed with economic needs, however, and the Dominican-inspired laws of 1542, abolishing slavery and all "forced labor of free Indians," very nearly reduced the Spaniards to indigence. The labor problem was solved by a practice which, whether the Spaniards actually knew it or not, was close to an ancient Indian custom called *tequío,* whereby every citizen was obliged to render public services. The Spaniards called their system *repartimiento,* and work under it included mining, masonry, road-building, and irrigation. Unlike the *tequío,* such work was paid for. Although theoretically a civilized institution, it led to abuses which the Franciscan, Jerónimo de Mendieta, denounced in 1575 in a letter to Philip II. Thirty-four years later a reformed law was drawn up which still influences government treatment of the poor agricultural and mining populations. It was laid down that Indians should not be forced to work long distances from home or in unaccustomed climates (an important rule in a country where a journey of only a few miles may bring a sharp change of altitude).

Although it was stipulated that wages must be fair, a wide gap grew up between the pay of the unskilled *repartimiento* worker and that of a skilled man in the silver mines. The silver kings could afford to pay.

At least three standards of wage-earning thus began to appear among the native population; and the gulf between them has not narrowed in spite of reforms and revolution. First there were the peons, ancestors of today's *ejido* peasant landworkers and small farmers. Above them were the skilled and semi-skilled miners, whose salaries were higher than those of the peon in much the same proportion as those of the modern factory worker are higher than the peasant's. Somewhere between, more independent than either but earning probably less than the miners, were the craftsmen who passed on their skills to children and grandchildren and established a self-sufficient economy in villages such as those around Guadalajara, Uruapan, and Puebla.

These widely differing wage standards were not altogether unjust, for the miners worked hard in often dangerous conditions, and the craftsmen were gifted and quick to pick up Spanish skills. It was due to them that by the end of the sixteenth century there were some four hundred monastery buildings and innumerable churches.

As time went by the Spanish Crown became well disposed toward the Indians, and Philip II's enlightened viceroy, Luís de Velasco (who freed 150,000 slaves and was known as Father of the Indians), made a statement that ought to be balanced against that of de Croix: "The freedom of the Indians is worth more than all the mines in the world, and the revenue which the Crown receives from them is not so important that the Crown will on that account crush human and divine law underfoot." When Velasco died poor and in debt in 1564 the Cathedral Chapter of Mexico wrote to the King: "His chief concern was to do justice, without fraud and without recompense, serving your Majesty and keeping the realm in peace and quiet." Had succeeding rulers been as upright, a different fate might have awaited New Spain.

Martín, the foppish son and heir of Hernán Cortés, arrived in the territory in 1563 to claim his father's estate and title. In spite of his extravagant ways, in spite of the fact that he was a full-blooded Spaniard and that two other sons of Cortés, born of his Indian mistress, Doña Marina, were in his retinue, he received full support from the native population. The Franciscans, always under threat of secularization from the Council of the Indies, also backed him. If Martín had been half as strong as his father, he would have wrested New Spain from the Crown and Mexico might have been an independent nation so much the sooner. A plot was hatched between him and two sons of another *conquistador*, Gil González de Avila; but owing to Martín's shilly-shallying the Avilas were caught and beheaded for high treason in Mexico City's central square in 1566.

The unsuccessful conspiracy brought a climax in the always strained relations between Crown and conquering soldiers (including by now their descendants). Philip II put New Spain into the hands of one of his most ruthless judges, Alonso de Muñoz, who arrived there in 1567 and initiated a reign not less terrible than Nuño de Guzmán's; only this time the sufferers were not Indians but Spaniards and Creoles. Martín Cortés was jailed but later released and his estate returned to him. He never went back to Spain.

After the conspiracy the power of the *conquistadores* was at an end. From now on the viceregal lands became a respectable outpost of Spain, where men could live graciously and riches could be gathered without resort to arms. The seeds of both hatred and devotion to the Spaniards had been sown. Hatred of Nuño de Guzmán was later to be transferred to Cortés, although for many years after the conquest and after his death he was regarded affectionately by the Indians.

The judgments of Alonso de Muñoz, the evil practices of some *encomendados*, and the punishments and censorships of the Holy Office (which did not begin to function in New Spain until 1571) were foci for accumulated bitterness against the Crown. Rancor was caused, too, by the *Index Librorum Prohibitorum* listing all supposedly heretical books. It is still cited, rather aggressively and not very plausibly, to explain why there have been so few Mexican authors of international repute.

Another cause for bitterness was the rigid caste system which the Spaniards established. Free unions were general in viceregal times and were frowned on neither by Church nor State, but the children of all mixed unions suffered discrimination according to a carefully graded racial scale. Children of Spaniards born in the New World were called Creoles and their social standing was only just below that of Spaniards born in Europe. The slight slur on the American-born caused a sense of inferiority to grow in the Creoles however, even in those who, like Simón Bolívar in South America, were to become heroes of American independence. And yet discrimination against Creoles was negligible compared with that against the *Mestizos* or so-called *Coyotes*. These were the offspring of Spanish fathers and Indian mothers, begotten of ephemeral lust and ranking therefore even below the *Castizos*, who, as children of Spanish mothers and Indian fathers, were assumed to be the result of something nobler than animal promiscuity—for no Indian would have dared to take a white wife without her full consent and presumably her love. Then again there were *Mulattos* (children of Spanish fathers and Negro mothers); *Moriscos* (the converse); throwbacks; *Chinos* (progeny of throwback fathers and Indian mothers); "Wolves" (children of *Chinos* and Indian women); and still other mixtures referred to offhandedly as "Stay-outsides" or "There you are."

It was the disdain of the Spaniards, Creoles, and *Castizos* that forced the lower castes into the psychology of bribery, toadying, and bullying. As the Jews in other parts of the world were obliged by circumstance to make their livelihoods by moneylending because the professions were closed to them, and were then taunted with having acquired the characteristics of moneylenders, so many New World people unfavored by birth were forced to live by their wits, and they came as a natural consequence to trust nobody—not even their own kind. Customs forced upon them by society came arbitrarily to be regarded as the result of innate defects in character, and the prejudice against these "lower castes" was thus perpetuated. It was broken only centuries later by the force of revolution, but it takes time to annihilate psychological traits engendered by long years of high-handed treatment from the privileged orders.

But if Spanish *hubris* was a breeder of hatred, this was far from the whole story. There was also love and devotion to the friars (themselves often opposed to the Crown); love for the memory of Cortés, or at least respect for his qualities of courage, leadership, and diplomacy; love toward the new religion and the art in which it was clad. In many of their loyalties the churchmen on the one hand and the Creoles on the other could sympathize with the Indians; in others they were on the side of Spain. Here was material for conflict; but for a time it slept.

SILVER, SCOURGES, AND GOOD LIVING By the end of the sixteenth century New Spain had become a comfortable place to settle. True, Cervantes had remarked that it was "the refuge of the poor devils of Spain," and the picaresque novelist Mateo Alemán would scarcely have been tempted to Mexico if he had not served two terms in Spanish jails.

Intellectually, nevertheless, the New World was looking up. In the seventeenth century there were already Creole writers like the dramatist Juan Ruíz de Alarcón, the poet nun Juana Inés de la Cruz, and the mathematician and astronomer Carlos de Sigüenza y Góngora, who could be placed almost, if not quite, on a level with their contemporaries in Spain. Engineers were drawing up plans for draining the swamps of Mexico City and for controlling the floods caused by indiscriminate tree-felling (the climatic problems were not so different then from what they are today). Among the technicians was Enrico Martínez, possibly of German origin, who in spite of jealous opposition from a Dutchman, Adrian Boot, succeeded in building canals and tunnels for controlling the unruly waters. An Italian, Juan Bautista Antonelli, drew up the first road map in the New World and traced a route from Veracruz via Córdoba and Orizaba to Mexico City. This route was followed almost exactly by the builders of the modern highway in 1930. There was a plan, too, for a canal across the Isthmus of Tehuantepec to join Atlantic and Pacific.

An English traveler, Thomas Gage, described the Mexican capital as it was in 1625, with its large marketplace where it was possible to buy stuffs and silks, fruits and herbs, pineapples, pomegranates, quince, and other exotic fruits. Opposite was the Viceroy's palace, and nearby the street of *Los Plateros* where gold, silver, pearls, and jewels were abundantly displayed. Mexico City held at that time between 30,000 and 40,000 souls. Men wore hat bands of diamonds, and even tradesmen could afford them of pearls. But the streets were crammed with thieves, beggars, and outcasts known as *leperos*. Water ran close under the city, and coffins moldered in the sodden foundations.[1]

Typical of the time was the pathetic viceregal Archbishop, Fray García Guerra, who made a fair show of asceticism in spite of his preference for music and bullfights. When he first entered Mexico City as a humble vicar of Christ it was on a mule; later, as Viceroy, he rode with pomp on a white charger. During the reign of this adept at reconciling earth and heaven, a subversive plot was put down with twenty-nine men and four women hanged.

On the whole, though, the Hapsburg dynasty ruled more or less quietly through the seventeenth century, a period when the New World seemed at last to be yielding up its fabled riches. In 1546 a Spanish captain, Juan de Tolosa, had discovered silver deposits in Zacatecas. He and his colleagues, Cristóbal de Oñate, Diego de Ibarra, and Baltazar Termiño, soon became the richest men in Mexico. A mint was established in the town (there had been one in

[1] For first-hand accounts by travelers in Mexico see Mayer, William, *Early Travellers in Mexico (1534 to 1816)*, published privately by the author, Mexico City, 1961.

Mexico City as early as 1535), and nomad Indians were hired to work the mines. An even more important vein, the Valenciana, had been discovered in 1558 in Guanajuato. In its seventeenth-century heyday the shafts reached 1600 feet underground, and Baron von Humboldt said of them in 1803 that they were "one of the greatest and most daring enterprises in the history of mining." This vein produced silver, gold, lead, copper, quartz, and amethyst; and, as Humboldt noted in passing, the wealth of mining activity helped to extend agriculture even to nearly desert regions.

The Hapsburg régime saw, too, the rise of a landed clergy. Church property was exempt from taxation, and many curates extorted considerable "tithes" from their parishioners. The poor were kept firmly in hand, and all groups strong enough to cause trouble were economically so comfortably placed that, except for hunger riots in 1692 due to the neglect of agriculture, there was little political unrest.

By the eighteenth century New Spain had reached its peak of power and prosperity and the Bourbon age of enlightenment found propitious conditions. Charles III was so sure of his prestige that he dared even expel the Jesuits, who had become what revolutionary Mexicans have more recently accused the clergy of being—emissaries of a foreign government poaching beyond their spiritual preserves.

Charles III encouraged education and overseas trade. At the college of San Francisco de Sales in San Miguel el Grande, a distinguished philosopher, Juan Benito de Gamarra, was among the first Mexican intellectuals to teach the philosophy of Descartes and to urge his students to apply themselves to mathematics if they wished to be conversant with science. Another center of new thought was the Royal and Pontifical Seminary of Mexico, one of whose pupils was tried by the Inquisition for being a disciple of the French Encyclopedists. In spite of such persecutions, philosophical-scientific thought prospered among Spaniards and Creoles alike, so that New Spain continued to advance intellectually even though the mother country was falling into a decline. Across the Atlantic, eighteenth-century Spain counted on such brilliant representatives of the Crown as José de Gálvez, Antonio María Bucareli, and the two Counts Revillagigedo.

Gálvez, colonial minister to Charles III, meted out some moderately cruel punishments (85 men hanged, 73 lashed, 674 condemned to jail, and 117 banished for protesting against the Jesuit expulsion). But he was able to beat off a Russian invasion (driving south from Alaska) and to extend his domain as far as the Bay of San Francisco. He discouraged smuggling, and saw to it that the government received a substantial revenue from two important industries, tobacco and gunpowder (used for blasting operations in the mines). His economic policies were so similar to those of the Mexican treasury today that he can be considered the first exponent of happy union between private enterprise and state control.

The first Count Revillagigedo, Viceroy of Mexico from 1746 to 1755, organized the treasury and was a good friend of the Indians. The more famous second Count, who ruled Mexico from 1789 to 1794, introduced the study of botany into the colony, encouraged agriculture, opened communications, and had a reputation for complete rectitude unusual in those times.

Between the Revillagigedos came Bucareli, Viceroy from 1771 to 1779, who opened a poor house, built forts, encouraged science and mining, and combated a serious plague of locusts.

Under Bourbon prosperity, silver kings such as José de la Borda of Taxco were building splendid private homes and neo-classical churches. Science flourished under men like José Antonio Alzate y Ramírez who continued the astronomical studies of Sigüenza y Góngora, classified plants, and was a keen zoologist and archaeologist. Working closely with Alzate was a Jesuit, Francisco Xavier Clavijero, who wrote a short history of Mexico before and after the conquest; and these two made common cause with the great mining technologists. A tribunal of mining was organized and a school of miners established with the help of Fausto de Elhúyar, Andrés del Río (both Spaniards), and the Mexican-born Velázquez de León. Elhúyar was the first worker to isolate tungsten. With del Río, who had been a pupil of Lavoisier and who himself discovered vanadium, he established such high technical standards that not only Spaniards but also German investigators, including Alexander von Humboldt, were attracted to Mexico.

Architecture flourished under Manuel Tolsá who also directed the art academy of San Carlos; but of all periods in Mexican history the short stretch before the independence is the only one in which science has equalled the fine arts in importance. Had it not been for the political upheavals ahead, geologists, botanists, and miners might have established the climate for a truly national technology. But in 1788 the almost imbecile Charles IV succeeded to the Spanish throne, and the ambitious upstart guardsman, Manuel Godoy, became virtual dictator of the empire. Before Mexico's scientific-technological pioneers had died, Spain had been broken and the Mexican republic born. Humboldt, who had fallen under Mexico's spell and had predicted prosperity for the country, was granted a letter of citizenship. Del Río joined the independence movement and became a congressman in 1820. But Elhúyar, loyal to his homeland, returned to Spain.

If we look back from the eve of independence over three centuries of Spanish rule, we are hard put to it to say who among the conquerors and settlers did most for New Spain: whether the friars in their poverty, the affluent officials from the central government, or the mining industrialists and technicians. There is no simple, black-and-white picture of exploiting imperialist and downtrodden peasant such as an early nineteenth-century Mexican deputy, Miguel Ramos Arizpe, tried to present:[2]

> It is a well-known and lamentable fact that the government of the Spanish monarchy . . . has through the centuries bent all its endeavors toward the aggrandizement, luxury, and extraordinary splendor of its governors. It is also well known that, since these aims were impossible to reconcile with the rights of the nation and the achievement of its prosperity, there resulted a terrible clash of interests between the latter and its rulers. Force triumphed, and the most sacred rights of man were brought low. Naturally systems were adopted which guaranteed that despotism, arbitrary actions, stupidity, and in thousands of cases vice itself ruled from the throne and its entourage. For this purpose, darkest ignorance was encouraged, and the study of natural rights and the rights of man was forbidden.

[2] Miguel Ramos Arizpe's views, and a balancing statement by Manuel González Ramírez, are quoted in *México en la Cultura,* supplement to the newspaper *Novedades,* of September 30, 1962.

Looking back upon history, a present-day Mexican commentator, Manuel González Ramírez, is driven by common honesty to balance this picture:

> Two races are mixed in our social being: one suffering the punishment of defeat; the other with the pride of victory. But we should not deprecate one in order to extol the other. . . . The conquest would have been unfruitful if there had not later come missionaries, businessmen, naturalists, metallurgists, and in fact all who from that time to this have by their work and blood renewed the old Spanish roots among us. However, though recognizing the very humane activities of the missionaries, we should remember also that in the mines, workshops, *encomiendas*, sugar usines, and fields, the treatment of the Negroes, Indians, and [lower] castes constitutes the classical exploitation of man by man.

Injustices and abuses there obviously were. Nevertheless, during three centuries of rule Spain had given of her best brains and shrewdest administrators to the colonies. Indeed, if she had kept more at home it is just possible that the break-up of the empire might have been delayed, although the factors working against this were many and complex. The new liberalism, the French Revolution, the increasing economic power of Britain and of Scottish masonry (which had a strong hold particularly in South America): all these were forces that combined with growing Creole self-assurance to make change inevitable. Americans like to think it was their own independence movement that triggered off rebellion throughout the New World. It would probably be truer to say that all the hemisphere independence movements arose out of profound changes in the climate of European thought. Latin American independence wars were fought not by the indigenous peoples but by Creoles. Spaniards were turning against Spaniards, churchmen against the reactionary elements in the Church.

In Mexico, as we have seen, there had long been irreconcilable differences between the friars and the powers of the Church in Europe; between the Spanish governors and the Inquisition; between soldiers and administrators; between honest men with a vision of what this new continent could in time bring forth, and fatuous parasites regarding it as their playground.

In 1493 the Spanish Pope, Alexander VI, had believed himself empowered by divine right to grant the territories of the Americas "out of sheer bounty" to Ferdinand and Isabella; and the following year the famous *Inter Caetera* had drawn an imaginary line a hundred leagues west of the Azores and Cape Verde Islands, dividing sovereign rights in the New World between Portugal and Spain.

In those days the legality of Papal Bulls, even when with such divine and arbitrary nonchalance they apportioned the wealth of the earth, went unquestioned. But between the fifteenth and the end of the eighteenth centuries a number of things had happened, including Martin Luther, Henry VIII, Galileo, Descartes, Jean-Jacques Rousseau, and the French Revolution. Spanish intellectuals who had emigrated or had served in office in the New World were not so out of touch with their homelands that they could remain unaffected by new trends of thought. The *Inter Caetera* line began to look man-made and faded. It could stand neither rational inspection nor attack from idealists emotionally enflamed by the new cry of freedom, fraternity, and equality.

INDEPENDENCE Throughout Latin America the independence movements began—nominally at least—with a royalist program of support for Ferdinand VII against Napoleon. Napoleon had imprisoned the reigning Spanish monarch, Charles IV, and also the heir Ferdinand. Charles abdicated in favor of his son. Joseph Bonaparte had been placed by his brother on the throne of Spain. The Council of Mexico City, mostly rich Creoles, took Ferdinand's side. It mattered less to them that the Bourbons were by now weak, reactionary, and completely under the thumb of Godoy, than that Ferdinand had been summarily removed from the Spanish throne by a despot who seemed to want all Europe for himself—and possibly the Americas as well.

By a curious twist which was less accidental than it seemed, for it showed how deeply the new thought had penetrated, the loyalist program of the Creoles became the excuse for insurrection. The *Audiencia* insisted that it had still power to rule in the king's name, but the Creoles argued that the *Audiencia* and the Viceroy had lost authority at the moment when Ferdinand was jailed. Spanish towns had set up committees to rule until Ferdinand could be restored to his throne, and the Mexican Creoles wanted to do the same. The

Viceroy, José de Iturrigaray, had a sneaking notion that it might be as well not to offend the Creoles, who looked powerful and might well be on the verge of establishing a new régime. He sat on the fence.

Alarm grew among the Spaniards, who approached a sugar grower in Morelos, Gabriel Yermo, to lead them in revolt against their Viceroy. On September 15, 1808, the rebels entered the palace, arrested Iturrigaray, and replaced him by a Viceroy of their own choosing, General Pedro de Garibay. Although it had no legal power to do so, the *Audiencia* recognized the change. Lesley Byrd Simpson[3] says that from this moment "the *coup d'état* was to be the thing, and legality merely a cloak to cover rule by force."

As we have seen, however, illegality had entered long before, with Nuño de Guzmán. What the *Audiencia's coup d'état* established was rather a hypersensitive emotional approach to law, whether to its observance or its flaunting. Conservatives and liberals alike became, so to speak, jurisprudence-minded, and the game of splitting legal hairs came to seem as gentlemanly as chess. Octavio Paz[4] says of the liberals:

> . . . their criticism of the order of things was directed less toward a change of reality than toward a change of legislation. Almost all of them believed, with an optimism inherited from the Encylopedia, that to transform reality it was sufficient to pass new laws.

Thus there grew up an ambivalence created by the pull between lawfulness and self-interest. It can be noticed today in the endless discussions about exactly who may exploit Mexico's subsoil resources, and on what terms; in the proud fondness of Mexicans for their Constitution and for such unique (they say) concepts as *amparo* (which in broad terms is a variant on *habeas corpus*[5]);

[3] Simpson, Lesley Byrd. *Many Mexicos*. University of California Press, Berkeley and Los Angeles, 1959, p. 185.

[4] Paz, Octavio. *The Labyrinth of Solitude: Life and Thought in Mexico*. Translated by Lysander Kemp from the original *Laberinto de la Soledad*. Grove Press, New York and Evergreen Books, London, 1961, p. 124.

[5] Oddly, at an international law congress in Mexico in 1964, not a single Mexican delegate produced a paper on *amparo*, though in debate they claimed it to be broader than *habeas corpus* since it applies not only to human freedoms but to all legal cases except the most serious crimes. Against this, *habeas corpus* can be put into operation more quickly than *amparo*. The feeling of non-Latin delegates was that the value of *amparo*, however evident theoretically, has still to be proved in practice in a country where arbitrary legal procedures are too often the rule.

in the baffling procedures involved in approaches to government departments, whether for simple information or a permit to import. The *mordida* (bite, bribe), and the blatant contravention of regulations by people who believe themselves sufficiently privileged to get away with it, are merely the converse of this overriding preoccupation with law.

Back in 1808 the *Audiencia's* coup became an excuse for a revolt that was only nominally loyalist, although it probably never occurred to the militant insurgent priest, Miguel Hidalgo, that he was aiding and abetting subversion. It was one of those moments when a blind urge to survival takes possession of an inarticulate people. Slogans and leaders were thrown up that would serve as makeshifts until somebody should think out more coherent aims. Octavio Paz[6] says:

> . . . the war began as a protest against the abuses of the metropolis and the Spanish bureaucracy, but it was also, and primarily, a protest against the great native landholders. It was not a rebellion of the local aristocracy against the metropolis but of the people against the former. Therefore the revolutionaries gave greater importance to certain social reforms than to Independence itself. Hidalgo proclaimed the abolition of slavery and Morelos broke up the great estates. The Revolution of Independence was a class war, and its nature cannot be understood correctly unless we recognize the fact that, unlike what happened in South America, it was an agrarian revolt in gestation.

This, of course, is retrospective judgment, and it is doubtful whether Miguel Hidalgo or any of the insurgents could have seen the war in that light in the troubled years between 1808 and 1811.

A military captain, Ignacio Allende, was to have given the first call to a royal, loyal, and thoroughly Spanish independence; but the news of the plot leaked out. Allende informed Hidalgo, priest of the little village of Dolores. On September 15 he raised the banner: "Long live Religion. Long live our Most Holy Mother of Guadalupe. Long live Ferdinand VII. Long live America and death to the bad government." This was too long-winded for the populace, who changed it, with results probably unforeseen by Hidalgo and

[6] Paz, Octavio. *Op. cit.*, p. 123.

much bloodier than he intended, to, "Long live Our Lady of Guadalupe! Death to the *Gachupines!*" (Spaniards).

At the head of 50,000 insurgents, Hidalgo and Allende together marched on Guanajuato, where a large granary, the Alhóndiga, had been converted by Spanish loyalists into a strong point. The insurgents had been crudely armed with home-made lances, swords, and machetes (only very few had carbines or pistols). They were accompanied by wives and children and were an unwieldy, rag-taggle lot. Such was the strength of their passion, however, that the Alhóndiga defenders were massacred; and Hidalgo, the obscure curate who ran a pottery establishment, grew grapes and mulberries for wine and silk, and taught the villagers music, found himself at the head of a victorious and vengeful army. In spite of his total ignorance of strategy he was a more inspiring figure than Allende, especially to the peasants who loved him for his bounty and thought of him as their priest and father.

But Hidalgo wavered. Instead of taking Mexico City he retired to Guadalajara. By the time Allende assumed command, strategic damage had been done. Besides, the Creoles became alarmed at the violence of the insurrection and left the peasant armies in the lurch. Hidalgo was unable to control his men, who plundered the crops and killed the cattle. Though the priest's brother, Mariano, tried to organize a treasury and to distribute provisions in an orderly way, there was little he could do against the force of the unschooled rabble. For lack of trained officers, unequipped soldiers had to be raised to high ranks. Such an army could not long endure against the disciplined Spanish regulars. Hidalgo and Allende were caught and shot. Before dying, the priest recanted of his "heresies," but it availed him nothing for he was posthumously anathematized.

It is said that a Bishop once inquired of Hidalgo what method he favored for selecting the best mulberry leaves for feeding to silkworms; to which the priest replied that he chose them haphazard since the silkworms would eat them all anyway. "Ah," said the Bishop, "the revolution is very like that."

Nevertheless, those who remained after Hidalgo's death were undaunted by the sanguinary turn of events. José María Morelos, friend and pupil of Miguel Hidalgo, continued the struggle. Lucas Alamán writes of this sturdy man that he had "only eternity before his eyes." With little of Hidalgo's fanaticism, with greater military skill, especially in guerrilla warfare, with courage to fight on through pain and adversity, and with sounder statesmanship than his teacher, he succeeded in formulating the principles which—as we have already seen—have motivated every Mexican reform and revolution since his day. America (not Mexico alone, be it noted) was to be declared independent of Spain or any other foreign power. No other religion was to be tolerated except Roman Catholicism, but the Church was to be supported by tithes only, and every other source of revenue must be abolished. Regular orders were to be condemned, and the only interpreters of Catholic dogma were to be the secular hierarchy. Sovereignty was to reside in the people and to be exercised by them through their elected representatives; and the government was to be divided into three departments: legislative, executive, and juridical. None but Mexican citizens could aspire to government employment, and in all walks of life the only foreigners who would be tolerated were skilled mechanics without political affiliations, who could teach necessary trades.

Slavery, caste distinctions, and torture under law were to end. Laws were to be applied to all alike. The right to possess property was declared sacred, and a man's home inviolate. Government monopolies must be abolished, together with sales taxes and tributes. An income tax of 5 per cent and a 10 per cent import duty would, it was hoped, fill the treasury coffers.

In 1815, abandoned by the Creoles, this hard-thinking priest who suffered from migraine and permanently wore a kerchief bound round his forehead, was in his turn captured, anathematized, and shot. But his principles were to survive the cynical, self-seeking leaders who came after him and were to be re-enunciated by Benito Juárez. They were to survive Porfirian positivism, and were to be resuscitated in 1910. In them we find the anti-clericalism, the nationalism, the total lack of color bar or color prejudice, and the idealistic yearning for an all-too-elusive freedom which continue to inform Mexican policies. The next 150 years were to sound variants on these impassioned themes.

General Vicente Guerrero took up the cause of Morelos, and the ambitious and conservative Colonel Augustín Iturbide persuaded him to join forces in the declaration known as the *Plan de Iguala*, published in 1821. It was a temporizing scheme designed to placate all parties. It proclaimed Mexico's independence under a limited monarchy, and it sought to retain close ties between America and Europe. It proposed equal treatment for Spaniards and Creoles. The army was to be the custodian of guarantees, and the Catholic Church the supreme ruler over morals.

The "three guarantees" (Spain, the Catholic Church, and national independence) were symbolized in the red, white, and green of the Mexican flag, though few Mexicans today care to remember the original significance of the three colors. The stripes of the flag were at first horizontal but were later changed to the perpendicular in order to widen the white band and make room upon it for the ancient Aztec symbol of the eagle on the nopal cactus. Thus today, with Spain in the doghouse and the Catholic Church officially non-existent, the flag may be said to stand for the two traditions that have blended in modern Mexico (European and pre-Columbian), for spiritual values, and for independence.

Nineteenth-century independence was achieved, ironically enough, through the efforts of a proud and ambitious royalist. According to Iturbide's plan, Mexico was to be turned into a monarchy under a Bourbon prince. It was a scheme similar to one projected between Bernardo O'Higgins in Chile and San Martín in Argentina as a gesture of fidelity to Europe and a snub to the meddling U.S. Ambassador Joel Poinsett, whose chief claim to fame is that he introduced into the United States the Christmas flower named after him—poinsettia. Neither the Mexican nor the Argentine-Chilean scheme prospered, and instead of becoming democratic monarchies (which they might by a hair's breadth have been), Latin American countries have been fated to suffer the despotism of pseudo-republican presidents more absolute in power than most royalty has been since the mid-nineteenth century.

Iturbide's plan was the signal for freedom movements in Central America, and the independence of the "kingdom" of Guatemala was declared on September 15, 1821. It was an uneasy victory, with so much dissension among the contending factions that the annexation of Guatemala by Mexico was accomplished before anybody had had time to notice what was happening. The whole Central American area was then given a choice, of remaining with Mexico or of separating into smaller units. Chiapas, now Mexico's most southern State, opted to remain. The rest split off and formed five—and later six—separate countries (Guatemala, El Salvador, Honduras, Nicaragua, Costa Rica, and Panama). For a variety of reasons—they have been too small, too weak, too quarrelsome—four of them remain backward and troubled to this day. Intermittently the United States and Mexico have tried to patch up their disputes, but with little success, the United States always at risk of being branded (with some justification) "imperialist" and "interventionist."

Under the Central American Common Market the prognosis for these countries is now more favorable. But if Mexico had had a more acceptable leader at the time of her independence, the unity of the whole territory from Mexico's northern border to the Isthmus of Panama might have been assured a century and a half ago. As things turned out, in May of 1822 Iturbide had been proclaimed emperor—Agustín I—and, much in the manner of Caesar on the Capitol, had coyly accepted the crown. There had even been portents and good omens at this self-appointed emperor's birth; but alas, for him, though his accession to the throne had been acclaimed with jubilation, the people were fickle as they had been in Caesar's day and by December of the same year he was in exile. When he tried to return in 1824, in spite of having been declared a traitor by Congress, he was shot. His conqueror was Antonio López de Santa Ana. Iturbide, a complicated character who might have done much for his country if he could have kept personal ambition in check, died proudly and well, probably sincere in his belief that he might have saved his country from radical extremes. His disciple, Lucas Alamán, who had witnessed the Alhóndiga massacres and the easy tinder of crowd emotions, certainly thought that a responsible aristocracy, and not an unruly democracy, could be Latin America's salvation; and he seems to have believed that Iturbide—ambition and all—was the man who could have established sane government.

Although Mexico had shown she would have no truck with monarchs, she was very far from having become rid of uncrowned tyrants. Indeed, in the figures that dominated the independence movement and the new republic, we find prototypes of Mexican heroes and villains for a century and more to come: Hidalgo, idealistic, unrealistic, with a streak of fanaticism; Morelos, upright and legal with great physical stamina; Guadalupe Victoria, a harmless figure-head set up as first President of the Republic; Iturbide, ambitious and vain; and Santa Ana, treacherous and posturing.

If Lucas Alamán, called "a Metternich in Indian lands," a sensitive, honest anti-Jacobin, had been able to oppose Santa Ana more effectively, the history of the next fifty years might have been different. Alamán, appointed Iturbide's Foreign Minister in 1823 at the tender age of twenty-eight, affected a Parisian accent and wore green spectacles to make himself look older, though his eyesight was good. He deeply admired British conservatism, British law, and British lawns (whose seeds he introduced into Mexico). He did not, however, favor the parliamentary system; and he thought that freedom of expression was an error since a free Press would merely deceive the gullible public. In spite of his general disapproval of the United States, he admired the way that country had established independence while yet retaining traditional institutions and ideals inherited from Europe. He was convinced that any attempt to cut adrift from Europe and from the *Plan de Iguala* guarantees, and to impose an exaggerated liberalism, would in the end be Mexico's downfall.[7]

Believing the United States to be already too powerful on the continent, Alamán opposed American plans for a canal through the Isthmus of Tehuantepec. He persuaded Canning to recognize Mexico's independence, and signed a commercial treaty with Britain: acts which did not endear him to Joel Poinsett who had appointed himself guardian of Latin America. In an attempt to balance power, Alamán pleaded for the importation of foreign capital and technologists (preferably not American). In spite of his personal affectations and vanities, he was too hard-headed, too realistic, to be popular; and though he was careful to keep strictly to the principles of Morelos he was charged quite correctly with being a monarchist —proclerical, pro-Spanish—and was forced to resign.

By helping to defeat Alamán, Poinsett secured a victory over Britain which was to leave Mexico extremely vulnerable to pressure from its colossal northern neighbor. Curiously, and perhaps with unintentioned and ironical naïveté, Adlai Stevenson on a visit to

[7] Alamán, Lucas. *Semblanzas e Ideario*. Prologue and Selection by Arturo Arnáiz y Freg. Mexican National University, second edition, 1963, p. 113.

Mexico called this scheming politician (who figures in the "rogues gallery" mural in the Mexican Senate), "the first example of the good neighbor policy."

Back in the government in 1831, with the pendulum swinging again to the conservatives, Alamán was partly responsible for putting General Vicente Guerrero before the firing squad. It was a sign of the times that a statesman of integrity should have believed that the old insurgent warrior's death was essential for maintaining order.

Opposed to Alamán stood Valentín Gómez Farías and Miguel Ramos Arizpe. In 1824 they drew up the first Mexican Constitution, largely inspired by that of the United States and in many ways unsuited to Mexico, as Alamán and Fray Servando Teresa y Mier both understood. (The latter, a Dominican friar who for his political views was fated to join the heroic little band of Mexican excommunicated priests, spent a large part of his life as a refugee from one kind of régime or another and finally, having renounced his vows, became a deputy in the Mexican Congress.)

The creation of nineteen independent States on the American pattern established an arbitrary and fatal sense of separateness in a country that needed unity first and foremost. Besides this, the ruling that the defeated candidate for the presidency should become vice-president was soon proved totally impracticable, and the office of vice-president was later abolished.

At the time, however, it seemed to the liberals that a federation of states and a division of control between parties would insure that power did not fall into the hands of the rich merchants and miners. Centralism became equated with reaction, and a form of government was thus established that still today retards the development of *cacique*-ridden areas far from the capital. With air flight shrinking distances, federalism becomes ever more of an anachronism, but it continues to be championed today for no better reason than that it has been written into the Constitution and must stand forever. For a revolutionary country, Mexico is often oddly tied to tradition.

The two planes of Mexican life—reality on the one hand, legislation on the other (which Octavio Paz notes and condemns)—were fortified by this first Constitution. "The effect," wrote Samuel Ramos,[8] "consists of an unfolding of our life on two separate planes, one real and the other fictitious." He goes on to quote the Peruvian Francisco García Calderón:

> The actual development of Ibero-American democracies differs remarkably from the admirable spirit of their political charters. These contain all the principles of government that have been applied by the great European nations, balance of powers, natural rights, liberal suffrage, representative assemblies. But reality contradicts the idealism of these statutes imported from Europe. The traditions of the dominating race have created oversimplified and barbarous systems of government.

The ideals were originally from Europe it is true, but they arrived in Latin America via the United States; and no provision was made for the entirely different psychology that prevailed south of the Río Grande.

The new idealism, however, was not always ineffective. José María Luís Mora, right hand to Gómez Farías, established in "the Imperial and Most Ancient College of St. Peter, St. Paul, and St. Ildefonso of the City of Mexico" the first course in economics to be given in the new republic. Though he began life as a priest, Mora's liberal views led him to become one of the most forthright critics of the clergy. "Every Mexican should ask himself daily," he said, "whether the people exist for the clergy, or whether the clergy has been created to satisfy the needs of the people"; or again, "In every country where social and religious duties are confounded, it is almost impossible to establish the foundations of public morality." Seven centuries after Becket and Henry II had confronted each other over the boundaries of Church and State, and three after the Reformation, Mora led an almost exactly parallel struggle to fix just bounds between human and divine law. It was a strange twist of fate that he should find himself on the opposite side from Canning and the British in the subtle contest being waged in Latin America. By all logic, Britain should have been with the liberals. Britain and the United States were struggling over Latin Amercian heads for control of the area's trade; but beneath this greedy battle

[8] Ramos, Samuel. *Profile of Man and Culture in Mexico.* Translated by Peter G. Earle, introduction by Thomas B. Irving, University of Texas Press, 1962.

there was another and more important, for principles. In the elections of 1828 the centralists won, apparently putting Britain in the ascendant. Unfortunately, it was Santa Ana who—after some judicious periods of retirement while knotty problems sorted themselves out—took command.

This tragi-comic figure thumps through Mexican history on a cork leg, one of flesh and blood having been lost to the French when they tried to capture the Veracruz customs house in lieu of payment for outstanding debts. The artificial limb had its uses. It aroused the sympathy and patriotism upon which its owner was able to call when, after a period of exile in Cuba in 1824, he returned to Mexico to lead the military campaign against the United States during the Texan war.

Together with California, Nevada, New Mexico, and Arizona, Texas was a part of Mexican territory. These were pre-oil days, and Texas seemed an arid and undesirable corner of the globe, fit only to be populated by religious minorities in search of freedom to worship as they pleased. Before Mexico's independence, it had been planned to found colonies of Roman Catholic Americans on this arid soil. In 1821 the Mexican government consented, and 300 families led by Moses Austin and his son Stephen, settled there on the assumption that they were to become Mexican citizens.

So far so good. But Protestants followed Catholics, and the Protestants were determined to remain American. By 1827 there were at least 12,000 U.S. citizens in Texas. Mexico passed laws to prevent further immigration. The American Texans, annoyed, declared their independence and asked the United States for help. On March 6, 1836, the tiny Alamo Mission Station of San Antonio was besieged by Santa Ana's troops and its defenders killed; but the Americans had their revenge in a battle on the San Jacinto River in which Santa Ana's army was annihilated in fifteen minutes. Texas, proclaimed the Lone Star Republic, waited nine years before being admitted to the United States on March 1, 1845.

At this the Mexican government, with 20,000 active soldiers and 24,000 officers (armies tend to be top-heavy in Latin America) declared war. Santa Ana, who after the Texas massacres had suffered another period of exile, returned again, and, in the guise of a liberal democrat, coyly accepted the presidency.

Though the Mexican coffers were empty, Santa Ana managed to lead his army 300 miles from San Luís Potosí to Buena Vista, where he met General Zachary Taylor on February 22, 1846. Four thousand Mexicans had been lost on the march from desertion, hunger, disease, and bitter cold. In the battle, Santa Ana's killed and wounded totaled 1500. Yet somehow he withdrew with the remnants of an army intact. His soldiering was remarkable.

Americans under Winfield Scott landed at Veracruz and marched on Mexico City, stormed the heights of Chapultepec whence the nine cadets known as the Child Heroes fell to their deaths rather than surrender; and by the Treaty of Guadalupe Hidalgo, on February 2, 1848, Mexico lost all claim to half her territory in return for 15 million dollars paid into the bankrupt treasury. In the museum in Chapultepec the loudspeakers still harangue the Americans for this act of spoliation, and Robert F. Kennedy has admitted publicly—to the fury of Texans—that the whole war was unjustified. According to Mexicans, "the only friends that this country has ever had in this shameful affair" are Robert Kennedy, Abraham Lincoln, and Ulysses Grant.

After the war Santa Ana retired in self-imposed exile to Venezuela. Benito Juárez, who was then governor of the State of Oaxaca, had refused him asylum and was to pay for this disrespect when Santa Ana returned still once more to Mexico in 1853. He came, it was supposed, to rescue the country from the chaos into which it had been thrown by the American war; but he forced Juárez to flee to New Orleans where the future president of Mexico earned his living making cigarettes.

Juárez and his supporters need not have worried. Santa Ana's days were ending and his posturing was hollow and pathetic. In 1855 he was defeated by an Indian rebellion. He conspired both against Maximilian and against Juárez, who banished him from the country in 1867. In 1874 he returned once more—he was nothing if not resilient—but his time was near its end and he died in 1876.

Since 1855 the liberals had been in the ascendant, and the moderate Ignacio Comonfort joined with the Jacobins in a ruthless anti-clerical campaign. Juárez, back from New Orleans but not yet president, formulated a law restricting the jurisdiction of ecclesiastical courts to ecclesiastical cases. The storm that followed led to still harsher measures in the *Ley Lerdo,* designed to force the sale of Church lands and to abolish communal holdings in favor of small proprietors. In 1867 Gómez Farías, now aging, was the first to sign a new Constitution introduced by Juárez. Congress had certain powers over the State governments; military and clerical immunities were abolished; corporations were forbidden to own land; nuns and priests could renounce their vows if they wished; and secular education was established.

Pope Pius IX complained that the Mexican Chamber of Deputies was corrupting manners and tearing away souls from religion. He believed he had the right "to condemn, reprove, and declare null and void the said decrees and everything else that the civil authority has done in scorn of ecclesiastical authority. . . ." Not for nothing have Mexicans accused their clergy of being emissaries of a foreign and meddling power. The Papacy, which had once distributed the lands of the New World, seemed now equally convinced of its divine right to alter a free country's Constitution. The town of Puebla, a Roman Catholic stronghold, championed the cause of Rome. Comonfort was elected president, but after an unsuccessful attempt to avoid controversial issues he fled from impending trouble, and Mexico was again plunged into war. Benito Juárez now led the anti-clerical, anti-army, left-wing faction. This Zapotec Indian, who had abandoned a theological seminary in favor of law, was to become the Abraham Lincoln of Mexican history, the backwoods boy made good, the champion of democracy, humorless but upright.

During his New Orleans exile he had sat at the feet of the liberal Melchor Ocampo, with whom he was later to quarrel and who, together with another great liberal, Santos Degollado, was to be shot by General Leonardo Márquez, one of Maximilian's supporters. Now, with Comonfort in voluntary exile in New York, Juárez took over the presidency of a government banished from its own capital. He strengthened the offending 1857 Constitution by announcing complete separation of Church and State (the date should be noted, for modern writers on Mexico sometimes talk as if disestablishment had resulted from the church wars of Calles in the twenties of this century). All male religious orders were secularized, and religious bodies were suppressed, together with novitiates in nunneries. In logical extension of the principles of independence formulated by Morelos, Church property was nationalized and tithes abolished.

From Veracruz Juárez fought and defeated the conservatives under Generals Miramón, Mejía, and Márquez, and on January 1, 1861, he entered the capital in a triumph that was short-lived. Trade and agriculture were ruined, Mexico's international standing was at low ebb, and France, Spain, and Britain were pressing for payment of debts. They formed an alliance with intent to seize and hold Mexican ports until their claims had been met.

However, plotting with right-wing Mexicans, and without the knowledge of either Britain or Spain, Napoleon III persuaded Archduke Maximilian of Austria to accept the non-existent Mexican throne. British and Spanish forces withdrew; and on January 7, 1862, a French division landed alone in Veracruz.

Maximilian seems to have been an idealist, duped by Napoleon and by his own wife, Carlotta, into believing that Mexicans needed and wanted him. But Juárez showed no mercy toward this madcap venture to rehabilitate a country whose only request for help had been made through enemies of the government in power. He declared war. One of the great battles in Mexican history was fought outside Puebla on May 5, 1862, and the French General Laurencez was defeated by the Mexicans under Ignacio Zaragoza. The French then reinforced their troops to a total of 34,000, and these were joined by 20,000 conservative Mexicans. The Juárez Mexicans resorted to guerrilla warfare, with such success that it was not until May 28, 1864, that Maximilian and Carlotta could safely land at Veracruz. Maximilian received a cold reception. Garibaldi sent a message to "the brave officers who fought for Mexican freedom" on the liberal side. Europe was far from being indifferent in a struggle that was clearly an extension of the profound schism between the new philosophies of democracy and the divine rights of kings. Maximilian labeled Juárez and his soldiers "bandits," and announced that all who took up arms in the outlawed cause would be put to death.

Just then the American Civil War came to an end. With the North victorious, a U.S. army sat glowering at the French from the

U.S.-Mexican border. Napoleon had reason to be nervous; and deciding that Maximilian was expendable he ordered his commander-in-chief, Bazaine, to retire. Puebla was captured by the young Porfirio Díaz, and Maximilian withdrew to Querétaro from where he watched his army massacred at Cerro de las Campanas. Together with the conservative Mexican generals Miramón and Mejía, he faced the firing squad on June 19, 1867 (Márquez and other imperialist leaders had fled to Havana).

Manet's retelling of the scene is economical. The broad, quiet brushstrokes are profoundly ironical, for Maximilian's death was a warning to Europe—and to the United States besides—that Mexico would tolerate no more crowned heads or foreign meddlers of any political persuasion whatever.

FROM DICTATORSHIP TO REVOLUTION By the time Juárez died in 1872 he had brought Mexico back to lawfulness and stability; but he had also—through no personal ambition—vested dangerously absolute power in the person of the President. He was succeeded first by Sebastián Lerdo de Tejada, during whose short presidency the British-built railway from Veracruz to Mexico City was opened. Accused of tyranny by Díaz (of all people!) he was forced to flee the country in 1876, and the long Porfirian "reign" began. It was to extend almost unbroken from 1877 to 1911. Díaz did not lack high qualities, but he stayed too long. Juan Sánchez Azcona,[9] an opponent of the dictator in his later period, wrote:

> Porfirio Díaz is one of the greatest personalities with whom I have had dealings. He was a glorious soldier . . . had great powers of statesmanship, and was a great Mexican. His continuance in power . . . caused him to commit such big and important mistakes, especially in his later period, that his retirement was essential to the nation. Although I in no way repent of all I did to bring about the defeat of Porfirio Díaz, I remember him with deep respect, and it vexes me that in our day there should be . . . revolutionaries who rant against him without cause. . . .

Like many Latin American dictators, Díaz brought fabulous prosperity to the upper classes, who lived in a state of drowsy euphoria,

[9] Extracts from memoirs published in *México en la Cultura (Novedades)*, September 30, 1962.

cushioned by the smug architecture of positivism, French chic, a foreign-dominated economy, and a foreign and prosperous clergy. Scientists, economists, and writers were encouraged, but the common people were dragooned by a band of thugs known as the *rurales*. Political prisoners cultivated *henequén* in Yucatán (where *hacendados* were amassing fortunes) and tobacco in Oaxaca; but it was not long before the massacres of the so-called "caste wars" in Yucatán and Chiapas had seriously depleted the labor force.

In Yucatán the wars led to tacit renunciation by Mexico of rights to the disputed British territory of Belice (British Honduras). In 1825 and 1826 treaties of "friendship, commerce, and navigation" had been drawn up between the two countries. In these documents there are suggestions that Britain acknowledged Belice to be part of Mexican territory, although Mexico conceded to British subjects the right to continue the timber-felling which had begun with a concession from Spain in 1783.

By Porfirian times, footloose adventurers from Belice were finding it profitable to carry on a traffic in arms with the discontented Indians. Complaints from Mexico led to the treaty of 1893, in which Mexico recognized a demarcation line between her territory and Belice; and the *hacendados* were lulled.

In 1910 the centenary of Mexican independence was to be celebrated with fitting pomp. Nobody heeded the mutterings of young liberals, of the Yucatecan Felipe Carrillo Puerto, or the quite unknown Francisco Madero whose little book called *The Presidential Succession in 1910* was causing a minor stir. It was absurd to think that a régime that had endured now for thirty-four years could be dislodged by nonentities.

Magnanimously, and with no intention of keeping his word nor any suspicion that he might be forced to do so, Porfirio Díaz had told an American journalist, James Creelman, that he intended to retire in 1910. The small, physically weak Francisco Madero, with a partiality for spiritualism, was seized with the convenient notion that if the office of vice-president were revived he himself might be a suitable candidate. Such near-seditious thoughts were motive enough for clapping him into jail, and a Díaz puppet, Ramón Corral, was given the job instead.

The causes of unrest went much deeper than even the little spiritualist realized. In spite of the lavishness of independence-day celebrations, there were signs of trouble. Pascual Orozco, the more famous Doroteo Arango (better known as Pancho Villa), and Emiliano Zapata were taking up arms. The following year Madero found himself almost reluctantly pushed into leadership. Díaz, threatened with a forced resignation, hastily recalled his Treasury Minister, José Limantour, who had been touring Europe. Limantour realized that the tide could no longer be held back, and he and Justo Sierra (another of Porfirio's Ministers and one of Mexico's most respected historians and philosophers) tried to persuade the old dictator that graceful retirement would be the sensible course. But Díaz, stubborn to the end, ordered the guards of the national palace to fire on the protesting crowds. Two hundred people had been killed before he would accept defeat and exile to the Paris he loved.

Madero was now President, but his triumph was brief; for the American Ambassador Henry Lane Wilson intervened to protect American business interests. The United States' tool was Victoriano Huerta, who was persuaded to rise against Madero, take him into custody, and have him shot while "attempting to escape."

If Huerta had hoped for American support, he was to be disillusioned. The revolution, which had begun as a genuine popular movement with Madero as a convenient figurehead, lacked any leader strong enough to hold together all the self-seekers who were crowding in for a share of the spoils. Pancho Villa campaigned in the north. The ascetic peasant land reformer, Emiliano Zapata, harried the gentry on the high central plateau and down into the temperate lands about Cuernavaca, until he was betrayed and shot by an opponent masquerading as one of his own peasant army. Venustiano Carranza formulated his "Plan of Guadalupe" to restore the Constitution of 1857, and joined forces with Alvaro Obregón who had been schooling the wild Yaqui Indians of the northwest into the semblance of an army. Jealousies were soon wreaking havoc among the various factions, with Obregón playing Carranza against Villa, and Villa making uneasy terms with Zapata. Carranza's role in the revolution has lately been called in question, and there is evidence that he had little sympathy with those who wanted agrarian and other economic reforms. He adopted a revolutionary program only under duress and to insure his own popularity.

Huerta lost his only ally when Ambassador Wilson was recalled to Washington. Wilson's replacement, John Lind, did not take kindly to Huerta, and the United States began passing arms across the border to the troops of Carranza, Villa, and Obregón in return for stolen cattle. In 1914 U. S. Marines landed at Veracruz in an act of intervention which in retrospect looks like a dress rehearsal for the colossal blunder of the Cuban invasion. Somehow or other, possibly through an erroneous assessment of the situation by Ambassador Lind, more probably because the United States has a weakness for regarding itself as a kind of knight errant to Latin republics in distress, President Woodrow Wilson had become convinced that the main revolutionary movement in Mexico would welcome U.S. intervention. Imagine Wilson's surprise when he was accused jointly by Huerta (still President of Mexico) and Carranza (self-styled First Chief of the Revolution) of violating the Treaty of Guadalupe Hidalgo. In July Obregón entered Mexico City with his triumphant troops singing the revolution song *La Cucaracha,* and Huerta fled to Europe. When he tried to return to the United States his American friends thanked him by jailing him in Fort Bliss, where he died.

Carranza, entering Mexico City on Obregón's heels, became President. The United States, who throughout the revolution was determined to be on somebody's side but never able to decide whose, withdrew support from Villa, and sent General John J. Pershing over the border in pursuit of him. It was another American blunder and for the time being it turned Villa into a hero. (A son born after Villa was assassinated by his political enemies was for a time a government official in Chihuahua. He talks reverently of his father and says he himself is "believing but not proclergy.")

The final outcome of the muddled active phase of revolution was the Constitution of 1917, drawn up largely by Obregón and General Francisco Mujica, with Carranza standing somewhat doubtfully in the background as convener of the meeting. This Constitution, which is still in force, returned once more to the principles of Morelos and also to the Constitution of 1857. Land is to be restored to the people. The nation must own all subsoil wealth, including petroleum. Article 123 recognizes the workers' rights to organize, strike, bargain collectively, and to receive adequate compensation and sickness benefits. A recent amendment tightens the provision ensuring that workers are not unjustly dismissed, and gives them the right to participate in the profits of industry. Both measures are regarded with the utmost suspicion by American and some Mexican right-wing businessmen.

An Article directed against the clergy has long since gone by default at least in its more rigorous aspects, but it is still on the statute books and presumably could be invoked if the Roman Catholic Church should ever again be regarded as a danger to the government.

Of course, this Constitution was quite uninfluenced by the Bolshevik Revolution. Later a Marxist-Bolshevik twist was given to the Mexican freedom movement, mainly by intellectuals (such as the Mexican muralists and the educationalist Narcisso Bassols) and to some extent by the austere and ascetic President Plutarco Elías Calles; but basically it was a document without any international political line, designed to correct specifically Mexican ills. The Mexican revolution had thus little affinity with the Cuban, dominated almost from the start by international politics.

Unfortunately, the 1917 Constitution was more difficult to implement than its authors had hoped. One of the immediate effects was the persecution of the clergy, the confiscation of churches, and the expulsion of priests. The result was the bitter war of the *Cristeros,* which broke out in 1926 when in Jalisco, Michoacán, and Colima the clergy took to the hills and fought a rearguard guerrilla battle while Calles herded the faithful into concentration camps. There are country priests who still use this war as an excuse for carrying a revolver beneath their surplices, though they fire only upward and innocently, adding to the noisy banging of fireworks on religious feast days. (Rockets have been banned of late in Mexico City, for too many fingers were being blown off.)

An important result of the new Constitution was the formation of a political party which, after several changes of name, survives today as the ruling Partido Revolucionario Institucional (PRI). It had been intended by Calles as an instrument of power through which he could rule under cover of puppets. But, unfortunately for Calles, one of the puppets rebelled and danced to his own tune. Lázaro Cárdenas was docility itself until he became President. Then, having strengthened his position by winning the support of the workers, he deposited his benefactor Calles over the U.S. border, and proceeded to make himself so strong that even today he is the only left-wing leader capable of inspiring general admiration. The Communist Vicente Lombardo Toledano can hold union men and farmers by marathon oratory, but it is Cárdenas, dry and untheatrical, who commands love from the left and the respect and fear of the right. Cárdenas is known for his nationalization of petroleum and railways and for his agrarian reforms, which somehow never quite came off. Land has been returned to the peasants, it is true, but Cárdenas himself admits that his "co-operative farms" have failed because of apathy. Toward the peasants he has a guilty conscience, believing that he should have been able to foresee that they would be released from their former masters, the *hacendados*, only to fall into the clutches of unscrupulous agrarian banks. Cárdenas himself is strictly upright, as humorless as Juárez, a man of tight-lipped integrity whose peasant mind is not always nimble enough to deal with the sly foxes of the right or his more unscrupulous colleagues of the left. Yet he has been able by devotion to his cause to stand his ground. Even his enemies concede him some dry and rather puritan virtues. He is patient, law-abiding, and self-controlled. He performed a service to Republican Spaniards when he gave asylum to 12,000 refugees. The exiles, 80 per cent of whom became naturalized Mexicans, helped the growth of their adopted country's intellectual and professional life through twenty-five formative years.

It was a more doubtful service to have allowed Leon Trotsky into the country after Turkey and France had received this explosive figure with something less than warmth. Trotsky arrived in Mexico in 1937. Together with a number of disciples he exercised an influence over Mexican intellectuals which lasted long after his assassination on the morning of August 20, 1940, when Jacques Mornard entered the closely guarded house in the Mexico City suburb of Coyoacán, and slugged him with an alpine ax. Mexican Stalinists have been cited as accessories in this crime, which did much to perpetuate the anachronistic myth that the Mexican revolution was an offshoot of Bolshevism.

The revolution, having usefully but somewhat haphazardly destroyed a number of withered institutions, was given a respectable front by Manuel Avila Camacho, who put a brake on the more radical reforms and prepared the country for the inevitable slowing down (some would say a direct reversal) of the impulse of 1910. He brought Cárdenas back into the government as Minister of Defense during the 1939–45 war, when Mexico joined the allies against the Axis; but Cárdenas stuck fairly to the job in hand and did not influence the political scene. He has returned as a political figure only in the sixties.

The next régime, that of Miguel Alemán, was criticized for its alleged graft and for too close a friendship with big business interests; but a left-wing Guatemalan refugee in Mexico admits: "We could do with some of Alemán's kind in Central America. He saw to it that money flowed."

Adolfo Ruíz Cortines pledged himself to end graft and corruption in Mexican bureaucracy; but reforms cannot be hurried, and after President Alemán's lavish spending it was not easy for his successor to balance the budget. The peso had to be devalued to 12.50 to the dollar.

Adolfo López Mateos (President from 1958 to 1964) encouraged Mexicans—after their years of introspection—to look further than their own frontiers, especially to the rest of Latin America in a search for economic unity; but also toward growing countries such as the various African nations, India, Indonesia, and Israel—and always, with a mixture of sympathy and resentment, to the United States. He continued to return land to the peasants, and his administration built social security centers that would be the envy of the staff of any Municipal hospital.

Between them the Ruíz Cortines and López Mateos régimes set Mexico firmly on the path toward the welfare state, and if little space is given here to post-Cárdenas Presidents it is because their achievements are an integral part of the new Mexico that will be discussed in all its aspects—political, economic, social, and artistic—in the following chapters. There are people who would put the influence of López Mateos even higher than that of Cárdenas in the shaping of modern Mexico. Certainly he worked indefatigably and wore himself out physically as he toured Mexico and the world, presenting a new image of his country as an important minor power. His wife, Doña Eva Sámano de López Mateos, was a social-welfaring first lady such as Mexico had never known before—selfless in her efforts to relieve the distress of cyclone victims and to give children, mothers, and cripples a better life. No future President of Mexico will be able to forget the example set by these two; and even if he leans slightly more to the right, Gustavo Díaz Ordaz (elected for the term 1964–70) will certainly respect and try to keep continuity with the efforts of his predecessor.

A mural by the Communist David Alfaro Siqueiros, on the National University Rectory building, leaves a date unfilled. After 1520 (conquest), 1810 (independence), 1857 (reform), and 1911 (revolution), there is an enigma: 19??. We are too close to events to tell whether 1960 began a new era. In that year, during the celebrations of 150 years of independence and of the fiftieth anniversary of the fall of Porfirio Díaz, the irreverent were saying that the best way to celebrate one revolution was to have another; but the only visible signs of unrest were a riot or two and some firecrackers exploded under Miguel Alemán's statue at the university. It turned out to be strongly built. It has been patched, and remains, artistically speaking, a blot among the pepper and *colorín* trees and the Mexican-style Corbusier architecture.

In August 1960, just before the anniversary celebrations, David Alfaro Siqueiros and a journalist, Filomeno Mata, together with other agitators, were jailed. Nineteen months later they were found guilty of the somewhat nebulous charge of "social dissolution,"[10] under an emergency law brought in during the Second World War and kept on the statute books precisely to deal with elements blocking the smooth progress toward the industrial-welfare state. It is a law regarded by responsible Mexicans as necessary in a growing country, although perhaps—they will add—the wording requires modification. Taking into account the necessity for curbing irresponsible agitation, freedom of speech is on the whole real; and where Mexicans seem to be muzzled it is not so much through gov-

[10] Siqueiros was released from jail on special pardon in July 1964.

ernment interference as through the timidity of journalists who prefer to display a sycophantic attitude toward their rulers than to exercise their brains on critical analysis. Many revolutionaries are at large and free to harangue the government in the rather scandalous and jejune fortnightly *Política* or in the pink-tinged *Siempre*. It is, however, a cozy characteristic of the intellectual left-wing that its members are the progeny of prosperous middle-class parents. They themselves live in luxurious suburbs, their houses high-walled and equipped with cocktail bars and swimming pools. The peasants, on the other hand, are conservative, disillusioned by politics if indeed they are aware of the meaning of the word. The lower middle-class Mexicans are attracted toward the bright new toys of modern civilization, toward intercoms and visual aids and transistor sets. Factories hum, though not always to full capacity, and there is a vested interest in prosperity. The young and the thoughtful, beset by *inquietudes*, are seized by pangs of conscience when they see the poor barefoot and illiterate, loaded like pack mules, living in hovels with earth floors, untouched by technological magic. But if material prosperity can be eased gently down the social scale till it embraces the humblest village, there is no reason why the bad consciences should once more breed the violence and inter-group hatreds that have been the plague of Mexican history. Mexicans are by nature a gentle people and want peace.

Toward the end of 1961 Miguel Alemán, Lázaro Cárdenas, and the other five living ex-Presidents were safely herded into the administrative fold and given tasks to suit their interests and experiences. General Cárdenas had been causing nervousness by his flirtations with iron-curtain countries and with Fidel Castro. At the head of the commission of the vast undeveloped Balsas River basin, he finds himself able to continue working for the peasants whose interests he has at heart. Miguel Alemán, at the other end of the political spectrum, lifted tourism out of mild depression. Abelardo Rodríguez, once left-wing, now a big business tycoon and said to be the only President to have spoken the U.S.-adulterated *pocho* Spanish of the northern border, is reorganizing the hitherto somewhat desultory fishing industry. Emilio Portes Gil, severely autochthonous and formerly Mexico's first Ambassador to India, is president of the National Insurance Commission. Adolfo Ruíz Cortines is with the government financing agency, Nacional Financiera, and Pascual Ortíz Rubio was government liaison officer to the architects and engineers until his death in November 1963. Roque González Garza, who is coordinating the public works in part of Hidalgo State, served his brief term in 1915, which shows remarkable continuity in government.

It is rare in Latin America for ex-Presidents to live, let alone work, with succeeding administrations. Mexico, with the caballistic seven safely herded into the fold of government orthodoxy, is looking impressively firm.

4 *Modern Mexicans and How They Live*

To the question "Who is a Mexican?" we have had a historical answer. There are full-blooded Indians, and Spanish descendants of those early soldiers, lawyers and swag-hunters who came with mixed motives to the New World; *Mestizos* derived from free union between Spaniards and Indians; Negroes and mixed Indian-Negroes; children of Spanish-republican and other European refugees of this century; ranchers, bureaucrats, teachers, small tradesmen, captains of industry, sweepstakes vendors, bootblacks with "Social Justice" written on their overalls; marketeers in brown holland overalls and forage caps; left-wing intellectuals; beatniks and bourgeois, rich and poor. It is a medley of race, creed, and color, with tolerance for all.

At the time of independence Mexico was a sparsely populated country of about 4.5 million including those living in the large slice of land later ceded to the United States. It was seventy or eighty years before the population had even doubled; but by 1895, the year of the first official national census, the count was 12.6 million. The population continued to increase slowly to 13.6 million in 1900, and to 15.2 million in 1910. During the active period of revolution it fell, but by 1930 it had reached 16.5 million, and from then on it accelerated abruptly. At the 1960 census there were 34.9 million people in Mexico, and Gilberto Loyo[1] calculates that by 1975 there will be 53.3 million.

Peasants have been crowding into the towns so that the urban population, which was only 12.2 per cent of the whole in 1900,

[1] Loyo, Gilberto. *La Población de México: Estado Actual y Tendencias, 1950–80.* Article in *Investigación Económica,* Mexico City, 1960, p. 28.

is now estimated at between 38 and 51 per cent. About one-third of the people are economically active, and this figure has remained nearly constant since 1900. In his 1963 state-of-the-nation report, President López Mateos said that only 49 per cent of the population are now engaged in agriculture, animal husbandry, forestry, and fishing, against 85 per cent in 1900. It seems likely that today about 17 per cent work in industries against 10.7 per cent in 1900. On the other hand the mining population has dropped from 2.1 to 1.2 per cent.

The 1960 census showed that there are about 3 million people who do not speak Spanish or speak it very imperfectly, and who produce only enough for their own primitive needs; 2.7 million people said they either wore no shoes or only the rough sandals known as *huaraches;* 10.6 million were illiterate, and the same number did not eat wheat bread; 8.1 million reported that they ate very little meat or milk and few eggs.

According to the 1960 census there are sixteen towns with more than 100,000 inhabitants,[2] and it is noteworthy that three of these border the United States; that in spite of Mexico's long coastlines only two are ports; and that in the whole southern and southeastern section of the country, in the great curve extending from Oaxaca to Yucatán, the only large city is Mérida. But we shall speak of the decentralization and general planning problem elsewhere.

Statistics exist classifying various social and color divisions in the population, but these are not very helpful because the dividing lines are unclear and it is possible to move with relative ease from one grading to the next. With perfect poise a pert shorthand typist, clad in nylons, atiptoe on stiletto heels, will pass the time of day with relatives ranging from a State governor to an unshod peasant

[2] Mexico City, 2.8 million (4.9 in the whole Federal District)

Guadalajara, Jalisco	736,800
Monterrey, Nuevo Léon	596,939
Puebla, Puebla	289,049
Ciudad Juárez, Chihuahua	261,683
Léon, Guanajuato	209,469
Torreón, Coahuila	179,955
Mexicali, Baja California	174,540
Mérida, Yucatán	170,834
San Luís Potosí, San Luís Potosí	159,980
Tijuana, Baja California	151,939
Chihuahua, Chihuahua	150,430
Veracruz, Veracruz	144,238
Aguascalientes, Aguascalientes	126,617
Tampico, Tamaulipas	122,197
Morelia, Michoacán	100,828

carrying *tortillas* in a basket on her head. A young man broadcasting on economics from the National University radio station recalls his childhood in a slum; and a future architect serves fizzy drinks between classes in his mother's store.

In spite of this lack of clear definition, however, Mexico is stratified by income and living habits into at least five groups. At the top are those old landed families who withdrew in time from their ancestral *haciendas*, now broken into small holdings or given over to cattle and forestry co-operatives. These one-time gentlemen farmers, some of whose names have made Mexican history, live today in the colonial suburbs of Mexico City where the houses of *conquistadores* have been refitted for modern life. They intermarry with the new industrial families, so that the cream of society, once Europeanized and urbane, is shot through with steel-and-concrete brashness. Beyond the mellow suburbs with their faded pink walls are new housing estates, "contemporary" and exclusive behind lava-rock walls.

Below the tycoons are the professional classes, the architects, lawyers, doctors, and engineers who are the overworked creators of modern Mexico and who give the lie to the myth of a "land of *mañana*." Their day may begin with classes at the university, where they teach for a pittance and the honor of it. Office hours stretch into the evening but are compensated by "English weekends" in country cottages, by boating or fishing on one of the artificial lakes created for hydroelectric schemes.

Below these still, among the lower middle-classes, we see the full impact of revolution. The people whose standard of living has risen most sharply are the factory workers, the new consumers whose grandparents or parents wore no shoes and slept on straw mats. They are crowding in from the villages to the towns, filling workers' housing estates, learning trades, thronging the football grounds and bull rings, taking their girls pillion-riding to the nearest green patch for a picnic barbecue. From birth to death they are protected by social security, which provides them not only with medical attention but also with marble-halled palaces where they may learn to sew and cook, to equip themselves for semi-skilled trades, to swim and knock a football about.

Somewhere between the urban proletariat and the peasant villages the revolution peters out in what the government hopes will be only a temporary dead end, though there is evidence that peasant living standards are actually deteriorating. Ifigenia M. de Navarrete[3] shows that between 1950 and 1957 the average family income had risen 23 per cent in real value, but that the lowest 20 per cent of the population had suffered both a relative and an absolute decrease. It must be remembered, however, that the more ambitious and prosperous peasants are moving upward while the fatalistic lowest level remains sunk in traditional apathy. To a villager, it is a sign of great wealth to possess a yoke of oxen, a horse, a litter of pigs, a chest of treasures which may include a crucifix and a change of clothes for Sunday. That is all. Planes fly above the tracks where mules and donkeys carry local produce to market, where barefoot women with toes like animal claws trot low under their burdens.

Finally, in the mountain fastnesses, are the unassimilated Indians who still preserve their ancient customs and speak their native tongues (of which there are about fifty). Types vary greatly from region to region, a Tarahumara being as different from a Chamula as a Shetland crofter from a Mediterranean fisherman. There are Nahuas, Otomies, Huastecs, and Totonacs; Mayas and allied groups such as the Tzotzil-Tzeltal-speaking people in Chiapas; Tarascans, Coras, and Huicholes in the west; and many lesser divisions besides.

The cruder aspects of Mexican life have been documented by Oscar Lewis, an American anthropologist using a tape-recorder for gathering firsthand accounts of families from different social groups. The innate artistry and humor of Mexicans persist through all the bawdiness and promiscuity that can be expected when many people share a single room, when dozens crowd into the *vecindades* (groups of apartments clustered round a *patio* with its communal washtubs and play space). These ingrown units are beset by violence, drunkenness, illegitimacy, financial instability, and other characteristics common to slums all over the world. Yet even in such cheek-by-jowl surroundings, where any relaxation in

[3] Navarrete, Ifigenia M. de. *La Distribución del Ingreso y el Desarrollo Económico de México*. Instituto de Investigaciones Económicas, National University, Mexico City, 1960.

the struggle for basic survival means death, there is still time for idealism and dreams. Hear, for example, Consuelo, poet of the Sánchez family:[4]

During the Christmas *Posada* [crib-singing] season, as evening would begin to fall, Roberto or Manuel would sit with Marta and me in the doorway, and would show us the three most brilliant stars in the Big Bear constellation. . . . I remember how every year a little before falling asleep I would look at the sky and it would really seem to me that the stars were coming closer. In my imagination I surrounded them with an intense light that dazzled me even after I was asleep.

There is time for philosophy too. "To me one's destiny is controlled by a mysterious hand that moves all things," says Consuelo's brother Manuel,[5] who can be incisively self-analytical:[6]

I am the kind of guy who leaves nothing behind, no trace of themselves in the world, like a worm dragging itself across the earth. Looking back over my life I see that it was based on a chain of errors. I have treated it frivolously. I have been content to vegetate, to survive in a grey twilight, without effort and without glory. . . . It sounds laughable, but if I could find the appropriate words, I would like to write poetry some day. I have always tried to see beauty, even among all the evils I have experienced, so that I wouldn't be completely disillusioned by life. . . . More than anything, I must win in the fight against myself.

Not altogether surprisingly, perhaps, Oscar Lewis's poor Mexicans are less psychologically damaged than his bored and uneducated rich. A family living in the luxury capital-suburb, Lomas de Chapultepec, is more sadistic, more pathetically self-tortured than the peasants of Tepoztlán; for the crudities of the latter are straightforward, the result of physical destitution and not of the self-inflicted and largely fictitious depravities. We need only attend a village *fiesta,* with its hubbub of guitar and song, its stalls selling charred meat, pork crackling, fuchsia-colored coconut, and ices dripping emerald green and shocking pink, with its floats of papier-

[4] Lewis, Oscar. *The Children of Sánchez: Autobiography of a Mexican Family.* Random House, New York, 1961, p. 100.
[5] *Ibid.,* p. 171.
[6] *Ibid.,* p. 370.

mâché, its laughing *Mestizo* boys and girls and the shuffling peasants in from the backwoods to buy themselves new hats, and its starry splendor of fireworks at night, to realize that no Mexican is too poor to spend money on life-giving nonsense.

Closer glimpses of the various strata composing Mexican society may help us to a completer understanding of the country as a whole. Visitors as a rule fall into one or other distortion: either they emphasize the squalid-picturesque, the Indian, the ancient; or they see only the modern capital city. Neither alone is true. The real Mexico is not a nostalgic dream world of simple peasants such as exist only in the minds of folksy tourists; neither is it the city façade. The mute Indians are ever-present, watching, rejecting, assimilating the new world at their door.

THE INDIGENOUS INSTITUTE In 1960, with the Indigenous Institute, I visited a colony of Indians in the Chiapas Mountains where everything went by old preferment. Mexican heroes looked down from the walls of the mountain school where posters drew the moral that alcohol makes a bad man of you. Into the clean wooden hut, strewn with pine branches, crowded the elders. The children cradled in their mothers' shawls slept quietly, unaware that the ancestral pattern of their lives was at that moment—after centuries of stagnation—being reshaped.

In this *paraje*, as the mountain settlements are called, the Indians had been aggressive and unresponsive to friendly approaches. Suddenly, under the influence of a schoolteacher and his wife, both of them educated Indians, the villagers were beginning to ask for improvements: a road, a co-operative store, a bakery for wheat bread, an orchard, a tile kiln, and a tailoring establishment.

Plans had to be discussed with the Chiapas Director of the Institute, at that time Professor Alfonso Villa Rojas. He made his points: "We will provide a bulldozer, which is equivalent to forty men's work. But you will work too. Whatever you invest in the store, we will invest half again. We will give bolts of cloth until you have learned to tailor. . . ."

Each announcement was translated by the schoolteacher into the long rhetoric of the Indian dialect. A few days later enthusiasm was translated into action when the Institute engineer drove up to

1. Mount Ixtaccíhuatl seen from the old Mexico City-Puebla road.

2. Copper Canyon on the Chihuahua-Pacific Railway in the Western Sierra Madre.

3. Sundial in the main court of Monte Albán, Oaxaca.

4. Detail of gesso work in the Rosary Chapel of the Church of Santo Domingo, Puebla: adoration of the infant Jesus by shepherds and kings. This chapel has been called 'the eighth wonder of the world.' It was completed in 1690.

5. Portrait of a friar, in wood: typical example of early colonial sculpture.

6. Chapel of Sisters of Charity in Coyoacán, Mexico City. Architects: Enrique de la Mora and Fernando López Carmona, with vaulting by Félix Candela.

7. Snail-shell historical museum for children on the heights of Chapultepec, Mexico City. Architect: Pedro Ramírez Vásquez.

8. Julián Carrillo, who split the notes of our Western scale and called his new tones 'Sound Thirteen.'

survey the road. A dozen Indians with pickaxes had kept the appointment and were able, by felling and laying logs, to fetch our Landrover out of the mud where it had stuck. In the *paraje*, as on all the days before, the morning's baking of wheat-flour bread was quickly sold although corn pancakes are cheaper. The boys were playing basket ball, obeying the teacher's whistle with the alacrity of trained sportsmen, their skirted and belted woolen *chamarras* flapping like birds' wings. Inside the school an Indian girl was showing her grandmother and her fiancé her newly acquired skill with the communal sewing machine. Down a green sward among the idyllic hills, a woman was weaving, the loom tied round her waist and a tree-trunk. In the farthest clump of huts a man with a face like mahogany and small wisps of beard was cleaning and setting in order various insignia of office, preparatory to some local feast; and off to leeward, in a hut blue with tallow smoke, a boy was ladling wax over wicks hung from a wheel suspended horizontally above the cauldron. The candles emerged as smooth as if they had been turned on a lathe.

It was to help thousands of settlements such as this that the Indigenous Institute was founded in 1949 by Dr. Alfonso Caso, Mexico's leading archaeologist and anthropologist. Aware of the abject cry for alms where well-meaning tourists have distributed largesse, the Institute established two principles. Everything must be paid for in part by the Indians themselves, either in labor or in money and materials; and any innovation must be the result of an expressed wish from the Indians. The latter principle tends to be theoretical, since the Institute inevitably coaxes the *parajes* in various ways, especially through its trainees in promotion work. Most of these are Indian, all are local, and they can thus gain the confidence of the villagers more easily than "foreigners" from Mexico City.

Though Chiapas is only one of a number of regions where the Institute works, it forms a particularly well-defined natural laboratory for studying a problem important not only to Mexico but also to Central and South America, where perhaps 15 million Indians are still living beyond the pale of modern life. Chiapas, southernmost State of Mexico, has until recently been out of touch with the federal capital. Even today the highland center of San Cristóbal is about four hours by air and two more by road from Mexico City. National newspapers arrive anything from one to several days late, though it is possible for London papers to reach Mexico City within twenty-four hours. So the whole State, about the size of Scotland, has remained unexploited. Its wooded mountains hide illegal liquor stills and its tropical valleys steam with malaria. Families once wealthy from cattle and sugar cane have been replaced by the new rich whose sources of income are coffee—a crop that suffers from chronic depression—and rum. The mass of the population is *Mestizo* or Indian.

The great valley of the Grijalva River, which holds the State capital, Tuxtla Gutiérrez, looks like a paradise where almost anything could be made to grow, but very few crops have yet been tried. Much of the land is divided into small holdings belonging to the highland Indians, who plant their corn sometimes two days' walk from their own less fertile homes.

San Cristóbal, where the Institute has its regional headquarters, is a town of 23,000. The pink and sugar-white stones of its baroque churches are as mellowed as the old streets, trodden by the hordes of anonymous Indians who come to sell their produce, and who provide a variety of picturesque styles of local costume: beribboned straw hats, woolen or cotton *chamarras* (or *ponchos*) falling over variously shaped shorts or loincloths, leaving brown legs free to the 6000-foot-mountain air, and *caites* or leather sandals with thick soles. Behind them trot the women more anonymous still, since the sheer physical magnificence of the men raises them into individuality. But the women are squat under their burdens, cowed by their servility to the men.

The basic division in Chiapas is that between Indian and *ladino*, the *ladino* being a white or a *Mestizo* who follows the customs of Western civilization. There is permanent hostility between the two groups. Apart from this broad racial division, the Indians are divided into two linguistic groups that bear about the same relationship to ancient Maya as modern French or Spanish to Latin. Many of the older people in the *parajes* speak no Spanish at all, but the children are learning quickly in government or Institute schools.

For this heterogeneous population the Institute supplies clinics and schools; trains doctors, nurses, and teachers; builds roads; improves water supplies; provides electricity to certain villages; encourages local trades; and introduces new methods of agriculture. A puppet theatre helps to teach Indians the importance of vaccination and hygiene, the *dramatis personae* being peasants and fat men, humanized microbes, soap, and combs.

The work of the Institute is fraught with difficulties. The bright boys picked and trained to act as mediators have a tendency to adopt *ladino* ways and a bourgeois mentality which causes them to spurn their own origins. The Institute, aware of this danger, is concerned that its students shall not undermine the prestige of the old men of the tribes, whose code of ethics is one of "dignity, serenity, prudence, tact, honesty, and courtesy," cultivated in order to foster the ideal of living "in harmony with men, gods, and things." In some parts of Mexico integration of the Indian into Western society has brought prostitution and other corruptions. Therefore, though the Institute directors want the women to be educated with the men, they are not hurrying to insist that the girls should go to school with the boys, or that the traditional segregation of the sexes should be broken down. While the boys play, little girls sit huddled close to their mothers, weaving belts or slapping *tortillas*. They are almost unnaturally good.

The Institute's official report says that its aim is to "raise the standard of living of the indigenous communities in such a way as to allow them to participate in the national and socio-economic development at the present stage of its history." All too easily the result may be to turn satisfied Indians into class-conscious *ladinos* drifting rootlessly to the cities and imitating the less desirable tendencies of modern life. But, says Professor Villa Rojas, "to be contented like a cow is not yet to be contented like a man, and to know the pattern of your life from birth to death is to be only half alive." He and the rest of Dr. Caso's competent team have been anxious to insure that material development shall go side by side with emotional and intellectual education so that the Indians shall maintain a pride in their traditions. They feel that if the Indians themselves can sift out their evident superstitions, their frequent witch-hunts and murders, leaving their wisdom unadulterated, the Institute's program will have been worth while.

CREFAL Many of those who work among the Indian communities have been trained at the Regional Center for Fundamental Education for Latin America, established in 1951 in Patzcuaro. The name has since been changed to Educational Center for Community Development, but as the initials had already acquired honor in the hemisphere, Crefal remains the abbreviated name.

Patzcuaro is an idyllic lakeside town surrounded by conifer-covered hills. With its tourist hotels and gentle rusticity it is reminiscent of the Rhine or Basses Alpes, rather than of the more untamed landscape of Mexico. But behind the prosperous façade there are villages that can coax only a marginal living from the meager wheat pushing through stones and from the fish-depleted lake.

Because the villages presented problems common throughout Latin America, Patzcuaro seemed a fitting site for a training center for rural workers. General Cárdenas donated the greater part of his lakeside estate for the purpose, and here the center works—not primarily to raise the living standards of the Tarascan Indians, though this is an important side result, but to train Latin Americans for carrying out community education in areas with like problems. After months first of theory and then of workshop practice, students go out to the villages and live as nearly as possible in peasant conditions. Without antagonizing the Indians they can apply what they have learned of the various techniques of community education, including basic health, rural economy, the use of audiovisual aids, recreation, and anthropology. The work is subject to continual trial and error. A premature effort was made, for example, to persuade peasants to raise their cooking hearths off the ground, and one ultramodern Tarascan housewife went so far as to build herself two raised ovens. These were soon discarded and the cooking pots again simmered on the earthen floor. The husband, who could not warm his toes at the newfangled stoves, had abandoned his custom of sitting with his wife after dark to discuss the day's events, and now wandered footloose about the village: which clearly would not do.

A similar case was the whitewashing of the adobe houses, which in their natural state are the warm reddish-brown of the local soil and not unattractive. Whitened, and then allowed by their owners to peel, they look sordid in the extreme.

A chicken co-operative, on the other hand, has been such a success that it has become the major occupation of one island, which sends to Mexico City about 35,000 eggs a week, representing a yearly net value of $300 per family. Women do much of the work, and they begin to exert an unheard-of independence by demanding a sewing machine or an electric iron to be bought out of the profits.

Graduates from Crefal work all over Latin America, in such centers as the Río Coco project in Nicaragua, the Andean Indian Mission extending throughout Ecuador, Peru, and Bolivia, and in smaller schemes in Honduras, Costa Rica, Guatemala, Colombia, Chile, Uruguay, and Haiti. Crefal is thus a kind of clearinghouse of knowledge and experience in educating the hemisphere Indians. Its graduates, and the many thousands of young doctors, nurses, teachers, and engineers prepared to go into voluntary exile for their fellows, are performing a task that cannot be too highly praised. The pleasure they derive from bringing a little knowledge to areas that have remained stagnant for centuries is its own reward. Apart from the rare misfits, these workers are not only educators but counselors and friends.

YALALAG It is hard to draw a clear line between the pure Indian village and the *ladino* settlements, even though the Indian himself may see a sharp difference. Yalalag, in the Oaxaca hills, is an example of a near-Indian village which is open to the outsider and is thus susceptible to closer study than more strictly Indian communities. Yalalag is many hours on muleback from a road. With two companions I made the first part of the journey in a truck crammed with peasants and stinking of dried fish, sour corn broth, and raw meat. Yellow marigold and wild crocus lined the path but gave way to fir and maguey cactus as the road climbed. It turned cold, and by the time we had reached the road's end and a lumber camp, a thick white fog had fallen. In mackintosh capes we rode in single file by muleback, with the sun setting and the moon coming up through shifting fog and fine rain, touching the curtain of ochre moss that hung from the branches above our heads. Peasants passed carrying swinging lanterns, and water tinkled overhead from a raised course made of hollowed tree trunks.

We reached a village called San Pedro Cajonas and were given a loft above the only store. Straw mats had been laid for us and there were freshly toasted *tortillas* and a pot of black beans. The village smelt of fresh leather from the cobblers' shops, and of baked bread that was being ladled out of ovens on long-handled paddles. A characteristic sound was the heavy uneven squeak of wooden wheels used for spinning maguey fiber, which would later be woven into girths, baskets, and halters. Barefoot children turned the foot pedals while their sisters pulled out the thread, chattering and flirting with the passing boys.

In preparation for market day, Indians as strong as oxen were coming into the village carrying tables and bedsteads on their backs, for everything had to be brought in either on mule or on foot, and human labor was about a quarter of the price of a beast of burden. The women wore white homespun with bright sashes.

Don Octaviano, who had hired us our mules, tried to overcharge us, and as he was too drunk to see reason we went looking for the municipal president. In the town hall, hat in hand, peasants were waiting patiently with petitions, but there is no hurrying time in the Oaxaca Mountains. It is necessary to extend courtesies, to eulogize the finely carved Renaissance doors, to insist that one is not a tourist, not a *Gringa* American. All this we did, adding that we belonged to the Land of the Holy Virgin of Guadalupe—to Mexico. That detail did the trick, and the president promised to arrange the price of our mules by morning.

Bidden farewell with fine courtesy, we left San Pedro Cajonas and rode on beneath massive crags, through pinewoods hung with spiders' webs and alight with butterflies. The Mexican landscape is too dry to be picturesque, too lacking in the sounds and the shimmer of water; but it is grand and seems to set mankind in perspective so that a muleback rider looks no more, no less, than an ocelot or a lizard in the waste. It is interesting to reflect on the influence of this impersonal landscape on the mind of the Mexican peasant. He is turned inward, imbued with a sense of magic, courteous and gentle to his fellow humans as if he appreciated their rarity, cruel only if crossed.

The sun had set before we climbed dustily into Yalalag, feeling ourselves shrunk to pebbles in the crumpled hills. We were in a large village standing on a spur and commanding the whole country. For lodging the municipal president, fat and with a mouthful of gold teeth, allowed us a hall in the "palace." This passage-shaped room opened on to colonial arches, and from there we had a view across tiled roofs, each with a wrought-iron cross, to the purple hills with their naked patches where indiscriminate wood-felling had left them clipped to the bone. "Nothing but mountains and vultures," said the federal schoolteacher, disgruntled, unattractive.

Luckily the village had an unofficial schoolmaster, Sam, who was a leader among the local intelligentsia that gathered each evening in the square for philosophical talk. He was a Methodist —rare in these parts—and he had his own view of civilization which led to some embarrassing questions: "What practical use is war? Why are your people against the Soviet today—I thought the Soviet was your ally in the last war? In the big cities, do you have time to think?"

Sam's philosophical foil was the *curandero,* the medicine man, who lived at loggerheads with the federal doctor so that the pretty nurse was constantly being called in to keep the peace. There was also the priest, round as an apple, who occupied a room that had once been the friars' library and still housed the monastery's books with their smell of pulverizing leather; a photographer who crammed his wife, child, and equipment into a single room so that they breathed and smelled of bromide; and the shopkeeper selling every need from church candles to lariats.

Yalalag's great day is the eve of All Souls, and we were able to watch the procession of women who every year bear the wooden effigy of a virgin from the village along a winding lane to the cemetery on the outskirts. They were dressed all in white, in *poncho*-like garments with two colored tassels back and front, and with heavy woolen turbans on their heads. Each carried a candle that made the brown faces glow a somber orange. They waddled barefoot like ducks, ugly in themselves, beautiful in their grouping. Behind went priests in lace cassocks bearing censers and a cross. A brass band clashed noisily enough to waken every corpse within miles. Through the open doors of the houses we could see altars piled with buns and fruit, and a carpet of marigold petals over which the dead might return to eat their fill, enough to last until next year, one hoped.

For nearly an hour, almost immobile, the women knelt under the full moon, while by the light of a lantern an old man read the prayers in Zapotec and Spanish.

Never mind that tomorrow the piles of bread would be found untouched. In spirit the dead had returned that night: men slaughtered in village vendettas, women who had died in childbirth, children for whom their parents rejoiced because they had gone to become little angels.

The solemnity of the occasion did not inhibit carousers, and by next morning the municipal president and his cronies were giving a fair imitation of the corpses they had been serenading; but the women were industriously back at work, laying out corn to dry in the sun, carrying pitchers to the well, combing nits from their children's hair. We ate tasty pork, beans, and *tortillas* in the house of an old man who showed us yellowed letters from President Venustiano Carranza commending his part in the revolution. "But," he said, "the revolution is over a long time since, and a good thing too for wars do no one any good. Why don't you settle here, and I'll help you set up a brandy factory?"

In spite of the tempting offer we said good-bye and set off with an army of boys to carry our luggage. It was always the smallest who was given the heaviest burden, but he never ceased smiling. That night, as guests of a municipal president who spoke no word of Spanish, we slept in a store smelling of grain-bags. One more day, and we were back on the road, but our truck's gasoline petered out at an altitude of 10,000 feet, and we were forced to attempt sleep on the sacks of lead it was carrying. Dawn rewarded us with a sunrise that dissolved mist and dew and showed us range upon range of mountains, the foreground all orchid and singing birds. The warmth stimulated our drivers to achieve what the night before they had declared impossible. On a dribble of gasoline the truck was started, and we hurtled downhill into Oaxaca, hours behind schedule but sufficiently negligent of time to stop again while the truck's pump inflated a football for some urchins on the road. It did not matter that we all had streaming colds: we had not, after all, gone over the precipice, the drivers pointed out.

THE COMMUNITY DEVELOPMENT FOUNDATION The average Mexican village is not Indian but a *Mestizo* blend that has grown up over the centuries, very often through admixture with blood from the big house—the *hacienda* that was until the time of the revolution the hub of all country life. The typical village is very poor, often sleepy and apathetic, and needs the help that many private charity organizations are providing. Some of these organizations are affiliated to the Roman Catholic or other churches; but perhaps the most important is the Community Development Foundation, privately devised in the United States but working in conjunction with the Alliance for Progress which distributes food through it to those villagers who will work for their supper. The Foundation started its activities in Greece, Peru, Korea and other areas before entering Mexico in 1963. Here it found a willing collaborator in the Ministry of Health and Public Assistance. The idea is to give peasants a helping hand so that they can improve their villages in ways that seem best to them. The Mexican program is proving so successful that it will probably be a pattern for others. When a group of journalists were taken to see typical schemes, we found ourselves—on the way to the villages of Guerrero State where the Foundation is working—in an old and nearly abandoned *hacienda* house that seemed to catapult us back through time; so that we were treated in a single day to a panorama of historical change moving from family charity to large-scale modern and highly organized benevolence.

Graciana Morena, who is as nut-brown as her name (*Morena* means brown), and who had a wart sitting like a bluebottle on the end of her nose, received us in the *hacienda* house that had once administered the agriculture of a valley stretching from horizon to horizon. Now scraggy bloodhounds lay sleeping in the living rooms and dust had collected over colonial paintings. Only the kitchen, with its circular brick stove and the copper cauldrons hanging from the walls, looked lived in. Outside, where wasps gathered round the sweet, sticky mill, farmers were bringing their sugarcane for communal grinding by methods that have not changed for a hundred years except that the old water-wheel—still standing —had been replaced by a diesel engine. The dark brown molasses was being melted and clarified in brick baths sunk into the ground, then ladled into earthen saucers to set into the cakes called *piloncillo* that make refined sugar look and taste anemic. Even the old name of the place, Tepechicotlán, defied the fashion of calling villages after revolutionary heroes.

The *hacienda* folk had been left for decades squeezed uncomfortably between old and new Mexico. Graciana Morena, for instance, spoke regretfully of the past and sorrowed for the neglected *patios* where orange and lemon and mango trees crowded unpruned among weeds. She described with romantic nostalgia how she had come to the place with the marauding Zapatista armies during the revolution and had stayed, protected by the estate owner whom she regards as the essence of gentlemanly refinement. She told how he gave his land to the peasants before the Government demanded it, and how today his sons work in collaboration with the *ejido* communal farmers.

Faintly oppressed by the drowsiness in the air, we could not help wondering what energetic life the young masters might have engendered if the revolution had not come to limit their scope. The old shell of the house had still in decay such dignified proportions that it seemed to symbolize all the best of a life that could be good or ill according to the conscience of each landowner. But not all the old dignity has gone since the Zapatistas passed that way, for when we visited the villages round about we were courteously invited into single-roomed homes with earthen floors. There was no television here as there would have been in town, but instead a touching courtesy and refinement mingling with penury. Such were the villages and the people the Community Development Foundation is helping.

The village of Papalotepec, for instance, had lived ingrown for centuries, a fortress topping a steep mountain whose sides prickled like a hedgehog with thorn and *mesquite*. There was no road nor any access to the outside world except by foot or mule. But one evening the men gathering round their transistor set heard an announcement that the Foundation was promoting essential public works; so they set out at once for the State capital, Chilpancingo, to ask for the road they had wanted for generations. The answer was that provided they worked they could have one. They did. Some of the journalists who had hoped to visit the site were defeated by the scramble through scrub up a sharp gradient in intense heat. The peasants, digging the road out of the rock face with their fingernails as somebody put it, needed plenty of fiber and sweat to cut the road by hand. Today the women and children are able to make sorties beyond their village as they had never done before, and the markets over the hills are open for their produce.

Another village was on the wrong side of a stream that is a harsh furrow in the dry season, a treacherous flood in the rains. It had no bridge. Now, with the Foundation's help, the men are building a handsome concrete structure.

The inhabitants of Guerrero have a reputation for being unruly and trigger-happy, but the success of the Foundation among them suggests that their aggressiveness was merely waiting to be channeled constructively. "They are tough! My, they are tough!" exclaimed Mr. Glen Fraser Leet who fathered the world program and counts himself no mean athlete. The Mexican Government gives his organization technical help and equipment. Local business firms provide materials at cost price. Stamped on the Alliance for Progress food sacks are messages of goodwill about which nobody seems to have reservations except some food suppliers who imagine they are being undercut. According to an American computer firm that keeps the records, in the first six months of work 115 miles of rural road were built (it sounds a modest figure but one had to see the roads); also 58 schools, 200 houses, 105 agricultural centers, 40 public health clinics, 25 sewing establishments, 30 sports grounds, 25 hospitals, and 20 soil conservation units. All this was achieved in spare time from regular peasant tasks. At the end of six months the Foundation's total investment in Mexico was about $160,000, but the value of the labor was calculated at another $1.2 million. The keen men work; the lazy object. Suddenly they find their lives enriched by clear water, or a market for their melons, or a swimming pool, or a main square with a flagpole. These things make a lot of difference, especially when you have elected to build them yourselves.

A PROVINCIAL TOWN Toddlers with their hair licked into topknots are dabbling their hands in the park fountains. Teenagers have gone to the movies. It is time for the men to gather under the *portales* where they drink strong coffee and play dominoes, banging the pieces on the marble-topped tables in a monotonous rhythm that is punctuated at every quarter by the church clock. The men wear loose cotton shirts falling over their trousers, and if it were not for the profusion of Cadillacs nobody would suspect the fortunes—in coffee or vanilla—that some of them have amassed. They live in suburban houses, the glass-paneled door of the drawing-room kept locked and opened only for special visitors. The rest of the living space is all Coca-Cola tops and broken toys. The money a European would spend on vintage wines, on the best schools for the young, or on books perhaps, is hoarded for holidays in the United States.

In the few blocks round the cathedral, behind the massive *zaguán* doors, semi-aristocratic families live in a state of proud decay. The door is opened a crack only, at a jangle from the bell, and the servant's nose will obtrude and withdraw again sharply, as if it feared the plebeian street air. If the master is not at home, the lock will click down gently but irrevocably. If he is in, the visitor must wait until the servant has slumped across the *patio* and back. Only then will the stranger, who might easily be a thief or an intruder, be directed past the chickens and the flower pots, up the stone steps to a veranda flanked by living quarters and bedrooms, shuttered and musty, for they have been sealed off a century and more from the sub-tropical sunshine that makes the town smell by day of orange blossom and spikenard, quince and coffee and tangerine.

The master may be there in loafers, unshaven, his shirt-tails hanging out behind. His wife emerges from the kitchen, wiping her fingers on her apron and complaining that most of the servants are out. The collective noun she uses—*servidumbre*—is intended to suggest that the house is normally overrun by lackeys and it is only by chance that one has caught her at the chores. The children are dressed—girls and boys alike—in faded pants, soiled and torn. In another room, chilly and dank, the grandmother rocks herself to semi-sleep. When she dies—and everybody feels it cannot be long now—the next generation will inherit the tattered remnants of her fortune and can perhaps cut loose from old ways and shape their life at last to the twentieth century. In the meantime she is the matriarch and there is nothing to do but wait. The chickens scratch. A parrot calls a naughty word. Nobody heeds it but the yard boy, who giggles. The scene is pure Balzac. Through one door the visitor may catch sight of a television screen with teenagers clumped round it, sucking ice cream off a stick and gaping at the American way of life let surreptitiously loose in this ancient town.

In still lowlier back streets artisans are working in open yards under electric light. One is making wicker furniture, another is hammering sandals. Their single rooms are occupied by badly sprung, brass-knobbed double beds that occupy almost all the space. An image of the Virgin of Guadalupe hangs on the wall by the first-communion photographs framed in plastic lace. There may even be a university pennant belonging to the eldest son, who has gone to the capital to study.

Dominoes continue to bang on the tables. Peasants who have come from the villages with their wares are moving softly, stealthily homeward, and skinny dogs are nosing among the refuse beneath the tables. Long-distance buses are drawing up in the main square, disgorging their fares into the restaurants. The poorer travelers will buy crusty rolls filled with chicken and chili from the wooden stalls or from itinerant vendors. Cripples and scavengers beg for alms, automatically and without hope.

The domino players light cigars and call for *café filtre*. They are too used to squalor to notice it at all.

IN THE BIG CITY Let us create an amalgam and call him Don Xavier. He is an eclectic. His house, paneled in cedarwood and with a private swimming pool and *frontón* (Basque *pelota*) court, is built into the shell of a colonial building so that from the street we see nothing but fortress-like walls. Inside, with its rather self-conscious modernity, it is saved from brittleness only by the exquisite collection of ancient Mexican sculpture and the colonial paintings of pink cherubs and blue virgins floating on cloud. There are Diego Riveras, too, and Chinese Chippendale, heavy carpeting, and a library stacked the height of two floors, filled mainly with leather-bound books on Mexican history which Don Xavier has himself picked up in his Saturday prowls round a secondhand market. A cocktail bar and hi-fi have been blended discreetly with the relics.

For Don Xavier's wife, life begins early with the passing of the school bus, colored bright orange to call the attention of the traffic police, lumbering through the elegant suburbs, dead slow at the traffic lights, stopping to pick up the children in their crisp gingham overalls, gradually filling with chatter. If nannie is lacking, Mother must see them off, so everyone is up betimes.

The servants hold a social conclave as they wait for the passing of the rubbish cart. The shoe-shine boys, the milk cart, the postman, the peasant selling vegetables, the regular beggar on her beat who fills a tin with crusts and beans for her babies, the young woman doing a survey of television tastes, distributors of sample crackers: it is an endless ringing of bells that requires one menial's attention full-time. The garden and the pavement must be watered and brushed. If the *Señora* were lower in the social scale she would depart for the "super," a maid trailing behind carrying the heavy basket. But Don Xavier's wife is patriotic, fond of traditional fare best bought in the local market. Here there are exotic fruits, *chirimoya, chicozapote,* pomegranate, and quince. There are pumpkins whose yellow flowers can be cooked like a vegetable and used to fill *tortillas* fried and doubled. There is fish already baked and broken in two to show the white flaky meat inside; pork crackling; strange-smelling herbs such as *ipazote*, a sprig of which is thrown in with black beans to make them tasty and more digestible; corn cobs overgrown with fungus which provides an excellent dish served with rice; mealy corn enclosing bits of chicken and wrapped in banana leaves (the Oaxacan *tamales*), chicken in chili-spiced chocolate sauce (*mole Poblano*).

Don Xavier will be at home for the main meal of the day at about four o'clock, but then back to his office to work late. The center of town shows no sign of the traditional Latin *siesta,* and activity is constant. The foreigner may be frustrated by delays it is true, but if someone important wants a thing done fast, there are no workmen speedier than the Mexican. A wasteful quantity of human flesh may snooze and dawdle and cool its heels in Don Xavier's antechamber, but inside his own office activity is feverish. It is essential to get things done fast if they are to be done at all.

As a government official his term of office will be six years only, and after that his magic power will suddenly shrink.

It is only on Sundays that he relaxes a little; but one cannot reach the inner sanctum of his home, the library where he will bring out matured *mezcal* for favored guests, without running the gauntlet of a couple of chauffeurs hung with pistols and a maid with long black plaits and the eyes of a Maya princess. For Don Xavier needs protection from sycophants, bootlickers, job-hunters, and small bureaucrats up from the provinces with petitions for this and that. The pistols of his henchmen are never loaded (at least not visibly or audibly so), but are a harmless symbol behind which he may exercise his temporary power.

In talkative mood, Don Xavier will expand on the subject of the Mexican revolution. He may inveigh against the clergy, but when his daughter enters to bid him good night he will cross her on the forehead just in case; for the priests are persuasive and it is as well to be insured.

If the foreign visitor is looking for a neatly docketed pigeonhole in which to place Don Xavier, he will not find one. At his parties atheists and Catholics, Marxists and steel tycoons, meet on friendly terms. Since they are all somehow interconnected by marriage or by the equally binding relationship known as *compadrazgo* (which means, perhaps, that two people have stood godparent to the same child), they will give each other the warmest *abrazos* and there is no reason to suppose that these outward signs of affection conceal hypocrisy.

Nor is there hypocrisy in Don Xavier's own explanation of why, as a revolutionary, he can still remain calm of conscience though he possesses estates as large, say, as Rhode Island. He has worked hard. He has given himself few pleasures beyond an occasional trip into the mountains to inspect a new dam. In spite of his sophistication he is essentially a countryman. Nothing pleases him more than to exchange anecdotes with his workmen in their own rough language. He may act the cosmopolitan and convivial townsman, but he distrusts the part, feels awkward in it, and is perhaps a little inhibited in the company of the intellectual who knows the answer to all problems. As a Mexican, he finds such logical facility suspect. He prefers methods of trial and error; and though he may sometimes try to be guided by a consistent philosophy, he has a sneaking admiration for British rule-of-thumb.

WOMEN Mexicans are agile and quick, not beautiful and graceful. Those who can see no charm in the ancient clay figurines will find them, probably, frankly ugly. The men have a predilection for absurd hats and loud ties, the women for frizzing their hair till it conceals the sharp outline of Indian bones. But it is quite untrue, of course, to suggest (as a lecturer on a foreign television station did) that they normally dress in *fiesta* frills and flounces, that they never go out, have no intellectual life, but just mind the babies and cook.

This kind of generalization affronts Mexican women who crowd the universities, who write and paint, practice medicine, and study nuclear engineering. Even those who, intractably feminine, are absorbed in the eternal problems of servants, shopping, and dress, must choose their wardrobe so that it stands up to the wear and tear of modern city life.

Sidesaddle, in a snowy tumult of flounced petticoat, the young girls can ride as swift and as strictly aligned as cavalry officers when they perform in the colorful Mexican rodeo called *charrería*. Changing petticoats for frilly panties, they win applause on the world's tennis courts. Mexican women range from bureaucrats high in the administration to servile Indians who are beasts of burden at the men's command. Peasants deftly turn ceramics with one hand while the other is steadying the inverted plate used as a potter's wheel. They arrange flowers, not perhaps with the sophistication of the Japanese, but with as much color sense and feeling for growth. The matriarchal Tehuanas, whose erect carriage is accentuated by flowing skirts and a traditional red and orange bodice, have a reputation for dominating the men. No wonder that if you ask Mexican women about their position in the world you will get contradictory replies. In the Ministry of Labor Señora María Cristina Salmorán de Tamayo has been president of the Federal Committee for Conciliation and Arbitration: a long-winded title but it gives her weight to deal with serious labor disputes such as crop up in the unions. There is not much doubt that she has earned the respect of the toughest workers.

Some Mexican families have a tradition of intellectual activity and public service. One of Mexico's leading sociologists is Professor Catalina Sierra, a descendant of Justo Sierra. In a busy office of the department of the Federal District, a tiny woman, Angela Alessio Robes—daughter of a Mexican statesman—looks after all public works in Mexico City, which is a mighty task indeed. In the López Mateos administration another administrator, Señora Amalia de Castillo Ledón, was appointed under-secretary for a newly created sub-secretariat to the Ministry of Education dealing with cultural affairs. When questioned about prejudice against women in public offices she retaliated: "Isn't it a matter of ability?"

There are those who disagree: the aggressive feminists who chill by being so unfeminine in their methods of demanding feminine rights. Thanks to the suffragette movements in other countries, earlier, aggression is hardly necessary in modern Mexico, and in 1958 women voted for the first time in presidential elections. Though cartoonists parodied them—"Do we wear our new sack line at the polls?"—their presence helped to create the calmest elections ever recorded. Nevertheless, there are still societies, universities, and magazines exclusively for women. Most have a jaded, outmoded look.

A balanced view on the position of women today was given by Señora Carolina de Fournier, who runs a medical publishing house and who described how ideas have changed in her own working life. Girls from the best families will serve today behind the counters of department stores. But Señora de Fournier added, "I think Mexican husbands still need educating!"

Cultured and landed families are no longer always rich, and their womenfolk are glad to have a profession and an income. Only on a lower level, where fear of losing a precarious social hold is a stronger urge than money, do anomalies still exist. A self-styled "good-family girl" says she cannot work because it would degrade the standards by which she has been brought up. Among the rising middle classes—readers of glossy magazines, watchers of television —there are husbands who carry on even their social lives so apart from their wives that it seems to be a "top secret" whether they are married or not. Such men marry intellectually beneath them and soon demote their wives to the position of cook-nannie, while they carry on their home and office lives in separate compartments. The fault is not altogether the men's. The wife of a well-known writer is capable of hiding behind the refrigerator to escape her husband's bookish guests. In a provincial town there is a local girl who serves her husband's meals as if she were the hired servant. If a guest offers her a chair, she takes fright, retreats to the kitchen, and does not emerge until the moment of farewell.

Women in the skilled and semi-skilled laboring classes have in some ways more social freedom than those clinging to the outer edges of the professions. In the proletarian suburbs it seems to matter less what the neighbors are gossiping, and an easy companionship between boy and girl comes naturally—as it does, now too, among university students. Indeed, many trends toward a completer life for women will show results in another ten years as higher education for them becomes more general. In a country where the customs of Spain, with its Arab-influenced cloistering of women, mingled after the conquest with those of the ancient Indians who had also a severe code of feminine behavior, old conventions cannot be broken down overnight. An ancient text in the Nahua language adjures the young girls not to cheapen themselves or they will never have "a pot or a stewpan" of their own; and to have a pot and a stewpan was evidently the highest ambition at which a woman should aim.

Nevertheless, the eternal mystery of love and of the seduction of a woman's charms is present in myth and in the figures of strange and terrifying goddesses. Ixtaccíhuatl, so legend goes, was a lovely princess wooed by Popocatépetl. When he failed to win her, he turned her to stone and then himself too, so that he might contemplate her forever. Ixtaccíhuatl presides over the valley of Mexico, her formidable mass of lava rock etherealized under snow and wispy clouds.

Coatlicue, the goddess, is another story: colossal, powerful, and uncompromising. With her petticoat of serpents, her bifurcated reptile head, and the skulls adorning her, she is a paradox representing all the contradictions of an immense cosmic process and perhaps of modern women too.

Ixtaccíhuatl and Coatlicue, Malinche, the brown Virgin Guadalupe, and the poet-nun Sor Juana: these are the prototypes of Mexican woman. If it seems fanciful to think they bear any resemblance to their modern sisters, one need only look at the sturdy little girls on their way to school in their starched and frilly pinafores, at the sculptural firmness of their heads, the hair pulled starkly back into pigtails; at the contradictory mischievousness which recalls all the elusive variety of mountain and goddess, lover-interpreter, gentle Virgin, and intellectual nun.

Mexican women would scarcely trouble to think of these prototypes as they pursue their daily tasks. Nevertheless, in a history-ridden country, it is not altogether fanciful to think that they still preside. Even while some women are overcoming obstacles to recognition in the professions, millions still suffer fate blindly. Like the Indian women of Yalalag, in the Oaxaca hills, they wend their tragic way each night of All Souls to commune with their dead. One poor burdened villager graphically described their fate: "We are always being used up so we wear out soon like mops." Then her wrinkles broke into laughter to prove her humble life had not embittered her. She could scarcely imagine another.

MASKS AND MIMICRY "The tragedy of Mexico . . . and therefore the tragedy of the Mexican," says Rodolfo Usigli, the playwright, "resides both in what he hides, because this is what he reveals, and in what he reveals, because this is what he hides."[7] Usigli describes the Indian who takes refuge behind a mask of silence, without contradictions, almost without lips, "as if his eyes were turned inward." But the Creole hides his nature too, though by another kind of subterfuge, and his concealment is shown in a sense of superiority. He is aloof, reserved, distinct from the *Mestizo* whose disguise of contortion and gesticulation disturbs the natural silence of the Mexican plains. Usigli reminds us of the tale of an Indian who refused to sell all his merchandise to tourists because, had he done so, he would have been idle for the rest of the day. The *Mestizo*, on the other hand, will sell everything in order to buy, in order to sell more, and more, and more, in an endless chain of purposeless activity. He is the inverse of the noble Creole, who would rather starve than be rid of his collection of shawls or colonial diamonds.

[7] Usigli, Rodolfo. Essay in *México, Realización y Esperanza.* Editorial Superación, Mexico, 1952, p. 47.

Octavio Paz[8] detects a disguise and a refusal to "let go" in the ritual complications of Mexican courtesy; in fondness for closed poetic forms such as the *décima* (but this, surely, is a simple and direct imposition from Spain); in the love for geometry in decorative arts; in the formalism of political institutions.

Paz describes how:

> In its most radical forms dissimulation becomes mimicry. The Indian blends into the landscape until he is an indistinguishable part of the white wall against which he leans at twilight, of the dark earth on which he stretches out to rest at midday, of the silence that surrounds him. He disguises his human individuality to such an extent that he finally annihilates it and turns into a stone, a tree, a wall, silence, and space. . . . The Mexican is horrified by appearances, although his leaders profess to love them, and therefore he disguises himself to the point of blending into the objects that surround him. That is, he becomes mere Appearance because of his fear of appearances. He seems to be something other than he is, and he prefers to appear dead or nonexistent rather than to change, to open up his privacy. . . .

Paz posits a certain Mr. Nobody who is

> . . . quiet, timid and resigned. He is also intelligent and sensitive. He always smiles. He always waits. When he wants to say something, he meets a wall of silence, when he greets someone, he meets a cold shoulder. . . . Nobody is afraid not to exist: he vacillates, attempting now and then to become Somebody. Finally, in the midst of his useless gestures, he disappears into the limbo from which he emerged. . . . Nobody is the blankness in our looks, the pauses in our conversations, the reserve in our silences. He is the name we always and inevitably forget, the eternal absentee, the guest we never invite, the emptiness we can never fill. He is an omission, and yet he is forever present. He is our secret, our crime, and our remorse.[9]

This view of the Mexican as a self-effacing Nobody seems at variance with the impression given by the town Mexican, with his loud necktie, his idiotic hats, his raucous laughter. But Mexican silence—the silence of the villages at dusk when men are wrapped

[8] Paz, Octavio. *Op. cit.*, p. 32.
[9] *Ibid.*, pp. 43 *et seq.*

to their eyes in *sarapes* and even to breathe seems an infringement of privacy—this silence is simply the inverse of the *fiestas,* the explosions, and the fireworks. Between twilight hush and the debaucheries of midnight there are no gradations. The neighbor turns on his wireless full blast, and if he is asked to tone it down, he switches off. There is for him no golden mean of sound. The Mexican laughs at near death. He gazes in mask-like silence at his lover, at the landscape which he feels to be a part of his being, at the moon and stars that have governed his conception of deity as far back as anyone knows.

Mexican *fiestas* are not so much a sign of high spirits as a denial of all ordinary logic, of all the rules of economy that have been fixed by Western civilization and then given the appearance and the sanctity of law. Mexicans feel instinctively that the presumed infallibility of modern economics—whether capitalist or Communist—is illusory. Therefore they spend money on fireworks and paper decorations, and even nowadays on transistor sets, when they cannot afford to buy sufficient calories to keep themselves in health. They know that death is implicit in life; and they know this not as a theory best relegated to some cobweb-hung corner of the mind, but as a minute-to-minute reality. Therefore they laugh at death, mocking it, depriving it of any power to wound. In doing so, they automatically deprive life of any power to hold them hypnotized. The shuffling walk of the Mexican peasant, his clothing loosely tied and slipping from his hips, the way he shrugs off time with a gesture of impatience as if he were ridding himself of a bothersome mosquito (and so perhaps it is): all these are the visible signs of a detachment both from life and from death. There is a sense in which the Mexican should be the envy of aspirants to eternal bliss. Unfortunately, his detachment is so thorough that in the process of reaching contentment he has annihilated himself. He has become like a stone or a tree and is unable to understand or make use of his instinctive sense of values. He does not want to become the champion of these values. He prefers to hold them in secret, even to mock them. And so he belittles himself.

The dichotomy of Mexican history aids and abets this belittlement. Malinche betrayed the Indians, and modern Mexicans are the sons of Malinche; therefore, they are traitors in their own minds.

Treachery is elevated to the rank of original sin, worshiped, and attributed both to the Spanish greed for conquest and to the Indian refusal to give battle.

Gilberto Loyo[10] reminds us that throughout history, though especially at the time of Santa Ana and during the Díaz régime, there have been *Mestizos* and Creoles who have felt uneasy for having been born Mexicans. They have shown this discomfort in various ways, some having betrayed their country, others having tried to import European princes to rule over Mexico, others having gone to live abroad, and still others vainly trying to imagine that Mexico is either the Greece of Pericles or a western-European power.

As Paz says:[11]

> The strange permanence of Cortés and La Malinche in the Mexican's imagination and sensibilities, reveals that they are something more than historical figures: they are symbols of a secret conflict that we have still not resolved. . . . The Mexican condemns all his traditions at once, the whole set of gestures, attitudes, and tendencies in which it is now difficult to distinguish the Spanish from the Indian. For that reason the Hispanic thesis, which would have us descend from Cortés to the exclusion of La Malinche, is the patrimony of a few extremists who are not even pure whites. The same can be said of indigenist propaganda, which is also supported by fanatical *Criollos* and *Mestizos*, while the Indians have never paid it the slightest attention. The Mexican does not want to be either an Indian or a Spaniard. Nor does he want to be descended from them. He denies them. And he does not affirm himself as a mixture, but rather as an abstraction: he is a man. He becomes the son of Nothingness.

The tape recordings of Oscar Lewis support the findings of Mexicans themselves. Paz, Ramos, Loyo, Leopoldo Zea, and others have underscored the quirks of national character, especially *machismo* (exaggerated emphasis on maleness, toughness); *Malinchismo* (treachery); the cult of death; the tendency to wear a mask, to mimic others and at the same time to appear *pelado*, plucked, or bare; the habit of lying for the mere pleasure of it and also to

[10] Loyo, Gilberto. *La Revolución Mexicana no ha Terminado su Tarea.* Article in *Investigación Económica,* Mexico City, 1959, p. 429.
[11] Paz, Octavio. *Op. cit.,* p. 87.

hide behind the lie which acts as a protection against intruders. "Since we attempt to deceive ourselves as well as others," says Paz, "our lies are brilliant and fertile. . . . Lying is a tragic game in which we risk a part of our very selves."

Mexican lying is self-mockery. Mexicans poke fun at everything: at time, at life, at death. But their fun is seldom constructive, it leaves them empty. Perhaps the day they come to understand this, they will know how to use, without being dominated by them, all the paraphernalia of modern time-bound living, the schedules and the clocks, the company profit-and-loss accounts, the radio jingles. Mexicans will retain their innate playfulness before these heavily serious inventions, in the same way that they now dangle skeletons before tourists and display sugar skulls in bakery windows. What the cartoonist Abel Quezada thinks today, may infect all Mexicans tomorrow. In this unembittered but incisive critic of the national scene we find Mexican humor at its most constructive and also at its closest to tragedy. There are cartoonists who draw better, including "Freyre" (Quezada's companion on the newspaper *Excelsior*), but none is so consistently and so acceptably a gadfly. One even suspects that Quezada's bad drawing is a carefully cultivated asset, a shorthand easily comprehensible to the "little Mexican." A horse's head sticking out of sand means drought; diagonal dashes, deluge; an inverted floor mop atop a boyish face used to be President Kennedy; a fat man minus a shoe, Mr. K., a shape like a banana, a nose—and if the nose is circled by a diamond ring, the character is the graft-rich Mexican millionaire Gastón Billetes (Gastón Dollar-bills). A skinny peasant propped up by two forked sticks is a potential beneficiary of the Alliance for Progress ("Hot cross credits for sale," cry the bankers) if only he could raise the necessary guarantees.

Quezada makes up for his "bad" drawing by plenty of text, and in this he seems to ape the garrulous little Mexican who, if only he could marshal his thoughts, would express himself in just such gently ironical language. Quezada was brought up in a beehive village, he says; but if he has bees in his bonnet they buzz some pretty good sense. Having drawn a moral from the hatred of one small village toward another, he becomes Andean, which would mean that he believed in the overriding need for unity in Latin

America, except that such a formulation sounds as if it implied disunity between Latin America and the rest of this quarrelsome globe. Quezada, like his government, wants to be friends all round.[12]

But Latin America is a handful. The latest coup, wherever it may be, is motive for Quezada to get down to the business of drawing inflated chests with lots of medals (shorthand for military dictators). The Communist peril in this area arises—he says ironically—because of the activities of those who want to further social justice, education, and tax and land reforms, thus jeopardizing the interests of the rich. Betrayal of the people takes subtle forms, and perhaps one day, if Latin America does not learn from history, it may learn from Quezada's A.B.C. In country A, Generalísimo B is dictator; Colonel C rebels; the country supports him; triumph of the revolution (drawn upside down); dictator B flees with dollars bursting his suitcases; the people (birds circle round one little fellow with a plow) are ruined and have to begin again; Colonel C promises elections; the U.S.A. recognizes him; the Army names him General but he raises his own rank to Generalísimo; Generalísimo C becomes a dictator; the cycle begins again like a children's round. The only difference is that, when we reach the people, the little fellow with the plow has a patch on his shirt which was not there before, the birds have become predatory, and a tree in the background has withered.

As a Mexican, Quezada finds it pleasant to dream up the "Quezada Doctrine," according to which Mexico is the strongest country in the world, all automobiles have Hispanic names ("There's a González in your Future"), and committees are organized to prevent discrimination against Americans by blond-persecuting restaurant proprietors. But then, of course, one wakes up.

Mexicans are in some ways Rip van Winkles, though their irrepressible vitality has kept them stirring restlessly in their long sleep. Now, like Quezada, they are waking to realize that it takes more than revolution and legal codes to become, not the strongest—they have no ambition for that—but a respected minor power.

[12] Quezada, Abel. *El Mejor de los Mundos Imposibles.* Joaquín Mortiz, Mexico, 1963. (Published first in somewhat different form by Prentice-Hall, New Jersey, in 1963, under the title *The Best of Impossible Worlds.*)

5 *Politics and Policies*

In a European or American sense, politics in Mexico can scarcely be said to exist. Nevertheless, there is not a single aspect of Mexican life that is not permeated with political implications.

The Partido Revolucionario Institucional (PRI) was established by President Calles under another name: the Partido Nacional Revolucionario. In 1937 Lázaro Cárdenas renamed it the Partido de la Revolución Mexicana, and it was not until 1945 that it received its present wholly illogical title. A contradiction in terms it may be, but somehow it fits. PRI has undergone periodic metamorphosis, has adapted itself to the changing needs of a country quickly emerging from feudalism, and has ruled with a fluidity that even the British parliamentary system has never perhaps achieved. PRI is the Establishment. It is an Academy for training the bureaucracy, the economists, the technicians who do the country's official and semi-official work in all walks of life, the arts and sciences not excluded. Anyone with an official appointment is, at least by implication, a supporter of PRI. Anyone among the professional classes who is a close friend or a relative of a high party member may possibly (one never knows) be wielding political power; and in this sense doctors, lawyers, bankers, and businessmen are politicians. Only the extremes of right and left remain outside PRI's ranks. It has been flexible enough to embrace the radical régime of Lázaro Cárdenas and the right-wing business autocracy of Miguel Alemán. Through all the twists and turns of presidential and ministerial policies since the 'twenties, PRI runs like a magic thread, insuring stability, creating a continuity in spite of the brusque ruptures and changes of personnel that have occurred every four to six years as one administration follows another. PRI is a rock and as long as its monolithic structure is not dynamited (which is unlikely) or eroded (which in the fullness of time it may be), there can be no politics.

Yet if a rock can be intangible and ineffable, that too is PRI. Who supports it? Active party members of course. But paradoxically the active members are often the least powerful. The critics of PRI may be more closely allied to it than the sycophants, provided the criticism is constitutional and constructive. All official appointments are made with at least the tacit approval of the government. Private business must rely on government permits and therefore on PRI. Everything that PRI seems to be, it is not; and wherever PRI appears most hidden, there it is.

Just how PRI came to wield this total authority is a mystery. Its secret has been precisely its elasticity. Perhaps its great strength has been its early dissociation from a military élite. Political generals still hobble onto the stage to make patriotic declamations or vituperative harangues; but they are looked upon with tolerant smiles. The active army is professional and nonpolitical, more concerned with highway patrol than with defense, though it may be called out now and then to quell sporadic riots at their source.

PRI succeeded in channeling the strong nationalist sentiments of the country at the precise moment when nationalism could be used to goad apathetic sectors of the population into corporate action. It has drawn for its talents upon all educated sectors of the community, so that many diverse young men have gained administrative experience. It has never been as exclusive as powerful political parties in other Latin American countries.

What other forces there are behind PRI, secretly strengthening it, nobody knows. Many high party officials are Masons, and Masonic Lodges have frequently exercised a balancing pull against Catholicism and the autocratic priesthood. But direct and detailed proof of Masonic influence is difficult to trace.

At all events, PRI has been Mexico's salvation; and there is scarcely a person in the small opposition groups of left and right who would deny that without it the country would have fallen into chaos. Studying PRI's history, it may be possible to draw a moral for the whole of Latin America and even for other have-not areas of the world. In Latin America particularly, those countries that have tried to mature politically too fast have become subject to periodic "palace revolutions" and military coups that have canceled out whatever progress has been made toward theoretical democracy. According to a study quoted by Howard F. Cline,[1] Argentina rated fourth as a democratic nation in Latin America between 1945 and 1960. Since then it must have dropped several places; and though Mexico may not rank as high as Uruguay, Costa Rica, and Chile, it has been able to combine a fair degree of democracy with an economic growth that inflation-troubled Chile cannot boast. PRI seems thus to have provided an acceptable compromise between anarchic instability and orderly but iron dictatorship. Under its rule, freedom of opinion has been able to flourish, and it has been possible to pursue a more or less constant aim. Revolutionary aims guide policy, and it is with policy rather than with politics that Mexico's rulers are concerned on any level above the petty, personal squabbles and vendettas that arise from graft and nepotism. Political voices, in a European sense, are raised during the eighteen months or so before presidential elections, when the PRI nominee (and therefore by implication the coming president) is chosen by a mysterious procedure of opinion-sounding and behind-the-scene maneuvers; but for the rest of the administrative term they are lulled to sleep by the fairly efficient humming of the PRI machinery.

Which does not mean that Mexican political life is all quiet purring. Storms, sudden and wayward, shake it constantly and fill the press with wildly exaggerated headlines. What is worse, in some provincial districts the old-fashioned custom of liquidating an opponent quietly but irrevocably is still practiced. There is a strange secretiveness, and reluctance to examine the circumstances in which people from time to time disappear from view. Criminals in rural areas are therefore rarely brought to justice. The federal government may blush to contemplate such a state of affairs, but does little to remedy it. There is an odd fear that the Constitution will be violated if the central authorities intervene in domestic affairs of each separate and in many respects sovereign State, even though the State may be grossly violating the Articles of Constitution.

[1] Cline, Howard F. *Mexico: Revolution to Evolution, 1940–1960.* Oxford University Press, London, New York, and Toronto, 1962, p. 173.

A case of this kind was the brutal murder in 1962 of an agrarian reformer—a kind of latter-day Zapata—together with his wife (who was pregnant at the time) and his sons. With a touch of melodrama the family was roused one morning, taken off to the archaeological zone of Xochicalco, and there shot. According to the left wing, Rubén Jaramillo was disputing the ownership of peasant lands that had been going up in value and were coveted by the local power group. According to the right, he was a bandit who seriously threatened law and order. Everyone was grieved at the cruel and itself lawless manner of his liquidation, but nobody seemed eager to investigate; and when a Mexican photographer working for the National Broadcasting Company of America was indiscreet enough to film a peasant demonstration against the local authorities of the State of Morelos (where the murders occurred), he was seized, cross-questioned, and then taken along a lonely road, punched in the stomach, relieved of his equipment, and left unconscious. NBC took the matter up with the central authorities; but though it was clear that neither the central nor the State governments had perpetrated the attack, the culprits were never found.

Incidents of this kind are apt to give an impression that stable, booming, industrializing, civilized Mexico is only a slippery step from post-conquest oppressions and the bloodier phases of revolution. Their occasional outcropping in a land of high ideals may be due precisely to the fact that the aims have been set—at certain stages in history—too high for practical effectiveness. Melchor Ocampo once drew attention to this tendency for Mexicans to believe that in order to transform reality it is quite sufficient to pass new laws. A gap has thus arisen between aspiration and reality, a gap that cynics and thugs have been ready enough to exploit.

It might be thought that the very difficulties experienced by PRI in making its ideals effective would give strength to opposition parties. PRI, however, has been clever enough to meet its critics more than half way. For example, the most important right-wing party, the Partido Acción Nacional (PAN), was mollified late in 1962 when President López Mateos put electoral reforms before Congress. According to the reform, which was at once approved, any party gaining a minimum of 2.5 per cent of the total votes cast throughout the republic would be entitled to between five and twenty seats in the Chamber of Deputies. These "party deputies" would occupy seats specially created in addition to those of the regular constituency members. At the time of the reform it was calculated that, even if PRI were to gain all 178 regular seats, the opposition might be able to have up to eighty deputies. PAN polled 9.5 per cent of votes in 1958, and 18.7 per cent in 1946 (the largest opposition vote in recent history). "Party deputies," it was evident, would be unlikely to muster enough strength to influence voting in Congress directly, but they could insure the opposition a hearing. Small parties, too, would have a chance to gain political experience.

In the presidential elections in July 1964 it turned out that over 9 million people out of 13 million on the electoral roll voted overwhelmingly for Gustavo Díaz Ordaz. The estimate of 80 opposition "party deputies" proved thus to be a long way out. For the office of president both the Communist-affiliated Partido Popular Socialista, and the nationalist Partido de la Auténtica Revolución Mexicana, threw in their vote with PRI. PRI also gained all Senate seats and all but 3 regular seats in the House of Representatives. PAN won 20 "party seats." Neither PPS nor PARM gained the minimum 2.5 per cent, but magnanimously the government allowed 10 seats to the former and 5 to the latter in order to give all opposition leaders a place in Congress. Elections were so orderly that one hotel put up notices suggesting that tourists visit the nearest polling booth "to watch how democracy works"; and a post-election television program featured leaders of all parties sitting amicably round a table and expressing themselves satisfied with procedure.

Those who fear that this reform is but a hollow gesture might note that, shortly after its passing, a minor but significant victory was won in the Chamber by a small group of PAN deputies. A "mewling and puking" little group perhaps it was; but under its instigation a congressional commission was set up to investigate and advise on measures for improving the efficiency of the *organismos decentralizados*. This is the clumsy title given to Petroleos Mexicanos, the Federal Electricity Commission, and other wholly or partly State-supported bodies, some of which are nonprofit-making, others acting very much like private business enterprises.

PRI, then, shows a genuine if timid desire to encourage opposition, and one would like to predict that some other Latin American countries may follow Mexico's example. In Mexico, the first party to benefit will of course be PAN, since the left-wing groups, including the crypto-Communist Partido Popular Socialista (PPS), are very much weaker and gain only a trickle of votes. Like the Cárdenas-supported "National Freedom Movement," which is not a political party at all and therefore puts up no candidates for election, they work mainly in the background, stirring up the more fractious elements in the population, especially left-wing university students and intellectuals, railway, petroleum, and other union workers, and agrarian "leaders." The rank and file of peasants are fortified against this kind of leftist propaganda by their simple-minded Catholicism and their innate conservatism. The PPS, which is the party of the Communist labor leader Vicente Lombardo Toledano, has incorporated into its ranks the Workers' and Farmers' Party of Mexico: as a first step, says Lombardo, toward forming a "great Marxist-Leninist party in our country." This sounds like wishful thinking, since genuine Communists in Mexico number only between 5000 and 10,000. Added to these there are highly articulate fellow-travelers, especially among intellectuals, and many young people with restless consciences to whom Marxist banners from time to time appeal. But even strict party followers are torn between national and international loyalties, and of late between China and the Soviet Union.

One sign of the weakness of Communism in the country was the inability of the left wing to secure the release of the muralist David Alfaro Siqueiros, the journalist Filomeno Mata, the railway leader Demetrio Vallejo, and others sentenced in 1960 for threatening the peace, damaging lines of communication, and similar offenses. Foreign intellectuals protested more loudly than Mexicans when these men were held without trial; and even allowing for the bias of a strongly right-wing Mexican press, protests against the final sentence of eight years for Siqueiros and Mata, sixteen years for Vallejo, and other periods down to one year for less prominent offenders, were surprisingly muted. Señora Siqueiros called the court's decision against the railway workers "macabre and unprecedented," but protest demonstrations were poorly attended.

Mata was allowed bail, but not Siqueiros, who was finally pardoned and released from jail in July 1964.

In spite of these severe punishments, there are other Marxist intellectuals who are tolerated and allowed to exercise an influence on the young: a fact that might be taken as support for the reiterated claims of the courts that they judged Siqueiros and his companions purely on the basis of civil crimes and did not allow their political sympathies to weigh in the balance. It may be, too, that the authorities are not seriously troubled by signs of disquiet in the young. Apart from cartoonists like Abel Quezada, university students have always been the gadflies, the conscience-prickers of Latin America. And "good luck to them" is the official view.

Among left-wing opposition leaders, Cárdenas (technically not "opposition" at all since together with all other ex-Presidents he holds a government post) is respected for the clear gains he brought Mexico during his own régime. He is evidently sincere in his desire to lift the living standards of large masses of the population, but many of his one-time friends have been nervous of late, due to his propensity to flirt with the Communists and with Cuba. He and other left-wing leaders have their following; but—as we have seen—their case has been weakened by the government itself, which has done much in recent years to meet the opposition's most valid criticisms: the allegations that there is still no effective suffrage, that the peasants are at the mercy of corrupt banks, and that the unions are ruled by false leaders. There are also signs that the left wing is quarreling internally. *Política*, the leftist bi-weekly which is abject enough to imitate *Time* in certain idiosyncrasies of style and format, has a hard job not to descend to the level of a parochial scandal sheet—and this in spite of the fact that it has an obvious and potentially important function in informing the public of facts often suppressed (whether by editorial policy or through insufficient news sense it would be hard to say) by the national dailies.

It seems clear from recent events that both extremes of opposition find it difficult to make effective attacks against a government that—as President López Mateos once put it—is "left wing within the limits of the Constitution," and at the same time anxious to encourage co-operation from big business so that the country can continue to industrialize. In a number of ways the government has pulled the planks from beneath opposition feet.

FOREIGN POLICY Foreign policy is ruled by the principles of self-determination and non-intervention, by adherence to the Charters of the United Nations and the Organization of American States, and by a desire for world peace and for closer ties with the rest of Latin America. Mexico has been particularly scrupulous in upholding the right of political refugees to asylum. As it once gave a home to anti-Batistas, so it now gives refuge to anti-Castro fugitives; and in neither case is any partisanship implied. Dr. Castro's sister Juana, for instance, was granted political asylum in Mexico almost at the same time that Mexico was refusing to implement the Organization of American States vote to apply sanctions against Cuba. Neither the one action nor the other was intended to show partisanship but only respect for correct legal procedure. Asylum is given to all political fugitives whose lives may be endangered if they return to their own countries; and the OAS was felt to have gone beyond its brief in applying sanctions against a country when its alleged meddling in the affairs of another (Venezuela) had not been (in Mexico's view) satisfactorily proved.

Although refusing to become aligned outright with the democracies against the iron-curtain bloc, and although refusing to be pushed into actively hostile measures against Cuba, there is scarcely a question that in any tight squeeze in which she was forced to declare her allegiance to one or other side, Mexico would be a friend of the West. Mexico's attitude toward Dr. Castro's Cuba, although it has been almost deliberately misunderstood by the United States, is clear and comprehensible provided it is looked at in its historical context. Mexico passed through a social revolution that was fought without the aid of any foreign power, Communist or otherwise. For years she was misunderstood, maligned, and cold-shouldered. The United States attempted to interfere in Mexico's internal struggle and was rebuffed. Therefore, when Dr. Castro overthrew Fulgencio Batista, a dictator who had exercised an iron grip at least equal to that of Porfirio Díaz, it was hoped that the Cuban revolution might follow the Mexican pattern and concern itself with essential agrarian reforms, keeping well out of international political controversies. Even when it became evident that the iron-curtain bloc was exercising its influence on the island, and even when Cuba was removed from the Organization of American States, Mexico felt that the door should be left open for the prodigal son's return to the Latin fold. After all, went the argument, there were other prodigals whose sins had been connived at, dictators who were tolerated because they represented no threat to the United States but were looked upon as friendly to the West even though they were dangerously Fascist in their tendencies. Why, then, should Cuba be marked out for special persecution?

Those who upheld this argument were considerably shaken by the crisis over the rocket bases in the autumn of 1962; but though there is no question that the Mexican government's heart is with the democracies against the dictatorships, there is still a feeling that the United States, in combating Communism, must avoid the other danger of propping up diehard, right-wing governments in the Americas. Moreover, in a country like Mexico, where the diehard super-right cries "Communist" at projects for reform that would not bring a blush to the cheek of a British Conservative, any stronger indictment of Cuba could put an undesirable brake on necessary internal reforms.

As a logical extension of Mexican non-commitment to either power bloc, President López Mateos and his closest associates traveled freely in Communist as well as in democratic countries. They visited Yugoslavia and Poland as well as Africa, Indonesia, India, the United States, and Canada; and, though Mexico consistently refused to join the neutral countries, there has been evident sympathy for the undeveloped and developing areas of the world. The readiness of President López Mateos to be friendly to all was in itself a reversal of Mexico's fifty-year policy of isolation and ingrowth. Among the newly modernizing countries, Mexico's voice began to be heard with respect, so that U.S. right-wing nervousness about such innocent voyaging seemed shortsighted and a little absurd. Absurdity bordered on the ridiculous when Americans began to see sinister motives in the visit of President Charles de Gaulle to Mexico in March 1964. The visit brought a wave of fellow feeling toward all Latin countries, but this did not imply antagonism to anyone else. If anti-U.S. sentiments were exacerbated in Mexico as a result of the visit, these were not the fault of President de Gaulle but of ex-President Harry Truman who remarked that the General should keep his nose out of U.S. affairs. "It's news to us that we're part of the United States," was Abel Quezada's comment.

Iron-curtain visitors have all been treated with punctilious friendliness but certainly not with any great public enthusiasm. When Russia's Deputy Premier Anastas Mikoyan was in Mexico in November 1959, the moderate newspaper *Novedades* attacked Russia directly and adjured the Soviet to "abstain from intruding in the domestic life of other countries and from maintaining an intensive proselytizing propaganda in them." In October 1963 President Tito of Yugoslavia, played up as a military hero, received a more spontaneous welcome. However, President López Mateos stated clearly at an official banquet that the ideologies of the two countries differed. Mexico, he said, had never been party to the view that nations with opposed political structures need quarrel, provided always that they respected one another's right to self-determination.

Though President Kennedy and other leaders of the democracies were received with more wholehearted approval, the West cannot assume that its policies will go uncriticized by the average Mexican. U.S. action to rid the hemisphere of the Cuban rocket bases was met by the skeptical comment: "And what about the bases in Turkey?" The lower middle-class city Mexican can be expected to be non-conformist and individual in his political views. The bootblacks, the taxi-drivers, the tradesmen and sweepstakes vendors may be uneducated but they are not fools.

THE GREAT NORTHERN NEIGHBOR Mexico's attitude toward the United States is therefore friendly but not uncritical. Inevitably there is much of cupboard love in this delicate relationship, especially when there is such enormous discrepancy in the standards of living on either side of the border. The average income per head per year in California is said to be $2800, the average in the Mexican northern border towns $655, and the average in the Mexican interior $280.

Americans are still curiously unaware, besides, that the Monroe Doctrine is unacceptable south of the Río Grande, where it is regarded as a unilateral attempt to impose United States policies on the hemisphere. Even the Alliance for Progress, though admittedly a generous scheme, is regarded as a makeshift measure. It has been suspected of being a camouflage to hide the fact that the United States has not yet reconciled itself to thinking of Mexico and the other Latin countries as anything but larders from which the U.S. can import the raw materials it needs, at minimum prices; as not-quite-sovereign states whose politics can and must be manipulated to suit the acknowledged arbiter of civilized standards.

Mexicans would feel happier about U.S. attempts to help the Latin American countries grow in social and economic stature if Latin countries were treated as responsible partners rather than as unruly children. A Mexico-U.S. round-table conference held in 1963 to discuss "problems of economic development and population growth" was an example of the kind of collaboration that produces more results than any amount of unilateral fingerwagging. At this conference the fingers wagged in both directions, and the gloves were off. Men of the caliber of Walt Rostow (author of *The Stages of Economic Development*), Paul Rosenstein-Rodan (one of the "wise men" assessing the Alliance for Progress), and Raymond Vernon (whose book on Mexico's development had just at that time appeared[2]) debated candidly with Hugo Margain (then Mexican under secretary of industry and commerce and more recently Mexico's Ambassador in Washington), Victor Urquidi (a brilliant economist in part responsible for planning the Central American Common Market), Emilio Mujica (director of the Mexican University's economic faculty), Juan Sánchez Navarro (President of the Mexican Confederation of Industrial Chambers), and others. Although organized with the help of the American Round Table Committee for the Advertising Council, the meeting held no hint of political or economic bias, Liberals, Marxists and industrial tycoons all had their say. Sparks flew, generating warmth and the hope of more such exchanges.

Meetings of this kind can help to air fundamental differences in philosophy. Border problems are another matter, being specific, transitory, and usually not serious. Chamizal, the disputed small territory in El Paso, was handed back to Mexico in 1963 in a gesture

[2] Vernon, Raymond. *Dilemma of Mexico's Development*. Harvard University Press, Cambridge, Massachusetts, 1963.

more symbolic than practical, after half a century during which the Mexican left wing had used the issue as a stick to belabor the U.S. The problem originated with the wayward Río Grande, which changed its bed in 1864, moving south, thus cutting away a portion of Mexican land. In 1911 an international court decided to support Mexico's claim, but the United States never complied, no doubt reluctant to cede an inch to a country then engaged in civil strife. As the years went by it became more difficult to alter the *status quo*, especially since land and property values in El Paso were rising. But in 1963 it was agreed that the river should be forced willy-nilly back to where it came from, with dykes to insure that it does not misbehave again. The total cost both to the United States and Mexico will be high, but the battle for Chamizal has been won. It would be a happy ending if Señor Antonio Bermúdez, head of the Mexican National Frontier Program, were to get his way and the area were to be turned into an international university pledged to culture and peace.

A problem that was far from symbolic was the salting of the Mexicali Valley in northwest Mexico by contaminated waters from the Colorado River. In the autumn of 1961 the Mexicali rural population began to complain that Arizona farmers, cleaning their own lands in a desert-reclamation scheme and then returning heavily salted water to the main river flow, were causing losses to alfalfa and wheat crops in Mexico. Mexicali grows cotton too, but this crop did not suffer so seriously. Although the United States was able to release more water to reduce the salt content on the Mexican side, the problem continued and Señor Manuel Tello, then Mexican Foreign Minister, called it the most serious that Mexico had confronted in twenty years. A recommendation by the Mexican National Farmers' Federation that a canal be built to drain the offending waters from the Colorado's tributary, the Gila, and that drains should be installed to catch the salts accumulated in the Colorado itself, was put before the U.S. authorities; but the estimated $80 million necessary was not found. Heavy snows in the Colorado head-streams during the winters of 1961–62 and 1962–63 diluted the salt, and serious agitation on the Mexican side was thus avoided by luck; but informed Americans agreed that the Mexicans were remarkably patient as they watched the chapping and splitting of their lands. They bore too with the cynical view expressed by U.S. farmers that the international treaty fixing the supply of Colorado water to Mexico (at least 1.5 million acre-feet a year and often up to 2.5 million) made no stipulation about quality. The relevant treaty, signed in 1944, specified that waters should be suitable for agricultural, domestic, and industrial use.

Mexico refrained from taking the case to the Hague Court, and instead, in the summer of 1963, President López Mateos decreed that 10 million tons of Baja California iron ore should be exported to raise funds for desalting works on the Mexican side. Mexico continued to hope, however, that the salting problem would be attacked closer to its source on the U.S. side. In January 1965 a joint commission studying the matter reached a rather odd agreement—that for the next five years dredging and irrigation of the Welton-Mohawk Valley in Arizona should be carried out only in winter so that Colorado waters should be pure during the Mexicali cotton season from March to October. It was a little difficult to understand just how the salt reaching Mexico in winter was going to be prevented from penetrating the fallow soil. More practically, in June 1965 the U.S. announced that a $200,000 canal would be built in Arizona to divert the salted water before it reaches the affected Mexican lands. Mexico has also undertaken works on her side.

The flow of casual harvesting labor which used to be recruited in Mexico for the cotton and fruit crops of the southern states was terminated by the U.S. authorities in December 1964. "If ever there was a slave labor piece of legislation, this is it," said a U.S. Congressman when the *bracero* (casual labor) law was being discussed. Farmers, threatened with a shortage of seasonal workers, did not agree. Nor did the Mexican *braceros* themselves, who for years had been queuing up for the privilege of joining this so-called slave-labor band. U.S. unions on the other hand complained of unfair competition from the Mexicans.

Picking time in the United States is usually slack in rural Mexico, and the chance to see a little of the world beyond the border, to earn dollars, and to bring back a sewing machine for the wife and maybe a television set for the children used to be eagerly sought by *braceros*, who in the United States could earn 70 cents to a dollar an hour, the equivalent of their daily wage back home. The Mexican government, though opposed in principle to the *bracero* system as diminishing the home labor force, was concerned at losing an estimated income of about $33 million a year in dollars that were once brought back by the harvesters to their families (American sources put this figure at nearly double). In the bad old days the Mexican government complained of discrimination against their laborers and of unsanitary conditions in the work camps. But an agreement signed in 1962 stipulated that the Mexican worker must receive no less than the prevailing wage among U.S. workers of the same type. This clause, plus the privileged position of Mexicans who receive free medical treatment and are entitled to unemployment insurance policy (which U.S. harvesters are not), was responsible for American union complaints. The big farmers, on the other hand, claim that, although there are white Americans who will willingly pick their fruit trees, there are few who will contract for "stoop" labor (bending to pick lettuce or beet). In Imperial Valley, California, the temperature may stand at 100° F. during the picking, and Mexicans bear the heat better.

Since the Korean war, when a million Mexicans used to enter the American harvest zones annually, immigration dropped steadily until in 1963 the *bracero* contracts were only about 200,000. Automation, whereby even lettuces can now be picked and packed by machine, was partly responsible for the decline. Final withdrawal of the *bracero* will force U.S. farmers to devise ever more ingenious machines, even for such delicate tasks as tomato and pear picking. In the meantime if the U.S. authorities decide to solve the farmers' labor shortage problem by importing reduced numbers of *braceros*, Mexico will certainly not object provided the terms of the new contract insure fair working conditions. Otherwise the Mexican government must somehow and quickly create jobs for the former immigrants during the Mexican farming off-season.

The *bracero* problem is not to be confused with that of the illegal harvester, or "wetback." In 1953, 800,000 of these foot-loose men evaded the migration authorities and crossed the border, but were later apprehended in the United States. In 1962 this figure had fallen to under 20,000, and it is now negligible, though the men when caught are treated well and are given the choice of leaving the country voluntarily with no jail record against them. Only after repeated offenses are they punished more severely.

Apart from agricultural laborers, there are also town Mexicans who have been used to crossing the border daily, particularly to El Paso and to Brownsville, to regular jobs in commerce, industry, and transport. The American Federation of Labor and the Congress of Industrial Organizations complain that it is easier for Mexicans to work at lower wages and have tried to stop this practice, though many of the Mexicans have had official working permits for a decade and more. Mexican workers have threatened, if they are cut off from their source of income, to cease buying over the frontier, a move that would put many El Paso shops out of business. But if they did so, the Americans could retaliate by cutting off border tourism, which earns Mexico in the neighborhood of $560 million against about $240 million for tourism in the rest of the country.

Border malaise arises chiefly from the discrepancy in standards of living on either side. This in turn has created the American image of a poor Mexican ready to make money by exploiting the weaker sides of human nature—by gambling, drugs (Mexico is accused of corrupting American youth with marihuana), and prostitution. The counter-accusation is that Americans and not Mexicans keep open the hundreds of night-life establishments in Tijuana, Ciudad Juárez, and the other frontier cities, and that it is the Americans who ought to keep their youth from freely entering Mexico in search of sensual kicks.

Whoever is to blame, neither side can feel happy about the unsavory reputation of the border. The Mexican police have tightened their preventive measures against drug traffic, but in order to do everything possible to eradicate the image of a disreputable border town, the Mexican government in 1961 created the National Frontier Program under the quiet, elegant and cultured former head of Petroleos Mexicanos, Antonio Bermúdez. Over the years, about $100 million will be spent in improving the area. The towns are having new and modernized customs sheds, shopping and exhibition centers, and museums in Mexico's most daring architectural styles. Matamoros, boosted in the early 'fifties by huge public works such as the Anzaldúas canal and the Falcón dam, and by petroleum and natural gas works about Reynosa inland, has already a new gateway befitting the style and size of the port it would like to become. Dutch and British companies have been interested in developing shipping there, but decision is constantly delayed, possibly because of resistance from Brownsville across the mouth of the Río Grande, for here and in Port Isabel to the north about 5 per cent of cargo moved is Mexican (Mexico is estimated to pay yearly about $42 million for overland freight, handling, and services in U.S. territory).

Ciudad Juárez has also a new bridge, and a museum where cultural festivals are held. Tijuana's somewhat shoddy places of entertainment are being replaced by supermarkets, exhibition halls, theatres, movie houses, municipal buildings, a modern bull ring (Carlos Arruza, the greatest of Mexican bullfighters, says that American bullfighting enthusiasts in Tijuana are among the most discriminating in the world), by *jai-alai* (Basque *pelota*) courts, a golf course, a residential area, and an up-to-date institute of technology; not to mention a turnpike of nineteen lanes for traffic entering the U.S.A. and five for traffic entering Mexico (over 60 million crossings are recorded yearly along the whole border, so the lanes soon become congested).

All this, together with the cleaning up of slum areas, will begin to startle any American tourists who still arrive on the border under the illusion that the typical Mexican scene is a cactus, beneath which a peasant in a *sombrero* takes his *siesta*. In spite of Mexico's architectural prestige, there are still Americans who cannot quite believe that Mexicans are capable of laying one brick on another; in spite of Mexico's industrial growth, there are still Americans who, south of the border, stare amazed when they see cotton actually being transformed into cloth.

But the problem of the northern towns will not be fully solved until more diverse industries are set up in the hinterlands. Tourism apart, the solid basis for the border economy is at present cotton and cattle raising, the nearest industrial center to the frontier being Monterrey, 200 miles from Matamoros. Communications along the frontier are bad, and the visitor can motor from town to town only via the U.S. side. Water supply is deficient, especially in Tijuana, and in some areas electricity comes from the United States with resulting high rates.

As material conditions improve, it is hoped that the most deep-rooted border problem of all will be solved. It is the problem of the Mexican who loses his own identity and becomes a caricature, a *pocho,* imitating the American and at the same time exaggerating his own rough maleness. The *pocho* psychology pervades a wide area on either side of the border. There is a large Mexican population living in the United States at least as far north as Los Angeles, and these disinherited Mexicans often feel that they are discriminated against. According to a special correspondent of *The Times* of London writing from Los Angeles,[3] the status of the million and a half Spanish-speaking Mexican-Americans living in California is no better than that of the Negro and may even be worse; but in contrast with the Negroes, the Americans of Mexican origin have so far tended to keep their troubles to themselves because they are more ethnically self-contained and more strengthened by their distinct language and culture. Nevertheless, for a breadth of 200 miles or so on either side of the border there exists a psychological no-man's-land far more barren than the physical desert. The typical lower middle-class border Mexican cannot even spell, let alone express himself with precision in his own language, because he is constantly talking in a hotch-potch of two tongues. He begins to lose what Salvador de Madariaga has called his strong individual being.[4] To restore self-respect and cultural dignity is one of the most important tasks of the National Frontier Program.

THE SOUTHERN BORDER The National Frontier Program aims to improve the few towns on the southern border also; but here the problem is not so much urban as political. It is a sparsely populated area traditionally occupied in contraband. Central American and Cuban political refugees are from time to time reported active here, smuggling arms or broadcasting from hidden stations. Such underground groups are a threat to Mexico's policy of neutrality, but so far she has been able to deal with them well, and she has also re-

[3] *The Times,* London, August 20, 1963.
[4] Madariaga, Salvador de. *Latin America between The Eagle and The Bear.* Hollis and Carter, London, 1962, p. 13.

fused to become involved in Guatemala's chronic squabble with Britain over British Honduras. Mexico's legal claim to part of the colony has never been withdrawn but would, it seems, be pressed only in the unlikely event of a Guatemalan victory over Britain in this lingering controversy. George Price, Prime Minister of British Honduras, visited Mexico in the summer of 1964 and, to the annoyance of Guatemala, received offers of economic and technical help and support for self-determination. Later the same year an international bridge built by Mexicans across the Río Hondo became the first road link between the two countries.

The difficulty of exact definition of territorial waters has occasionally caused trouble in this area, and in 1959 Mexico and Guatemala broke off diplomatic relations because of an incident in which Mexican fishermen were killed by machine-gun fire from a Guatemalan military aircraft. Mexico behaved with dignity, and harmony between the two countries was later restored.

A NOTE ON THE CONSTITUTION There is one sin no good Mexican will allow himself to commit—to deny the importance of the revolution and of the principles now contained in the Constitution of 1917. A brief outline of its most important Articles may therefore help us to understand Mexico's foreign and internal policies.

Like most documents of the kind, the Constitution begins with a series of individual guarantees including the prohibition of slavery, the protection of foreigners, and the right of free expression. It describes the aims of education as tending "to develop all faculties of a human being harmoniously and at the same time to encourage in him a love of country and an awareness of international solidarity in independence and justice." It announces that education will be kept strictly apart from any religious doctrine, and it therefore forbids any religious bodies from taking part in primary, secondary, and normal (teachers' training) education. This clause has often been misrepresented through having been taken apart from the general principle of tolerance toward all religious beliefs. In fact it follows logically from such tolerance, which is guaranteed in a later article (24): "Every man is free to profess the religious belief that best pleases him and to practice the ceremonies, devotions, or acts of the cult in question, in temples or in his private home, so long as these do not constitute a crime or fault punishable by law."

Another misconception revolves round the passionate subject of expropriations. Foreign indignation over Cuban expropriation policies has recalled Mexico's expropriation of petroleum and railway companies in 1938 and of foreign electric power companies very much later, in 1960. Fears that foreigners may receive unjust treatment in future should be allayed by a reading of Article 27 of the Constitution, which specifies that expropriations can be made only with indemnification. Mexico has always paid her indemnities fairly and on time. The last installment of over $8 million to Eagle Oil shareholders was handed over on August 31, 1962.

Mexico believes that the wealth of her subsoil can be fairly claimed as her own; and though she is prepared to give concessions to foreigners from time to time, she is not prepared to see such wealth exploited mainly for foreign benefit. Like most democratic nations, she believes also that public utilities are best managed by government agencies. She is jealous of her frontiers, and forbids foreigners to own lands on the borders or seacoasts. She insists on her right to extend territorial waters to a nine-mile limit, which she considers more realistic in the modern world than the three-mile traditional limit still favored by some countries.

The Constitution delineates the powers of the three sections of government: legislative, executive, and juridical. Since the time of Benito Juárez the powers vested in the president have been almost dictatorial. It is he who names or dismisses his ministers and ambassadors, and he who promulgates laws. Neither the president nor his ministers are obliged to consult Congress before taking action, and overt criticism of them is regarded as close to rebellion. The president may not, however, leave the country without Congress permission. There is no vice-president, but Congress has power to elect an interim office-holder if need be. The presidential term is six years, and every government official signs his letters over an affirmation of the principles of "effective suffrage and no re-election."

Below the president are fifteen ministers, three government departments headed by secretaries of state, the public prosecutor, and a proliferation of partly government-controlled but in some important respects autonomous bodies such as the petroleum agency, the government financing agency, and the federal electricity agency (*Petroleos Mexicanos, Nacional Financiera,* and the *Comisión Federal de Electricidad*). The ministers do not hold regular meetings,[5] nor do they sit in Congress; but once a year through the president they report on the progress made by their departments.

Congress consists of an upper and lower house (Senate and House of Representatives). Until recently its powers have been nominal, but there are signs of change and some new laws and revisions to the Constitution have been the subject of heated debate. It can be assumed, however, that once the president has presented Congress with a new law, this will go through at least in broad outline.

The Supreme Court of Justice and its local subsidiaries have the power of granting *amparo,* the much-cherished right of the Constitution which resembles habeas corpus although Mexicans believe that it goes further. In theory, it allows for "stay" against legal action taken against private citizens, and through it even the most humble may question the constitutional legality of new laws. Under its protection, there has been an interesting trend lately for business enterprises to call in question the dictates of ministers and even on occasion to override ministerial rulings on the grounds of unconstitutionality.

Legal proceedings in Mexico have a tendency to proceed on the implicit assumption that, once a person is accused, he is guilty until he is proved innocent. Judges are poorly paid, so that they are recruited mostly from the ranks of unsuccessful lawyers, though there are noble exceptions to this generalization. There are too few judges for the accumulation of work, which has to be done hurriedly. These and other failures in the judicial system have been exposed often enough by eminent Mexicans,[6] who seem to believe that respect for law will not increase until its custodians are able to be a little more painstaking.

In spite of the discrepancy between legal principles and legal

[5] It looks as though President Díaz Ordaz will encourage them to do so. At all events he wants their work to be more closely coordinated.

[6] See for example an interview quoted in *Excelsior* of March 6, 1963, with Manuel G. Escobedo, who was educated at Oxford and is President of the Mexican Law Association.

practice, however, prison administration and prison rules are in some respects more civilized than in Europe. Much depends on the governor in charge of each prison, but in general the authorities aim at educating, rehabilitating, and keeping prisoners well and happy. In the men's prisons there are conjugal cells (with sofa, hatrack, and washroom) where they may receive one wife—but not more—in strict privacy once a week. All tasks performed by the prisoners are paid for, so that men can earn from $80 to $125 in a space of six weeks, and their only obligatory outlay is for new underwear; but some of the money is held back to be sent to their families or for presenting to them on their release. Amenities of this kind compensate in part, possibly, for the very long sentences judges are fond of imposing.

One section of the Constitution lays down the federal rights of the twenty-nine States. It is open to doubt, however, how long the States can continue to go their separate ways in an age of quick communications and integrated planning. There are jurists, such as Manuel Escobedo, who believe that the modern tendency toward centralization should be resisted; but their arguments seem to be based on the sacred character of the Constitution and are not very rational.

In Mexico City and in many towns of the republic there are streets named after Article 123 which deals with the rights of workers. After fixing maximum working hours, standards for health and safety, minimum salary, and the conditions in which women and minors may be employed, it lays down that industrialists must in certain circumstances provide housing and other amenities for their employees. Employers are responsible for accidents at work and for industrial illnesses. Trade unions and professional associations are declared legal. Workers and owners have the right to strike provided the aim is to reach a fair adjustment of all the factors involved in production.

Workers may not be unjustly dismissed, and here there has been some cause for complaint from factory owners, since there has been a tendency for the courts to side with the employee, the underdog. An amendment to the Constitution now gives workers the right to choose between re-employment or compensation in cases of wrongful dismissal. Protests from management have been met with an assurance that the government has no intention of protecting the dishonest or inefficient worker, but it remains to be seen how the new law will be interpreted.

Workers have also the right to participate in the profits of industry. American industrialists are apt to see in this ruling a dangerous tendency toward totalitarianism. It is obvious, however, that there is no such nefarious intent, the government being anxious only to protect sectors of the population that have been underprivileged for too long. The Mexican Constitution, in fact, does no more than acknowledge principles formulated by the United Nations and by most welfare states. If the Constitution could be fully upheld, it would surely be unexceptionable; and if some of the wording seems a little uncompromising, so also do the actions of those who have been prepared to scoff at its underlying aspirations toward maturity and justice.

6 Economics

A Oaxacan Indian was given 100 pesos to buy some goods which she could sell in the market. Thrilled at being thus unexpectedly transformed into a capitalist, she bought a chicken, which she sold for eggs, which she sold in turn for *tortillas*. After a day's work she returned home with a heavy deficit. She scarcely noticed. She had been rewarded by the excitement, the human exchanges, the bargaining and—as she thought—the sharpening of wits. But after a week her stomach began to grumble and her mind set to work on the balance sheet: seven days' entertainment and an empty larder. She had had no time to feed her pigs or to water her plot of corn. Her assets were dwindling.

There are about 210 million Latin Americans, and most of them are on the same economic level as this Oaxacan girl. They have been given agricultural credits, elementary medical services, and primitive schooling. Because of this slight upward leverage they have begun to ask questions their forefathers did not. They cannot be expected to go on living at almost animal level. Unless something is done to help them further there will be more Castro-type revolutions, more frequent left-wing agitation, more repressive coups by the right. This is the thesis behind the Alliance for Progress, which sadly failed at first to come up to expectation. Those who believe in it ask for patience, but Latin America may not be in the mood to wait.

Within the area the two countries that have set the pattern for reform are Mexico and Cuba. Mexico was lucky in passing through her critical revolutionary stage before 1917, before two world blocs had risen in threatening opposition. She was able to keep her struggle untainted by imported ideologies.

Whatever the first motivations of the Cuban experiment, the result has to date been otherwise, and the rocket-base crisis in the autumn of 1962 showed to what extent the island had lost identity and become a pawn. Whether the iron-curtain countries decide at any moment to protect or to sacrifice the Cuban revolutionaries will depend on the tactical value of the island. At present such value can be rated high, because Cuba represents a bridgehead in enemy territory. Its importance is scarcely so great that the Russians would risk total war on Dr. Castro's behalf; but it is certainly great enough to make some expensive cherishing worth while.

The counterattack from the West—it is generally agreed—must be to support non-totalitarian, democratic social revolution in Latin America. Mexico has had such a revolution and can be taken as the pattern. It is useless for American scaremongers to attack this country for nationalism, socialism, or any of the other wicked nonconformisms that periodically put United States residents in Mexico into a state of schizophrenic panic. Mexico's economic policies are calculated to answer the Cuban-Sino-Soviet threat in terms that potential or actual supporters of the latter will be able to understand. If Mexico moved over to the extreme right, if the government became a dictatorship propped up by the United States and without any effective independence of its own, this would create a situation disastrous to the Western cause. Latin American political unrest will be cured by raising the standard of living and in no other way; and Mexico is the key.

From being traditionally a country dependent on agricultural and mineral raw materials, Mexico is advancing toward full industrialization at a speed that makes foreign observers dizzy. Youthfulness, readiness to experiment, vitality, unorthodoxy, and above all, impatience to get through the transition stage: these are the characteristics that make Mexico a fascinating study and also—or so newspapers in France said on the eve of a state visit there by President López Mateos—"the most promising risk in the world today." Timid collaborators are out, together with all those who fear government participation in industry, nationalization, and Mexicanization.

The Mexican revolution has passed through two economic stages and is in the midst of a third. The first stage was one in which "social justice was given precedence over other considerations, including that of economic efficiency."[1] In the second, the trend was reversed, economic efficiency becoming more important than nationalism or social justice. Thus, says Arnold Toynbee,[2] "the most Díaz-like feature of this second phase . . . has been the extent of the foreign participation in it and contribution to it. And, this time, the United States has been by far the greatest single participator and contributor."

This stage began with the presidency of Avila Camacho (1940–46) and was brought to a peak by Miguel Alemán (1946–52). Since then the revolutionary pendulum has been slowly swinging back. In the third stage, which Toynbee does not note, the emphasis has been on economic independence even at the expense of a decelerated rhythm.

In the early fifties the gross national product was rising at the rate of 6 per cent per year, while the population rose by 2.5 per cent. This created the hope that the standard of living would double in twenty-five years. However, by 1962 the increase in the gross national product was falling and registered only 4.8 per cent a year, whereas the population growth rate had risen to more than 3 per cent. Investments from the private sector had dropped by 18 per cent. Home consumption of many manufactured goods has not been keeping up with production capacity. A recovery was made in 1963, however, the gross national product rising by 6.3 per cent, and private sector investments showing more confidence. An issue of government bonds, the first to be placed on the international market in fifty years, were oversubscribed and were soon selling above their face value.

The foreign debt[3] is growing by about 25 per cent a year, largely due to massive loans for electricity, petrochemistry, and heavy industries. The whole economy is still so much geared to that of the United States that any recession in the latter country has an immediate adverse effect on Mexico, and any unorthodoxy in Mex-

[1] Toynbee, Arnold. *The Economy of the Western Hemisphere.* Oxford University Press, London, 1962, p. 15.
[2] *Ibid.*, p. 16.
[3] It stood at nearly $1,505 million on December 31, 1963.

ican politics brings the threat of withdrawal of U.S. investments. Moreover, the efforts to establish independent and highly nationalistic policies have at times caused the withdrawal of American capital.

Any adverse factors that may curb Mexican economy, however, must be balanced against other achievements: a speeded-up agrarian reform with more large estates broken up and more land made over to peasants;[4] the beginnings of a genuinely national industrial production; a build-up of infrastructure including electrical and petroleum supply, roads, and railways; nationalization of a number of public utilities which, though inefficiently run at this early stage, should eventually allow for fully integrated national planning; more social security facilities; income tax and labor laws revised.

These measures have not yet had a chance to yield their full potential, but provided no brake on social reforms is imposed by the extreme right, they can be expected to further the aim of distributing the national income more equably.

In the meantime the following figures given by José Hernández Delgado,[5] Director of the government lending agency Nacional Financiera, testify to the country's achievements in the last three decades.

The employed population has increased as follows:

	Inhabitants	
	1930	1961
Total Population	16,553,000	36,369,000
Labor Force	5,166,000	12,226,000
Agriculture, livestock, forestry, and fishing	3,626,000	6,520,000
Industry	743,000	2,074,000
Commerce and finance	274,000	1,124,000
Transport and communications	107,000	437,000
Services	206,000	1,610,000
Unspecified activities	210,000	461,000

[4] In his 1964 state-of-the-nation report President López Mateos said that in six years over 16 million hectares had been handed over, whereas between 1915 and 1958 the total figure was 43.5 million.

[5] Hernández Delgado, José. *La Confianza como Factor Decisivo en el Progreso Económico y Social de México.* Nacional Financiera S.A., Mexico City, 1963.

At 1961 prices, national production rose from $1792 million in 1934 to $10,132 million in 1961, with increases in the different sectors of the economy registered as follows (in millions of dollars approximately):

	1934	1961
Agriculture, livestock, forestry, and fishing	356	2,058
Petroleum	62	507
Manufactured goods	246	2,592
Commerce and credit institutions	395	2,108
Transport	76	518
Other activities	431	2,133

The only sector which showed a decline during the period was mining, which fell from $227 million to $213 million.

In 1934 the country had 395,500 acres of land under irrigation. In 1962 it had nearly 10 million. In 1934 there were 2500 miles of road, and by 1961 there were over 28,000. Registered motor vehicles had risen from 108,421 to 902,029. Cargo transported by rail rose from 2495 to 8113 million tons per mile. Installed electrical capacity in 1937, the year of the creation of the Federal Electricity Commission, was 628,980 kw. By August 1962 it was 3.6 million. In 1944, when Altos Hornos de México, the largest steel works in the country, entered production, steel ingot output was 181,352 tons, and by 1961 this figure had risen to 1.7 million.

Banking and finance showed the following rises (in millions of dollars approximately):

	1934	1961
Assets of credit institutions	53	4,528
Assets of insurance companies	8.4	291
Circulation of fixed-interest shares	.8	1,532

Foreign trade had increased, in millions of dollars, approximately as follows:

	1934	1961
Exports	179	801
Agricultural products	28	389
Minerals including petroleum	158	168
Other goods	2	244

	1934	1961
Imports	924	1,140
Foodstuffs, drinks and tobacco, oils and fats	8.4	59
Chemical products	11	174
Raw materials except fuels	36.4	87
Fuels, lubricants, and electric energy	3	39
Machinery, tools, and vehicles	25	602
Other goods	8.4	179

Mexico's adverse trade balance has been due to the import of capital goods required by an industrializing country. With home manufacture of cars, trucks, and tractors, aluminum and steel, the situation is changing and the prognosis for a balance between exports and imports is improving. Although government expenditure has been rising rapidly, from $35.6 million in 1940 to over $1,274 million in 1964, a tightening of income-tax collection, more taxes on manufactured goods, and above all, increased revenue from tourism, have allowed the budget to be balanced in recent years. The negative trade balance has fallen from nearly $420 million in 1958 to over $302 million in 1963.

PETROLEUM A toad hopped from under the pipes and blinked. It looked dazed, as surprised as we were to find itself there, the only sign of natural life besides man himself in a wholly man-made city. Towers and tubing, many-colored and glittering in the tropical heat, rose on all sides from this island in the Tabasco marshes. From Ciudad Pemex to Mexico City, 600 miles of pipeline carry the fuel on which Mexico runs; yet around this fabulous refinery, which can treat 300 million cubic feet of gas and yield 15,000 barrels of absorption liquids daily, peasants still push their hollow tree-trunk canoes through the sluggish, weed-choked waterways.

Petroleos Mexicanos, Pemex for short, is the symbol of modern nationalism. There has been graft, inefficiency and gross overstaffing, at which the Mexican Press periodically inveighs; and yet 92 per cent of Mexico's total power supply—probably a higher percentage than in any other country in the world—comes from petroleum and gas. In 1962 Pemex paid off its expropriation debt, and the following year celebrated its silver anniversary with the announcement that it no longer needs to import.

Twenty-five years before it had been left by the foreign companies without adequate equipment and without technicians. It had endured hard years, and yet, when the country began to boom and modern industries demanded more and more power, Pemex was able to meet the 7 per cent yearly increase in national consumption. All told, its record has been an example to Latin America, too often timid of what may happen if foreign aid is withdrawn, and therefore needlessly dependent on foreign countries with their habit of imposing unwanted and often curiously contradictory political pressures. Pemex shows that when necessary a Latin American country is able to tighten its belt and learn from its own mistakes.

Attempts to exploit petroleum in Mexico date back to 1869, but not until 1901 was there successful commercial exploitation at Ebano in the State of San Luís Potosí; and British and American companies were soon virtual owners of this industry. Although Mexico's claim to the wealth of her subsoil had been established at the time of independence, a Mining Code drawn up in 1883 had ruled that petroleum was the property of the surface owner. Under this Code Sir Weetman Pearson (later Lord Cowdray) and the American, Edward L. Doheny, were able to establish their Mexican oil dominion. Until 1910 exploitation was on a small scale, and Mexican petroleum began to attract international attention just about the time when Porfirio Díaz was overthrown and the Mexican revolution began. Antonio Bermúdez,[6] Pemex Director from 1947 to 1958, alleges that with the discovery of the famous wells, Potrero del Llano and Cerro Azul:

. . . stakes rapidly became so high that politicans were bought and sold, insurrections were made and unmade through the direct or indirect influence of the oil companies and allied private interests, a situation which hampered and delayed the realization of the revolutionary objectives until the expropriation of the oil companies and the nationalization of the petroleum industry on March 18, 1938.

[6] Bermúdez, Antonio J. *The Mexican National Petroleum Industry: a Case Study in Nationalization*. Hispanic American Report, Stanford University Institute of Hispanic American and Luso-Brazilian Studies, California, 1963, p. 4. (The main bulk of this study was published privately in Mexico in 1960 under the title *Doce Años al Servicio de la Industria Petrolera Mexicana.*)

The first revolutionary president to make a serious attempt to curb the power of foreign oil companies was Venustiano Carranza. By his decree exploitation of the subsoil was allowed only by means of titles issued by the Federal Department of Industry, Commerce, and Labor; companies, moreover, must pay a royalty of 5 per cent of the gross production, and operations could not be suspended without good cause for more than two successive months. This decree, and subsequent laws and amendments all tending to bring the international companies to heel and to force them to continue oil exploitation under conditions agreeable to Mexico, led on the one hand to frenzied extraction of oil (just in case activities should become impossible in the future), and on the other hand to transference of some companies from Mexico to Venezuela.

In the meantime Mexican petroleum workers' unions were formed and became powerful, but the oil companies persistently refused to sign collective contracts with them. A series of conflicts came to a head in 1936 with the threat of a general strike. President Cárdenas counseled patience, and the strike did not break out until the next year. The workers asked that the controversy be submitted to the federal arbitration board, which fixed the terms of a collective contract, but the petroleum companies refused to agree and sought *amparo* (stay) from the nation's supreme court. On March 3, 1938, the court refused *amparo*. There were only two possible courses, to allow the foreign companies to override the Constitution and the decree of the supreme court, and thus to lay Mexico open to similar high-handedness in future, or to expropriate. In full knowledge of the difficulties ahead, President Cárdenas chose the latter course and expropriated the fourteen companies then working, including Eagle Oil, the Sinclair Piers Oil Company, the Richmond Petroleum Company, California Standard Oil, and Consolidated Oil.

The companies were shocked. They had not expected Mexico to risk such a drastic move, and they hoped that all foreign interests would assume a united front against Cárdenas. Opinion abroad, however, was almost equally divided between fury and approval. The British government was angry, but the United States took a more moderate view and noted particularly that the British Labor Party was congratulating Mexico for "refusing to supply the fascist aggressors [Germany] with petroleum and for having supported Republican Spain. . . . The Labor movement should strongly oppose any attempt on the part of the British Government to protect the interests of the oil companies."[7]

In the U.S. Congress, a Democrat attacked the companies for refusing to pay their employees anything more than a "mere pittance," and Mr. Cordell Hull declared that his Government could not doubt Mexico's right to expropriate her own national assets. President Roosevelt put the seal on American assent when he announced that the United States would not allow peace on the continent to be threatened by extra-hemisphere aggression.

It was absurd, of course, to suggest that there was ever any question of either Britain or the U.S. using armed force against Mexico, and short of that it is difficult to see what any foreign country could have done to reverse Mexico's decision. The companies had been presented with an accomplished fact, not with an offer for negotiation. However, Roosevelt's friendly statement was a clear rebuke to Britain for her intransigent attitude—so unrealistic as to be almost Quixotic—and there is reason to suppose that at that moment the United States was glad to seize an opportunity of appearing to support the removal of powerful British interests from Mexico, even if U.S. companies were out on their heels as well. British prestige had already suffered one blow when the railways were taken over in 1937. Now, once the excitement of oil expropriation had subsided, perhaps the United States might be able to re-enter the country with more absolute control than it had ever before wielded.

Whether or not these were indeed Roosevelt's thoughts on the matter, events worked out in favor of the Americans. Cárdenas, not very experienced in assessing the finer points of international politics, did not foresee the twist history would give to his action. Petroleum remained in Mexican hands, but with the coming of war, and with Europe fully occupied elsewhere, the United States was able to establish a hold on the Mexican economy that it has maintained to this day, to Mexico's gain in massive investments and in the patronage of a powerful neighbor, but to her cost in a far more complete economic dependence than the foreign oil com-

[7] *Revista de Revistas,* Mexico, December 24, 1961, published by the Mexican daily *Excelsior.*

panies had ever imposed. Thoughtful Mexicans have had reason since to wish that—though it was evidently necessary to put a stop to exploitation (even the accuracy of the bookkeeping of the foreign companies had been called in question[8])—the balance of foreign economic power had not been tampered with so hastily. They have been trying to redress it by seeking markets, loans, and investments in other parts of the world—in Europe, Latin America, the Far East, and Africa—but the overwhelming dominance of the United States remains.

However, in March 1938 Mexicans could see only the rosy side of expropriation. General Cárdenas was able to report that university students, workers, peasants, the army, and even the clergy and the women and children of Mexico, had all joined in spontaneous applause.[9] The terms of indemnification were drafted, and though many companies complained that these were not good enough, they took their cue from the Sinclair group which was the first—in 1940—to reach agreement with the Mexican government. The foreign companies were not entirely out, for Mexican Gulf Oil continued to work in Mexico until 1951, selling its products to Pemex for refining. It was then finally expropriated. When the Alemán government began to allow foreign concessions again, the first company privileged to return was the Pauley Petroleum Company, which has since given valuable help with underwater exploration in the Gulf of Mexico.

One of the chief complaints of the Mexican government against the foreign companies was that they had depleted the country's reserves. The year 1921 had seen the peak of exploitation, with 193 million barrels of oil extracted, of which 172 million were exported. After that, the original and fabulous Golden Lane near Poza Rica went into a decline, partly through depletion of reserves but also through the entry of salt into the wells. In 1937, the last full year before expropriation, only 50 million barrels were extracted, and in the year following, the first of Pemex rule, the figure dropped further to 18 million. Yet by the end of the Bermúdez

[8] Bermúdez, Antonio J. *Op. cit.*, p. 13.
[9] See speeches of Lázaro Cárdenas at the time of expropriation, reprinted and recorded by him in 1962 for *Voz Viva de México,* a series of phonograph records produced by the National University.

administration Pemex was a national power with international standing—and this in spite of the "oil barons" who were amassing fortunes in Poza Rica. Drilling had been resumed in the known oil-bearing areas, and by 1963 the new director, Pascual Gutiérrez Roldán, was able to announce that production had reached 122 million barrels a year.[10]

The cost has been high. Pemex income is about $600 million and does not meet expenditure which must be made up by heavy loans, mainly for expansion and exploration. In twenty-five years since expropriation the government invested $20 million, excluding investments made by Pemex itself. It is estimated that $1,800 million is needed for exploration in the next twenty years, when Pemex must find reserves equal to 8,900 million barrels of petroleum or twice the reserves between 1901 and the end of 1962. There are something under 58,000 square miles of oil-bearing lands, and another 27,000 square miles of continental shelf that can probably yield oil.

Helped by private enterprise, Pemex has established petrochemical centers in various parts of the country: in the Federal District; in Minatitlán, a boom town on the Gulf coast; in Salamanca in the central plains; in Tampico; and in Monclova in the State of Coahuila. There are more than thirty plants operating or under construction and providing mainly materials for fertilizers, detergents, chemical processing, industrial plastics, and synthetic rubber.

Foreign companies are still apt to underestimate Pemex, and Pemex itself is something of a strutting peacock, so it is not easy to assess its precise worth. Mexico runs on her own petroleum, however, and one is inclined to forget sometimes that only just over a quarter of a century ago Eagle Oil accounted for 70 per cent of the industry. Today, Pemex has control not only of petroleum and also of gas extraction, but of the oil and gas ducts extending for 7000 miles, as against less than a thousand when the foreign companies went out. Although Pemex invites private collaboration in the petrochemical industry, and has received strong support, especially from France, it must by law control the first stages of processing.

[10] In 1963 the average daily production was 345,000 barrels of oil and absorption liquids; this figure allows a margin of 50,000 barrels daily over and above immediate needs.

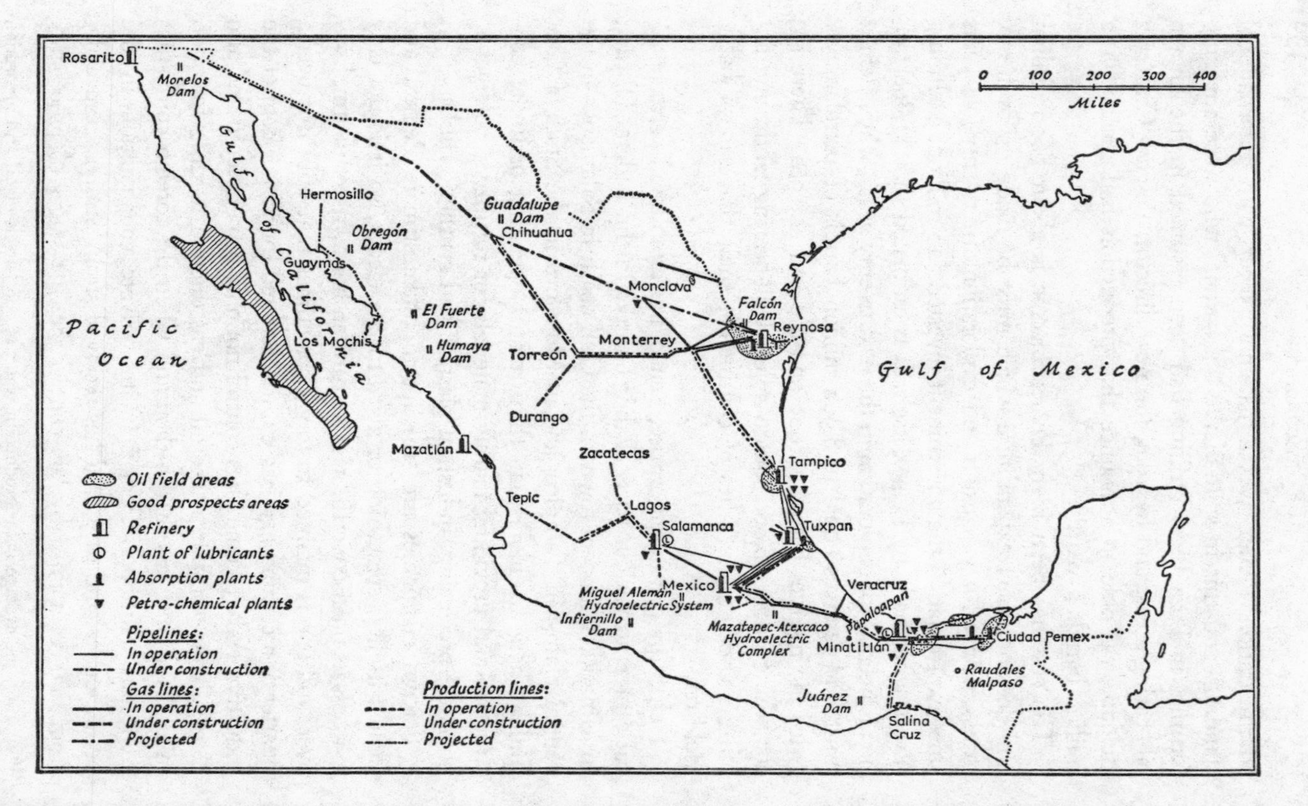

3. Petroleum Installations and Large Dams

In 1959 the Secretary General of the Mexican Oil Workers' Union referred sarcastically to the series of loans from foreign sources to Pemex as a "new foreign invasion"; but although these at the present time total about $209.6 million, all tied to the purchase of equipment, foreign participation had been strictly controlled.[11]

Mexico is unlikely ever to achieve the importance of Venezuela as an international oil producer, but the Pemex experiment is so interesting that it is curious how little attention it receives in foreign publications. J. E. Hartshorn,[12] industrial editor of the *Economist*, gives it scanty reference. Edward Ward[13] devotes a friendly but brief chapter. Pemex still awaits thorough and sympathetic analysis by a foreign expert; but any fair criticism must take into account Mexico's own aims for the industry. As Antonio Bermúdez says:[14]

Mexico is not a major exporter of petroleum, and it is not the national policy that it should become one. It is illusory, and would be harmful, to pretend that petroleum produced and exported in large quantities could become the factotum of Mexico's economy or the panacea for Mexico's economic ills. Mexico does not wish ever to be forced to export such an indispensable energy and chemical resource. Neither does it wish to compete with or join a world oil combine which does not and could not have Mexico's best interests at heart.

ELECTRICITY AND PEASANT REHABILITATION Electricity went the way of petroleum and was nationalized on Independence Day (September 16) 1960, when the Mexican Light and Power Company (owned by the international Société Financière de Transports et d'Enterprises Industrielles) was bought by the government. "Electric Services Have New Social Meaning from Today" said a headline, but the first noticeable effect was a rise in tariffs. Like Pemex, Luz y Fuerza is learning the hard way.

Electricity expropriation was, however, less important than the

[11] The French loan is for $150 million, the U.S. for $40 million, and two British loans total $9.8 million each.

[12] Hartshorn, J. E. *Oil Companies and Governments, an Account of the International Oil Industry in its Political Environment.* Faber and Faber, London, 1962.

[13] Ward, Edward. *Oil is Where They Find It.* Harrap, London, 1959.

[14] Bermúdez, Antonio. *Op. cit.*, p. 115.

petroleum take-over, since it merely marked the logical conclusion of a long process begun twenty-three years earlier with the formation of the Federal Electricity Commission; and the Commission had already done notable work in building vast hydroelectric-irrigation-rehabilitation complexes in potentially productive but undeveloped valleys.

From the days of the poet-king Nezahualcoyotl, whose aqueduct continued to be used long after the Spanish conquest, Mexicans have been builders. Their engineering has the élan of art, as if this land were looked upon as a pliable block of clay to be shaped for the fun of it. Lakes have been tossed in among mountain defiles, returning to the majestic landscape its missing element—water—and completely changing the habitat of thousands of peasants. Three of Mexico's most urgent problems—the control of its erratic water supplies, the adjustment of the poor Indian to modern techniques, and the stepping up of its power potential—have been solved simultaneously in some parts of the country.

In one Chamula Indian village in the Chiapas highlands, the chieftain stubbornly opposed a proposal from the National Indigenous Institute that electricity should be installed. It was against the will of the gods, he said. A neighboring village, with a more forward-looking chief, got its light. On foot and on muleback people rode to admire the new wonder. "You can see our homes from far away," cooed a Chamula boy, and the resistance of the conservative neighbor chieftain was broken down.

Consumption throughout the country has been rising at the rate of 84 per cent in 10 years—from 171 kilowatt-hours per inhabitant in 1951 to 315 in 1961. The López Mateos administration raised installed capacity to 5 million kw. at the end of 1964. About 57 per cent of electric energy is provided by thermic plants and 43 per cent by hydroelectric complexes. Geothermic power is also being developed in the State of Hidalgo, where a pilot unit of 3500 kw. has been installed.

Of the large hydroelectric schemes, the first was in the Gulf Coast river basin of Papaloapan (land of butterflies). The whole catchment covers over 15,000 square miles, the river itself being 300 miles long and navigable to about half its length. Two of its six tributaries—the Santo Domingo and the Tonto—have been subject to heavy inundations since at least the sixteenth century, and a particularly bad flood had taken place in 1944. Thereupon the Ministry of Hydraulic Resources, the Ministry of Health, the Indigenous Institute, and the young Federal Electricity Commission pooled resources in a sevenfold program including electricity supply, irrigation, and rehabilitation of the three different groups of Indians inhabiting the area. Unfortunately some of the plans have stagnated; but even as it stands the Papaloapan experiment can serve as a model for similar schemes.

About 20,000 Mazatecan Indians (probably belonging to the Chichimeca group, wild and hostile) had to be moved from the floor of the Miguel Alemán reservoir, which now circles several hills, is 20 miles long, and covers 118,000 acres. The electric plant is generating 774 million kilowatt-hours per year, partly for the benefit of the government steel and aluminum complex near Veracruz. Below it, flocks of heron and widgeon whiten the rocks of the river Tonto. A broad-beamed motor vessel waddles across the lake carrying supplies to the villages that are otherwise cut off from civilization. Before the Commission began its work, sugar and coffee were the region's chief crops, which were bought in advance according to prices fixed by local merchants. The Commission now helps to negotiate better terms for the peasants, a hybrid corn has been introduced, and rice, sesame, and beans are grown.

Miguel Alemán also gave his name to the hydroelectric complex of Valle de Bravo. Though it lies over the western watershed, it sends electricity to Mexico City and to villages in seven surrounding States. Three large and seven smaller lake-reservoirs have been formed at heights from 8600 to 2500 feet above sea level, one of the prettiest being Valle de Bravo itself, which is a fashionable boating resort. Toltec paintings have been preserved on cliffs high above the power plants in this region where puma and iguana still roam.

The Santo Tomás reservoir was formerly the site of an Indian settlement, which has been moved to what local people like to call the "newest village in the world," though this title must by now have been wrested from it many times over in Mexico alone. The new Santo Tomás is high on the cliffs, and the change in climate must have caused some hardship to the formerly tropic-dwelling peasants. Farm holdings are some distance away, the new concrete houses being packed close together. There is nowhere to put animals; and donkeys, goats, and even pigs have had to share modern quarters with their owners. But the Commission has learned a lesson and rehabilitation techniques are being perfected.

Among other schemes there are the El Fuerte reservoir in Sinaloa —an inland sea providing energy for a market-garden area that supplies Mexico's canning industry; the Humaya also in Sinaloa; the Guadalupe on the river Papigochic near Chihuahua; the Atexcaco and the Mazatepec northeast of Puebla where the fall of water to the hydroelectric plant is 1640 feet; the Raudales-Malpaso on the Grijalva River, the largest complex of its kind in the world—it is said —and destined to irrigate 875,000 acres of arable land and the same again of pasture; the Juárez dam on the Tehuantepec River in the State of Oaxaca; and hundreds of smaller multi-purpose schemes that must be gladdening the heart of Tláloc and Chac, the old rain gods so scurvily treated during long centuries of haphazard wood-felling.

One of the most controversial of the hydroelectric schemes, known as *Infiernillo* and claimed to be the most important project of its kind in Latin America, is nearing completion. It lies almost 200 miles west and slightly south of Mexico City, on the Balsas River near the junction of the Tepalcatepec, between the States of Guerrero and Michoacán. This is a jagged landscape of mountain and mostly desert plain, with some rice paddies and poor-grade cotton edging the Tepalcatepec: not a propitious place for a hydroelectric complex since there will be only limited possibilities for irrigation. *Infiernillo* itself is exclusively to provide electricity for the distant capital and its surrounding Federal District, where the demand is increasing by 70,000 kw. per year. But the long defile must have lured engineers, for it stretches sixty-two miles. A lesser arm of the reservoir will spread for about half that distance along the open valley of the Tepalcatepec. The whole reservoir will be double the size of Mexico's largest natural lake, Chapala, and the electric plant, tunneled into the mountain and as deep as a twelve-story building, will have 600,000 kw. capacity. For two years every eighteen seconds a truck dumped rubble to form the 510-foot dam wall—and woe to anyone late. Mexico can hardly be called a land of *mañana*.

DECENTRALIZING FROM THE TOPHEAVY CAPITAL Mexico has power in abundance, and well distributed over most parts of the country. Yet about one Mexican in seven lives in the topheavy capital or its surrounding area. The 5 million people concentrated here are using so much water that by 1980—when the population may well be more than 15 million—the situation will have become disastrous. The traffic congestion in the narrow streets about the National Palace is almost as bad as along Fifth Avenue—though Mexico City is better endowed than most European capitals with parkways.[15]

Mexico City accounts for more than half the country's total industrial output. The figure will be 60 per cent by 1980, says Dr. Paul Yates,[16] who, like the Mexican, Ernesto López Malo,[17] has made a series of recommendations for industrializing zones particularly well endowed with communications, power, and raw materials. Dr. Yates would like to see agricultural areas marked off as "green belts," for Mexico has a chance now to avoid such terrors as Britain's "black country" or the German Ruhr.

But the policy of decentralization meets with all kinds of obstruction, such as unwillingness of the new middle classes to live in provincial obscurity, surrounded by a countryside that has none of the cushioned rusticity of Europe. Dr. Yates lists a few of the forces tending toward concentration in the Valley of Mexico: the lower electricity rates, cheap natural gas, good communications, growing mass-production methods which make it difficult for small family-type provincial businesses to continue, an experienced labor force, good social services and housing, and—not least—the ambition of wives who want to show off their clothes and marry their children well. In 1958 the Federal District's annual income was a little

[15] There is a scheme, attractive though probably it will be condemned as unpractical, to turn this old center into a "museum city" with cobbled streets and no wheel traffic.

[16] Yates, Paul Lamartine. *The Regional Development of Mexico*. Bank of Mexico Industrial Investigations Department, Mexico City, 1961.

[17] López Malo, Ernesto. *Ensayo sobre Localización de la Industria en México*. Mexican National University, 1960.

under $20 per head of population, whereas most medium-sized towns averaged considerably less than $3. Factories contribute nothing to their municipalities, and State governments have lost revenue by tax exemptions in a vain effort to attract industry. Other important forces are the concentration of financiers in the capital, federal export taxes that discriminate against the provinces from which export products emanate, and ever-increasing centralized bureaucratic control.

Although the government is doing much to encourage decentralization, directing international bank loans toward regional schemes and setting up heavy industries in new towns such as Salamanca in the area known as the *Bajío,* or Ciudad Sahagún, north of the capital where the government has its railway wagon and automobile factories, it remains a mystery why some of these towns boom and some remain enveloped in an atmosphere of sunbaked drowsiness. Examples of the latter kind are the twin towns of Gómez Palacio and Torreón, in what is known as the *Laguna* area of the northwest. These towns were created by the revolution, more especially by Lázaro Cárdenas who developed this unattractive, dusty plain—a dried up inland sea—as a cotton-growing center. European refugees and Arabs set up family businesses which flourished until overproduction of cotton brought an end to the dream. Then came years of drought and cold, so that now the iron bridges spanning the waterless river beds look queerly redundant, trees are withering under the dust, more than half the irrigation water comes from underground wells and is costly to pump, and the government has been reduced to moving part of the peasant population to the Yucatán peninsula—a heroic measure since the innate conservatism of peasants makes projects of this kind delicate to handle. The Federal Government, too, has urbanized nearly 600 acres of desert land to form an industrial zone fed by a pipeline from Reynosa; but factories have been reluctant to rent sites at the high prices demanded.

Chicken farms and vineyards are supplementing the uncertain cotton production, and a local planning committee has enlisted the help of industrialists from New Orleans to recommend suitable industries. The Durango State government is waiving taxes for twenty years and giving worker-management guarantees.

But the whole area is sad and chromium-plated, Americanized but unprosperous, a slut living on the slum fringe of mass production and with none of Mexico's traditional charm. Perhaps these two towns were artificial creations doomed to failure from the start; for as a contrast there is Monterrey, booming on beer and bottles and steel, even setting the pace for the capital.

In a sense Monterrey ought not to exist at all. It, too, is in a barren plain. It is unendowed with water, raw materials or, until recently, good communications. Its bungalow buildings are set among hills that yield only lime and clay for cement, and an occasional pseudo-baroque cupola emphasizes the newness. There is nothing to suggest, at first sight, the canny business sense of its 600,000 inhabitants, grown from 72,000 in 1900.

In the early part of the century a farsighted state governor waived taxes to industrialists and gave them surplus land on which to build. But along came the revolution, industry closed shop, and Monterrey stagnated. In spite of chronic droughts, there were disastrous floods in 1901 and again in 1938, and many companies lost their capital several times before they could establish themselves. The barley for the pioneer industry, beer, had to be brought from afar. Czechoslovakian technicians were called in to make bottles. Bottles needed machinery, and machinery needed steel, so a special porous "sponge steel" that could be manufactured with cheap Texas gas instead of coal was developed. It was a little like the House that Jack built. Initiative invited initiative until today, except for electricity plant and the heaviest steel foundries, the town runs on home-made equipment. It looks deceptively impermanent, with much of the work done in the open air, as if this were a frontier encampment that might fold its tents and move westward in the night.

What has Monterrey got that Torreón, for example, has not? One important factor in its development has been the realization that no industry is possible without sound technicians and contented workers. The Monterrey Technological Institute was founded by private enterprise and has a high reputation. Students are driven hard but they are taught the graces of living too, and learn to keep the flowers of their campus blooming. Besides the more mundane textbooks, the library contains volumes on sixteenth-century Mexican history, rare books printed in Indian tongues, and 2000 editions of *Don Quixote* in most languages under the sun.

Before Mexico had any free medical services or social security, Monterrey businessmen had provided clinics. Profits from beer built a club where workers can get cheap meals, learn crafts, or join in theatrical and sports activities. They can buy their own rate-free bungalows on the never-never plan, and the particular Monterrey virtue—thrift—is encouraged by savings schemes. In Mexico City before each national holiday there are queues outside the government pawnshop, *Monte de Piedad,* where people convert their watches and sewing machines into ready cash. In Monterrey—its citizens boast—there is always something put aside.

The example of Monterrey seems to indicate that charity toward underdeveloped areas can be but a poor substitute for local initiative. Its exclusive clique of business magnates, accused of being tight-fisted, can justify their apparent niggardliness (and it is only apparent) by claiming that they have raised the living standards of a whole area. A diplomatic mission from behind the iron curtain was incredulous, but the system works.

It seems that in Mexico each town must go its own original way. Guadalajara, for instance, slightly larger than Monterrey with over 700,000 people, but less industrialized, has been trying without success to attract heavy industry. Its relative industrial failure is precisely this old colonial town's salvation. There are plenty of light industries that need the artist's touch, and their promoters are bound in time to discover the virtues of this region and its talented people. In the meantime Guadalajara should feel happy in its craft tradition, which it shares with the third of the important provincial towns, Puebla. But Puebla is nearer Mexico, to which it is connected by an extravagant new highway skirting the two snow volcanoes. So it has been able to set up cement and motorcar factories to supplement its tourist trade.

It seems reasonable to suppose that in future decentralized industry will follow the oil-gas-duct network. Heavy industry will thus trace a line from Minatitlán and the Isthmus petrochemical centers, to Veracruz where a rural Sheffield, turning out seamless steel tubes and aluminum, already squats amid fields where cranes perch in the treetops. Thence the line of industry will rise to Puebla and Mexico City, from where it will fan out in a general northwesterly direction to include such towns as Querétaro, Irapuato, Celaya, and Salamanca, before tapering away into the craft industries (including shoe manufacturing) of Guadalajara. An industrial park development in Querétaro has been sponsored by the important Mexican group, Ingenieros Civiles Asociados (ICA) and its subsidiaries. Loans have been obtained from the Interamerican Development Bank, from France, Sweden, and Denmark; and U.S. and other foreign firms are entering the area in joint-capital enterprises to build heavy machinery for the construction industry, dam gates, and the like.

Another industrial zone will embrace Reynosa on the Gulf, Monterrey, Monclova, Saltillo, and perhaps even Chihuahua in the northwest, with an extension at the coastal end of the Chihuahua-Pacific Railway in Los Mochis and Topolobampo, suitable centers for vegetable canning.

There will be ample space for Dr. Yates's "green belts" in the areas between. Some industrialists are encouraging the replacement of trees in eroded areas, and a complex of factories making electrical appliances is being set up on a famous ranch—Pastejé—that once bred fighting bulls. Together with the architect, Enrique de la Mora, Alejo Peralta (director of the Polytechnic Institute at the time of its greatest expansion) is planning a factory community in which each family will still keep roots on the land, and will continue to own and work its *ejido* holdings. The peasant girls, who decorously wear skirts over their jeans, will bicycle home at nights to their farm cottages surrounded by plots tilled by the old folk. These muscular peasants make good solderers and conveyor-belt workers, but they belong to the out-of-doors and are to remain there as far as possible.

COMMUNICATIONS Though Mexico's highways straddle the mountains with a nonchalance that makes their steep gradients seem like gentle slopes, there are still many areas of the country that must depend on air transport if they are not to be isolated from national life. Small planes hopping like crickets from valley to valley keep

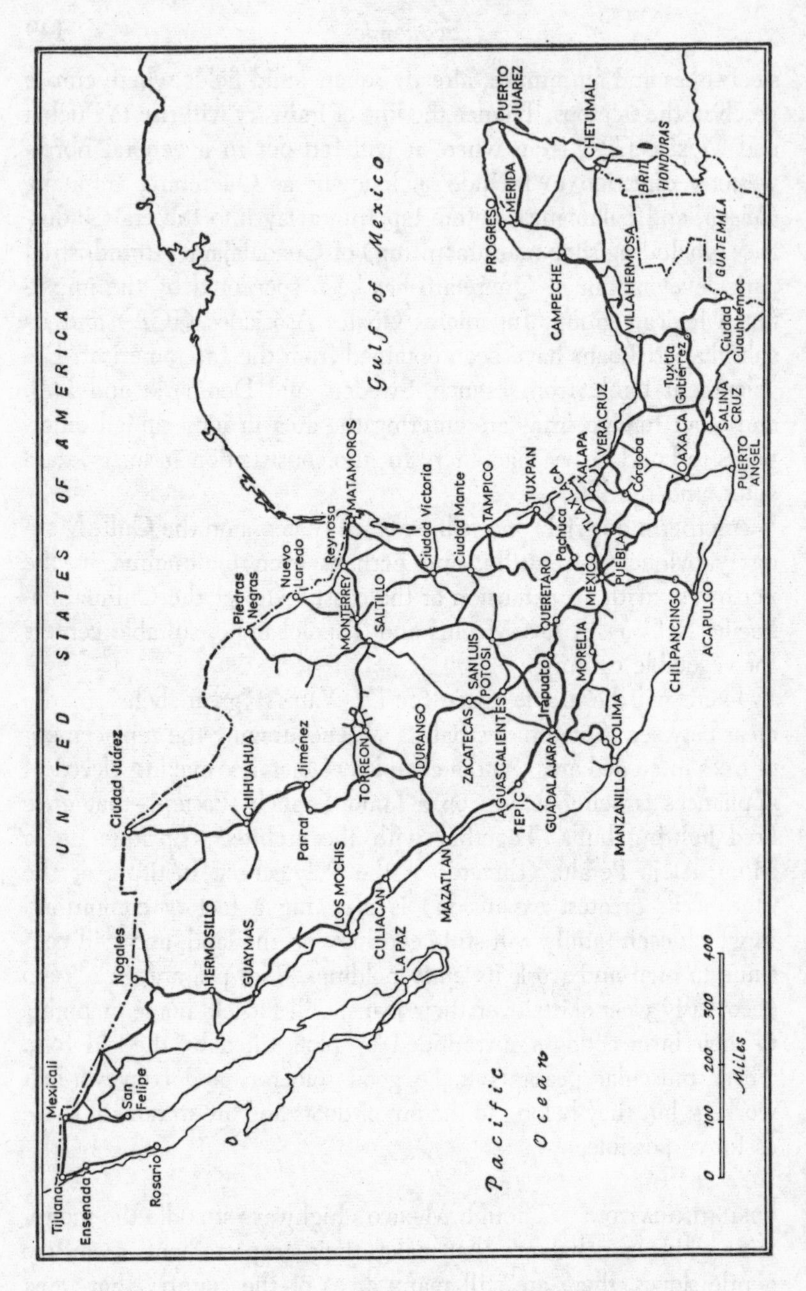

UNITED STATES OF AMERICA
Gulf of Mexico
Pacific Ocean
Tijuana
Ensenada
Mexicali
San Felipe
Rosario
Nogales
HERMOSILLO
GUAYMAS
Ciudad Juárez
CHIHUAHUA
Parral
Jiménez
LOS MOCHIS
CULIACAN
LA PAZ
MAZATLAN
TORREON
DURANGO
Piedras Negras
Nuevo Laredo
Reynosa
MATAMOROS
MONTERREY
SALTILLO
Ciudad Victoria
Ciudad Mante
TAMPICO
ZACATECAS
SAN LUIS POTOSI
AGUASCALIENTES
TEPIC
GUADALAJARA
Irapuato
QUERETARO
Pachuca
TUXPAN
TLAXCALA
XALAPA
VERACRUZ
Córdoba
PUEBLA
MEXICO
MORELIA
COLIMA
MANZANILLO
CHILPANCINGO
ACAPULCO
OAXACA
PUERTO ANGEL
SALINA CRUZ
Tuxtla Gutiérrez
Ciudad Cuauhtémoc
GUATEMALA
VILLAHERMOSA
CAMPECHE
PROGRESO
MERIDA
CHETUMAL
PUERTO JUAREZ
BRIT. HONDURAS
0 100 200 300 400
Miles

4. Roads

banking, business, and industry moving between Mexico City and the hinterlands. The two national airlines, Aeronaves de México and Compañía Mexicana de Aviación, operate under financial difficulties but are doing essential work in keeping out-of-the-way corners of this diverse country knit together. Though their international flights are a luxury maintained for the sake of prestige, their national flights are vital.

The road network, which links all main population centers, has recently been augmented by three important arteries. One is the Mexico City-Puebla highway. Another is the 194-mile road from Durango to the Pacific port of Mazatlán, where the first west-coast oil refinery is to be built. This crosses the heights of the Western Sierra Madre at a point where, since 1943, engineers have dreamed of driving a road through the trails of illegal woodcutters. Now, at a cost of over $11 million, this has been done. A 1160-mile road, too, stretches unbroken except for several ferries from Mexico City to the northeastern tip of the Yucatán peninsula. The coastal section almost completes the Gulf circuit, which will eventually extend 1524 miles from Matamoros on the Mexico-U.S. border to Quintana Roo.

At a time when most countries are closing down obsolete railways, Mexico is building new lines. The government believes that the cost is justified by the need to give access to areas that have remained practically untouched since preconquest days. The spectacular mountain sectors of the Chihuahua-Pacific Railway, which runs 563 miles from Ojinaga, on the Texas border, to Topolobampo, on the California Gulf, were completed in 1961 and follow a tracing laid down by two Mexican brothers, Francisco and Ramón Togno, who later busied themselves planning the Mexico City-Acapulco line.

The original scheme for a Chihuahua-Pacific railway dates back to the last century. In 1872 an American socialist, Albert Kimsey Owen, dreamed of establishing an ideal city bordering the ample bay of Topolobampo and connected to New York by rail. His project received a sympathetic hearing from U.S. President Ulysses S. Grant but no money was forthcoming. In 1881, however, Mexico gave Owen a concession for a transcontinental railway and for his "city of peace." He floated a company and issued co-operative bonds which were bought by idealists of diverse nations, tempted by his premature scheme to found a welfare state. With more enthusiasm than talent the settlers sang:

> Beyond the lofty peaks of snow,
> In the sunny land of Mexico,
> Where purest, sweetest waters flow
> Adown a lovely bay . . .

The reality was different. Typhoid sapped the physical and moral strength of the settlers and they made tracks for home. Owen blamed their lack of understanding, but they could hardly have been expected to exist on hope. No housing, food, or drinking water had been provided.

A railway was later built from Ojinaga to the down-at-heel mining and lumber town of Creel. Another went from Topolobampo to San Pedro, where the coastal plain meets the mountain wall. Between Creel and San Pedro the land drops from 8000 to 400 feet in 150 miles, and this stretch of line remained unlaid until the Togno brothers surveyed the area between 1940 and 1942. Today the railway has been built with French techniques, including elastic line and concrete sleepers; but all the engineers on the job were Mexican. The completed railway should revive the area's stagnant mining, permit timber exploitation, and give an outlet to the Pacific for Mexican cotton, of which Japan and Indonesia are buying large quantities. The cost of the line was over $87 million, but the track brings this backward area to life. Between Chihuahua and Creel there is a cellulose factory and a creosote-treating plant for sleepers. Near Ciudad Cuauhtémoc in the highlands, Mennonites have tamed the landscape until it becomes an example of wise husbandry; they can be seen, pale and puritan in their bonnets and pony-traps, like extras in a western movie. After passing their farms, journeying westward, one reaches the wild Barranca del Cobre (a gorge that Mexicans like to compare to the Grand Canyon of the Colorado) where Tarahumara Indians, their skins almost ebony, their hair bobbed, and wearing loincloths and full-sleeved satin blouses, live in caves on its steep walls tangled with vegetation. Some of the Indians were employed laying the track, and one saw

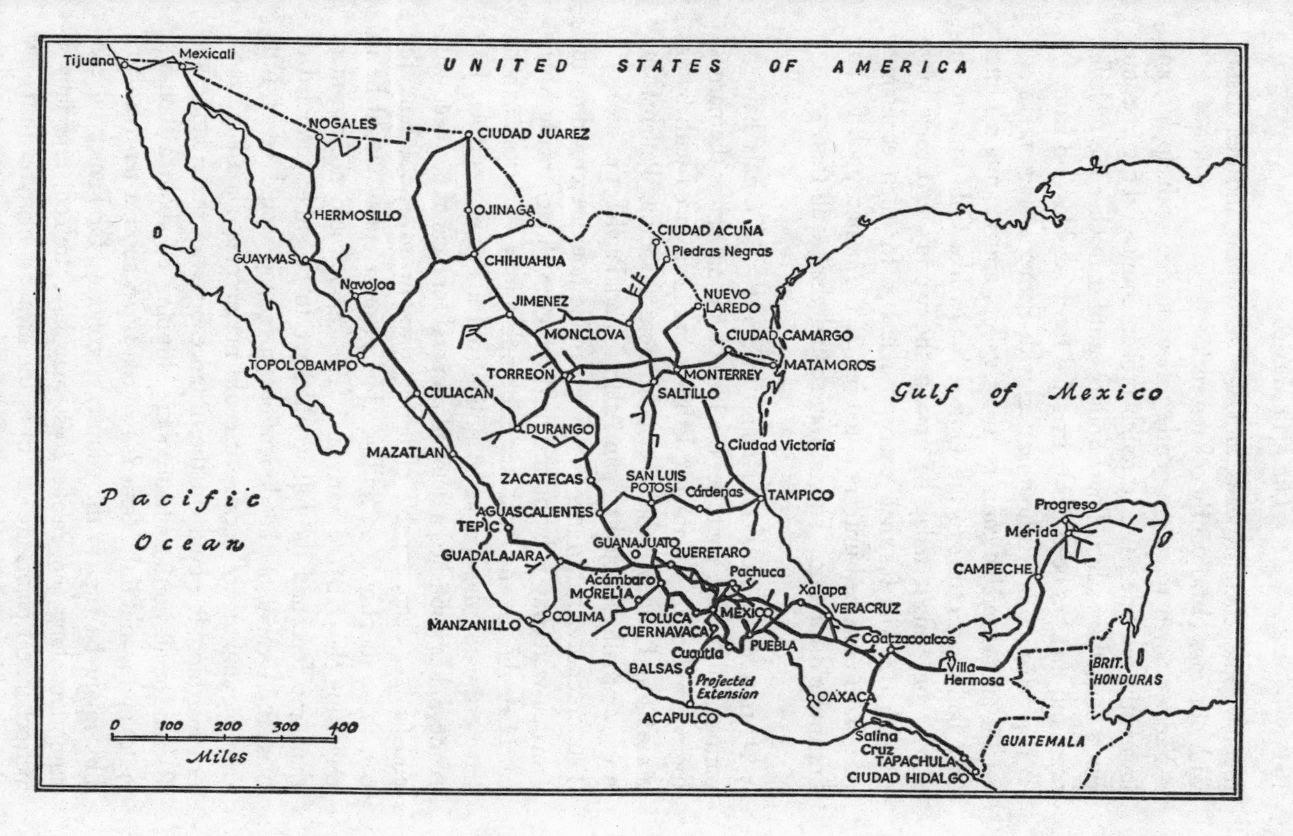
UNITED STATES OF AMERICA
Gulf of Mexico
Pacific Ocean
Tijuana
Mexicali
NOGALES
CIUDAD JUAREZ
HERMOSILLO
OJINAGA
CIUDAD ACUÑA
Piedras Negras
GUAYMAS
CHIHUAHUA
Navojoa
NUEVO LAREDO
JIMENEZ
MONCLOVA
CIUDAD CAMARGO
TOPOLOBAMPO
TORREON
MONTERREY
MATAMOROS
CULIACAN
SALTILLO
DURANGO
MAZATLAN
Ciudad Victoria
ZACATECAS
SAN LUIS POTOSI
Cárdenas
TAMPICO
AGUASCALIENTES
TEPIC
Progreso
Mérida
GUANAJUATO
QUERETARO
GUADALAJARA
CAMPECHE
Pachuca
Acámbaro
Xalapa
MORELIA
VERACRUZ
COLIMA
MEXICO
TOLUCA
MANZANILLO
CUERNAVACA
Coatzacoalcos
PUEBLA
Cuautla
BALSAS
Villa Hermosa
BRIT. HONDURAS
Projected Extension
OAXACA
ACAPULCO
Salina Cruz
GUATEMALA
TAPACHULA
CIUDAD HIDALGO
0 100 200 300 400
Miles

5. Railways

them working there in jeans, amid forests of pine and ilex slashed with outcrops of brilliantly colored rock.

Farther down there are gentle valleys loaded with apples, and lower still the line passes through broken country, the gorges and rivers crossed by tall, willowy bridges, until it reaches the table-flat coastland that has been partly irrigated for vegetables and fruit.

Topolobampo is a fishing center, with Pemex storage tanks and a fruit and vegetable cannery. If its valleys and mountain hinterland had been ceded to the United States like California to the north, they might today be among the world's expensive playgrounds. Luckily for their peace, but less so for their economies, they have remained until now too far off the beaten track for any but intrepid travelers. The railway should change all that.

A TEHUANTEPEC CANAL? Dreams of great ship canals have an ominous allure. For centuries the idea of a canal across the narrowing waist of the Tehuantepec Isthmus has been toyed with by engineers, and though the obviously more favorable Panama site was eventually selected to join Atlantic and Pacific, the idea of a Tehuantepec canal to take the excess traffic now overcrowding the Panama waterway is by no means dead, even though many Mexicans fear the international strategic implications. American experts have estimated the cost at $8 billion, but a Pemex engineer, José Noriega, has published a detailed proposal for a canal 600 feet wide and 60 feet deep, capable of taking ships up to 35,000 tons, the cost to be roughly $600 million. The greatest outlay would be in traversing the 720-foot watershed. The canal would not rise more than 400 feet, and the hill would have to be either tunneled or blasted. A canal of the dimensions suggested would be of little strategic importance because it could not accommodate large modern warships. It would cut the distance between the Atlantic and Pacific for all northern-hemisphere shipping by about a thousand miles and would link Mexico's two coasts. In another ten years this link might be vital to the country's economy, for Pemex oil consumption along the Pacific coast may have trebled, especially if petrochemical plants are set up in the area. As many as thirty-five ships could pass daily through the canal—an annual tonnage of 60 million, or slightly more than the present capacity of the Panama

Canal. The calculated financial value to Mexico is $400 million a year at least, possibly even double that amount. Almost all the engineering works could be put to multiple use, including electricity generation, irrigation, and protection of the lowlands from flood.

A four-stage building program is recommended, so that if for any reason the canal were not completed the preliminary works could still be fully used. By dredging, and with one or two cuts, the Coatzacoalcos River flowing into the Gulf could be made navigable to about half way across the Isthmus, so that the canal proper would not be more than about fifty-eight miles long. A reservoir would be built on the lower reaches of the river for electricity and irrigation.

Stage two would be to dredge the Great Lagoon on the Pacific, east of the port of Salina Cruz, so that ships could navigate about eighteen miles inland. A second reservoir and dam on the Gulf side of the watershed would allow shipping to penetrate as far as Matías Romero, which is almost at the watershed and might become a refinery center. There would remain only about eighteen miles, the most expensive to build. This stretch could be left pending without prejudice to the usefulness of the other two working stages. In the meantime cargo could be transported by rail by what the Americans call the "piggy back" or "sea train" system.

No concession to the United States for building a canal is or would be contemplated. Rights granted to the U.S. in 1853 for a canal were repealed in 1937, so that although foreign capital would presumably have to be found to help finance such a venture, the canal would remain Mexico's sovereign territory: a possibility that does not altogether appeal to the United States, which prefers a second canal in Panama or through the lake district of Nicaragua. Nicaragua, however, also appears to be insisting on maintaining sovereignty over any canal built there.

While Mexicans in general continue to regard the canal proposal with grave doubts, they are nevertheless eager for good communications across the Isthmus. The obsolete existing railway is being brought up to date and will have facilities for transferring containers between ship and rail. This railway forms the only direct link between Mexico's two coasts, and at either end of it the free ports of Coatzacoalcos (sometimes known as Puerto México) and Salina Cruz allow goods from the U.S. Atlantic seaboard to reach her Pacific cities tax free by sea (or *vice versa*) with only the small overland journey across the Isthmus. Movement of merchandise in the port of Coatzacoalcos has increased by over 2000 per cent since 1954; and if this trend continues the building of a canal here may be the logical sequence.

MINING Throughout Mexico's post-conquest history, mining has been a focus for passionate controversy. When in the early nineteenth century Alexander von Humboldt made a detailed investigation of the industry, he found that the methods of ore extraction were absurdly primitive. Ladder shafts sometimes 1800 steps deep had to be climbed by Indians loaded with anything up to 350 pounds of ore. Mercury was being imported from Spain for the process of extracting precious metals by amalgamation, and this was raising costs. Nevertheless, pay was good, there was no forced labor in the mines as there was in Peru, and vigilance was so lax that workers could loot metal and thereby augment their salaries.

Humboldt's report roused interest in Europe; and Lucas Alamán —who in 1822 was Minister both of the Interior and of Foreign Affairs and who himself owned gold and silver mines—persuaded a French group to invest in a Franco-Mexican company which had hoped to cajole Humboldt into accepting the position of chairman of the board and European consultant—his reward to be $5600 in shares. Humboldt refused, and Alamán assumed the directorship of the Franco-Mexican Association which was floated with a capital of $672,000. French shares were later transferred to London where the company was reorganized under the name of the United Mexican Association, and Mexican mining fell mainly into British hands.

One of the chief British mining engineers, John Taylor, forecast that between 30 and 50 per cent clear profit might be expected in Mexican mining, but he also counseled speculators to use prudence. His warning was ignored, and disaster followed. In spite of this, Mexican mining continued to attract foreign investors, who were soon being accused of exploiting the subsoil riches. Much later, when President Cárdenas was forced (by the obviously logical demands of foreign companies) to agree to fair compensation for the petroleum expropriation, he deemed it opportune to clap on to foreign-owned mining a series of exorbitant taxes. From his régime onward foreign companies worked under an almost intolerable burden. In spite of the taxation, they seemed determined to remain in the country, although they did little exploration and were reluctant to modernize their equipment or to provide decent conditions for workers. Today there are mining towns in the north where workers live in homes that are little better than caves, or in lean-to constructions on the slopes of slag heaps.

When, in 1961, the Mexican government drew up new laws designed to "Mexicanize" (not nationalize) mines, the foreign companies (notably American Smelting and Refining, American Metal Climax, the part-British Fresnillo Company, and the British San Francisco Mines) were on the whole happy to co-operate in making 51 per cent of their shares available to Mexican purchasers. The government hoped to encourage Mexican participation in mining by allowing a 50 per cent tax reduction to majority Mexican companies. Concessions, it was agreed, should in future be granted only to companies with 51 per cent Mexican capital (which meant in effect that foreign mining concerns would be working under conditions already recognized as normal in most Mexican manufacturing industries). Present concessions were to be allowed to lapse, and new ones would be for twenty-five years but could be extended if the government was satisfied that the mines were being adequately worked.

Unfortunately for the Mexican treasury, the first attempts at Mexicanization resulted in flight from the country of capital paid to foreign shareholders, and in a distressing loss of revenue from taxation. The burden on the budget had not been accurately calculated. The government back-pedaled, foreign shareholders were left in doubt about the legal situation, and prospective Mexican buyers were scared off.

This situation lasted until at least mid-1963, with a consequent serious mining recession relieved only by two promising factors: the rise in the world price of silver, and the increased demand for iron due to expansion in Mexico's steel industry. At that time, however, the government—seriously concerned at the miscarriage of what had appeared to be a soundly conceived reform—was able to negotiate with the United Nations Special Fund, which has promised to help in exploration. Foreign shareholders have also been persuaded that money from the sale of their interests in Mexican mining might be profitably reinvested within the country.

More recently Zacatecas, a typical mining town with its parallel terraced streets connected by steep alleys, and today the capital of one of the poorest States in Mexico, is at the center of a new movement to revive the economy of north-central Mexico. The drive began when a Lebanese archaeologist, Joseph Tanous, transferred his interests from the Mediterranean to Mexico and went searching for a lost Aztec city in the Zacatecas *Sierra*. He did not find one, but came instead upon sixteen abandoned gold and silver mines. A national company, Minera La Bonanza de México, was formed in collaboration with the American and Southern Corporation of Miami, Florida. The State government is driving roads and electric lines through to the town of Pinos where the mines are centered. Pinos, in pre-revolution days a city of 30,000 living on silver and gold, is reduced to 3000 inhabitants whose annual income is calculated at about $80 per family. Bonanza will give Pinos a $400,000 ore processing plant with a capacity of 350 tons a day. This will augment another and slightly smaller plant established by the State government near the capital to help miners who were previously forced to send their crude ore to Pachuca nearly 500 miles away, so that their meager profits vanished in transport.

At the moment both the mining and processing are primitive but methods will be improved as profits permit. Peons climb the shaft ladders with loads of up to 180 pounds slung in sacks from leather bands round their foreheads, just as they are portrayed in colonial prints. They receive the minimum wage for the area: 11 pesos or somewhat under a dollar a day.

Amid the nopal cacti, the rock and red sand of Zacatecas, there are everywhere cracks and holes where peasants have burrowed hopefully but with little profit. There could be no landscape more exactly matching the foreigner's idea of what is Mexican. As its native poet Ramón López Velarde noted, it is at once cruel and luminous; dun-colored but with a marvelous range of tints at dawn and dusk. In this harsh and beautiful land the villagers sit in rags on top of precious metal, waiting with new hope that something is at last going to be done for them. When the Governor, José Rodríguez Elías, made an inaugural trip from Zacatecas to the mines of Pinos, at every hamlet paper streamers had been strung across the route by people who can barely scrape together the coins for their daily meal of *tortillas,* beans, and chili. He received the full treatment: pretty girls, rockets firing, confetti and a brass band playing the popular *Marcha Zacatecas* that dates from a victory gained hereabouts by Pancho Villa's troops in 1914. Local militia, in ordinary peasant dress but with rifles, stood to attention as well as they were able amid the jostle of *sombreros*. "Long live the Governor, God willing," old men muttered as they listened to the speeches, seizing with touching faith on whatever words they could catch that seemed to promise work and bread.

As the Governor has told the mining company, if the peasants are treated fairly they will work loyally. If not, with their hopes raised it is anybody's guess what can happen next in this area of proud, sinewy people. Joseph Tanous, however, looks like the kind of foreign capitalist who will not be too aloof to understand the improvisations and sudden spurts of enthusiasm, the volatile changes Mexicans make from hard work to riproaring play; and it is no good coming to this tatterdemalion, friendly area if one does not.

Mining will never again, presumably, be the fabulous source of wealth that it was in the seventeenth and eighteenth centuries; but it must continue to provide the country with a considerable revenue and with the raw materials for its factories. Whereas the average annual growth rate of mining throughout the world has been 3.2 per cent in the last two decades, the Mexican figure is only 1.1. Import of metals has increased, especially of iron ore and iron-elaborated products (this trend is already being checked by increased local steel production).

Although Mexico remains the world's chief silver producer, exports of silver and gold together nowadays amount to only a little over 4 per cent of Mexico's total mining sales abroad. Gold mining had its heyday about 1910 and has since declined. Industrial metals have been gaining importance, lead and zinc together accounting nowadays for over 40 per cent of mining production and over 16 per cent of the country's total exports—and this in spite of depressed world prices and protectionist policies in other countries.

Iron is less affected by the international market, since over 80 per cent of Mexico's annual production (about 690,000 tons) is absorbed inside the country. Copper, of which about 50,000 tons are being mined yearly, is also needed in Mexico's own industries, which absorb about 45 per cent of the output. By far the most important of non-metallic minerals is sulphur, of which Mexico is the second biggest producer with 1.8 million tons mined a year, nearly all of which has hitherto been exported. Early in 1965, however, the government clamped down on exports with a ruling that in future only 10 per cent of the new reserves discovered each year may leave the country. Companies have been assured that their interests will be safeguarded, and new companies entering must have majority Mexican capital. There is still pressure from important groups in the country for sulphur to be nationalized.

Other industrial minerals found in Mexico are antimony (of which Mexico is the third world producer), cadmium (second world producer), arsenic, bismuth, coal, cobalt, tin, graphite, manganese, mercury, molybdenum, selenium, tungsten, fluorite, fluorspar (first world producer, most of the output going to the United States), barite, and dolomite. There should also be about 3 or 4 million tons of uranium reserves within another ten years.

AGRICULTURE, LIVESTOCK, FORESTRY, AND FISHING Mexicans have had to wrest an agricultural livelihood from an often hostile land; but they have had also the advantage of an almost infinite range of climates. If the chain of the Sierra Madre, the central volcanoes, the fissured gorges, the deserts of the north, and the swampy tropical forests of the Gulf are all inimical to farmers, and if hurricane, flood, and drought are constant threats, there are also compensatory rain slopes, valleys, and plains at almost any height a crop may need from sea level to 10,000 feet above.

The revolutionary agrarian reforms, upon which modern agriculture is based, aimed at breaking up the *latifundios* or large estates and on restoring to peasants their *ejido* landholdings. The *ejido* is common village ground, strips of which are apportioned to each peasant according to the number of his dependents and the quality of the soil. Strips may vary from 24 to just under 200 acres, and with them goes a share in the common grazing ground, woods, and any mineral deposits. Today most of the *latifundios* have been split into units between the two extremes of size. These are known as the "small property," and modern Mexican agriculture is thus based on three types of holding. Whether any one of them is well fitted to the new conditions of mechanization is a subject for debate. The less dogmatic agronomists are in favor of experimenting with fairly large units that can be more economically run and more easily mechanized than the small strips, but there is still an old guard that would uphold the traditional *ejido,* which has acquired a symbolic status. It is possible that the name *ejido* will be extended gradually to include types of corporate farming only distantly related to the original village commune. Forestry and fishing co-operatives, for example, set up as village-owned industries and with fairly sophisticated capital assets such as sawmills, refrigeration plants, and the like, are nowadays known as *ejidos.* The *ejido* may thus evolve to meet new requirements while still retaining its honored name.

From independence to the present day, agrarian reform has been a declared aim of all Mexican governments. Setbacks in the process of restoring land to the peasants have come as much from miscalculations and overoptimism that untried theories are somehow going to be made to work, as from any actively villainous intent on the part of great landholders. The efforts of Lázaro Cárdenas, for instance, were frustrated by ignorance on the part of the peasants, apathy, and corruption among the personnel of government loan banks.

In spite of very serious blunders, however—and the results can be seen in great tracts of scarred, eroded land—the revolution reforms were the beginning of a slow, painful improvement in the legal status of peasants in relation to the land. In agriculture, as in the petroleum industry, Mexico has learned by mistakes. Free criticism of a situation that is still far from ideal is expressed in an editorial in one Mexican newspaper.[18] Rural backwardness is attributed to:

. . . *caciquismo* and the abuses of *ejidal* authorities, connivance and carelessness on the part of federal and State officers and employees . . . carelessness and dishonesty of officers and employees

[18] *México en la Cultura,* January 7, 1962, p. 1.

of official organizations charged with distributing credits, collecting harvest produce, or looking after forest patrols; lack of control in the price of agricultural and livestock machinery. . . . It must be understood that so long as State authorities, including governors, use and manage agrarian questions and problems as political seesaws, the Agrarian Code, however well drawn up, will be ineffective. The farmers, *ejido* workers, and small-property owners will continue to be victims of deceptions, extortions, and robbery . . .

When the Spaniards arrived in Mexico they found a system of landholding by families, with certain lands also tilled communally by villagers, from whose produce tribute was paid to Aztec overlords. Under the post-conquest system of *repartimientos,* the villages and their surrounding lands were allotted to conquerors, the latter thus acquiring lordship over sometimes as many as 25,000 square miles and 115,000 people.[19] The land tenures of indigenous Indians became extremely confused, particularly because many of them migrated away from their ancestral holdings as they fled ever farther from Spanish dominion. The Church, too, began to acquire large estates estimated by some authorities to have embraced as much as three-quarters of the viceregal domain. This trend was arrested to some extent in 1765 when Jesuit holdings were confiscated by the Crown, but the agrarian problem remained so acute that it played a dominant part in the policies of all Mexican independence reformers from Morelos onward. Independence itself led to the abolition of the legal—but not of the economic—inferiority of the native Indian population.

In 1856 the Ley Lerdo dealt another blow to the Church, its lands being either sold or allowed to go to rentees at a 6 per cent capitalization. The next year it was decreed that no civil or ecclesiastical corporation might own land.

None of these measures did much to relieve the lot of the peasants, most of whom had no title deeds. In 1883 Porfirio Díaz ordered a survey of lands with the object of discovering which belonged to the nation. Survey companies, mostly foreign, were allowed to keep one-third of the land they assessed, with the result

[19] See Tannenbaum, Frank. *The Mexican Agrarian Revolution,* Macmillan, New York, 1929.

that villagers found themselves driven from their holdings or incorporated into large estates. Soon about a quarter of the republic had been appropriated by private companies. Indians, ignorant of the value of their patrimony, were often induced to sell whatever deeds they possessed in exchange for *aguardiente*, the local brandy.

By the end of the Díaz régime fewer people held land than at any time in history and contempt for the Indians had grown among the upper classes. The gigantic *latifundios* were worked largely by unpaid labor. For the privilege of living on estate lands, where they had to build their own homes, peasants were required to perform chores about the great house. Such wages as were paid were wretched and much of the payment was in kind. Peasants were continually overdrawing their wages by running up accounts at *latifundio* stores. Constantly borrowing money for a feast day, a wedding, a birth, or a death in the family, the poor were tied by a kind of unofficial serfdom from which there seemed no escape. Frequently it was the peasants themselves who had to bear the risk of an uncertain harvest, and in a bad year their debts mounted. The landowners were uninterested in improving either the lot of their workers or the methods of cultivation. They were doing quite well under the system of *laissez faire*. Mexico's internal revenue increased, and exports greatly exceeded imports. Foreign investments were entering the country, ports were being developed and cities modernized, and water power was harnessed. But the feudal system remained, and footloose bandits who had once been a threat to life and property were enrolled into the hated *rurales* police in order to keep the populace where it belonged—well at the bottom. Under good masters the life of the peasant was perhaps more comfortable and more colorful than it is today, for life revolved round the "big house" and its chapel, with saints and gilded cherubs to delight the peasant heart. Elegance could be glimpsed at least from afar, and the poor could take a vicarious pride in the social life of their overlords.

Today, old hacienda houses are in ruins. Political slogans are painted across their crumbling walls. The once green land surrounding them is dusty and chapped. Only an effective improvement in living conditions of the masses can justify this loss in gracious living, architectural beauty, and green acreage. The improvement is coming, fast in some areas, but still too slowly in the hinterlands.

Francisco Madero, himself a member of a land-holding family, had wanted to go cautiously with reforms. The peasant Zapata was more impatient. Carranza, a middle-class *ranchero,* would have liked to sit on the fence, uttering revolutionary platitudes but doing nothing. He was, however, forced when expelled from Mexico City in 1914 to make some concessions to the more radical of the revolutionaries. In Yucatán Felipe Carrillo Puerto, called the red devil by the landowners, was murdered after he had made a rather dubious attempt at land reform. It was not until the régime of Calles that land repartition really got under way, and not until the time of Cárdenas that it reached sizable proportions. The régimes previous to his had distributed altogether rather under 20 million acres of land. Cárdenas alone distributed nearly 45 million. After his term of office the pace slackened again, but President López Mateos speeded it up in an effort to abolish the remaining large estates, especially those on the U.S. border. By the end of his régime over 15 million acres of land had been distributed to peasant farmers but it is estimated that there are still nearly 700,000 agricultural workers without land. In October 1962 the new Director of the Mexican National Farmers' Confederation, Javier Rojo Gómez (a disciple of Cárdenas) outlined a twenty-year program aimed not only at returning land to the peasants but also at reorganizing the *ejidos.* He is one of those who believe that it is now necessary to form larger units combining a number of small farms.

One of the most interesting experiments undertaken in the López Mateos régime has been a farm colonizing nucleus in the State of Veracruz. In twenty-five new villages, nearly a thousand families have been settled from nine different Mexican States. A number of small reservoirs, used among other purposes for breeding carp, have made it possible for the settlers to cultivate 20,000 acres of land and to keep about 800 head of cattle besides beehives, pigs, turkeys, and chickens. The villages have been provided with iron foundries, carpenters' shops, brick kilns, electricity for domestic use and for light industries, roads, schools, a central hospital, and clinics. Each family has built its own house with government help and has been given 62 acres of land which the peasants themselves have leveled and cleaned.

Each colony will function as a co-operative, the *ejido* system thus having been adapted to modern conditions. In the future Mexican agricultural policy will almost certainly be to encourage such co-operatives rather than to perpetuate the obsolescent *ejido* system as such.

A vast scheme designed eventually to resettle 2.5 million peasants from northern deserts and depressed central plains, is for instance run on a very modified *ejido* system. The first of these settlements, on the Candelaria River in Campeche, close to the Guatemalan border, has been much criticized, especially since a few malcontents began spreading tales of distress and Governments bungling. One economist described the plan as magnificent but cruel. Such talk would be dispelled if people could see the pioneers and talk to them.

Early in 1963, 600 men were sent in advance of their families to the tropical forests. Each settler received, besides the land for his house, a plot for private cultivation, a portion of collective cattle pastures, and some permanent irrigation tillage. The water will be channeled from the Candelaria with its broad, deep reaches. Holdings cannot be sold and become family property in perpetuity and part of the village collective wealth.

In this valley the soil is so rich that fence posts sprout into trees and everywhere one sees rows of prunus or the yellow "wild cotton" festooned with purple convolvulus. Where the forest has been cut or burned, thickets of bamboo spring fifteen feet high. Candelaria, the last town on the jungle rim, is little more than one straggling street and the river, which is the single highway to the new settlements. For fifty miles and more the only habitations are scattered huts belonging to Indians who live by hunting and fishing or gathering the sap of the chicozapote tree, the chicle used for chewing gum, and from felling mahogany, teak, and cedar. (It is said that even toothpicks are made of precious woods in these parts.)

It is disconcerting when one arrives at the settlements to be met by a radio broadcasting the inevitable advertisements for hair oil and sedatives; and by an ex-harvester to the United States complaining "there's nothing to see here but an occasional satellite passing over." But he agreed cheerfully that he had little time to bewail the lack of civilization's pleasures.

Nevertheless, in spite of the abundance of natural amenities in the Candelaria Valley, about 10 per cent of the original settlers deserted and another 8 per cent had to be sent home because of illness. Some feared the night howl of monkeys, easily mistaken for lynx or coyote. Others complained that instead of an eight-hour day with union rules, they now worked from dawn to dusk, doing their own washing and darning on Sundays.

The Government answered that in the bad old days they had been hired hands; now they were in business for themselves. Those who did not get the point were replaced by keener men, and there was soon a waiting list for each village. The law of natural selection seems to be at work, and one notices that the intelligence of the settlers is higher than the average for a Mexican peasant village, so often bogged down by apathy.

On the basis of self-help, houses can be built for $600 each, and the plan is costing the Government an estimated $1600 per family, in contrast to a project financed by an international aid organization which will need twelve times that amount. The peasants will pay the Government back over the next ten years.

It may not be possible to assess the success of the Campeche plan for at least a generation, but the present enthusiasm is infectious, and the scheme may well serve as a model for other Latin American countries, since there is no doubt that Mexico is looked up to as the pioneer agrarian reformer of the area. Even so, the Mexican authorities would be the first to admit that the agrarian aims of revolution have been achieved only in part, and that the first task of every new administration is to continue improving the peasant's lot.

Today agriculture is the chief occupation of 52.8 per cent of the economically active population, and to this percentage must be added the great mass of non-economically active peasants who subsist on produce from their own small plots. Manufacturing industries, however, account for a little more than a quarter of the gross national product, with agriculture and livestock contributing only a little over one-fifth and slightly less than commerce in general.

With an exploding population agriculture cannot be allowed to fall behind. Fishing (a grossly undeveloped sector of the economy) could become a much more important source of food for the peasants, and a more versatile source of income for the country as a whole. It is recognized, too, that wasteful and often illegal timber felling must be replaced by rational exploitation.

The amount of land susceptible to cultivation is at present about 75 million acres with another two and a half million of grazing land and 87 million of forest, of which 10 million are authorized for exploitation.

The chief agricultural exports in very approximate figures are: cotton $227 million; coffee $91 million; cattle $56 million; sugar $42 million; *henequén* (sisal) $28 million; processed meats $14 million; tomatoes $11 million; rice $8 million; melon $8 million. Figures are very general as agricultural exports vary considerably according to the yearly crops, but they give some idea of the relative value of the different products in the country's total exports. Other less important agricultural exports are *candelilla* wax, some fodders, chick-peas, vanilla, vegetable hormones (of which Mexico is the world's largest supplier), *ixtle* (Tula or Tampico fiber); honey (mainly from Yucatán); oranges, strawberries, and other fruits; and canned vegetables.

The main crops for internal consumption are corn, wheat, barley (for beer), maguey cacti for distillation of *tequila* and fermentation of *pulque* (Mexico's two national drinks), beans, and chili.

Of the resources of the long coastlines, only turtle and prawns have been exploited on a large scale for export, almost the whole catch going to the United States.

Cotton. Cotton cultivation was encouraged by President Cárdenas, especially in the northwestern States. A boom period was followed by a slump due largely to overproduction, but one of the chief complaints of Mexican growers is that they depend upon foreign financing and distribution, mainly through Anderson, Clayton and Company which established its Mexico City office in 1923. The credits this company was providing for cotton farmers were curtailed in 1958 because a depression in the cotton industry seemed imminent. As a result, production dropped from 2.3 million bales to 1.6 in 1959, since when it has risen slowly again to around the 2 million mark. Outlets for excess cotton are being sought in Japan, Indonesia, and Africa, through direct or barter sales. Anderson, Clayton, one of the butts of the Mexican left wing, claims to have invested over a million dollars a year in Mexico during the last six years. Though its activities are mainly in cotton, in 1950 it built an industrial plant in Monterrey for producing lards, oils, peanut butter, and margarine; and in 1961 it acquired a plant in Mexico City for elaborating flour and pastries. It also holds shares in a chocolate factory.

Since 1958, 24 per cent of Mexico's total income from exports has come from cotton. There are about 420 cotton gins and 34 mills for grinding the seed and preparing fodder for livestock. One quarter of the national cotton production—about 500,000 bales yearly —is elaborated by the national textile industry.

Coffee and Rubber. In 1962 the coffee crop was 144,000 tons; it had more than doubled in ten years.

The United States buys over 80 per cent of Mexican coffee exports, and Germany over 10 per cent. Although this crop is Mexico's second agricultural dollar-earner, it has for long been depressed due to low world prices and overproduction during and immediately after the Second World War. Uneconomic farming, especially in Chiapas, has not helped. In 1949 President Alemán created a National Coffee Commission, and an experimental station was set up in Veracruz to increase the yield; but the National Coffee Growers' Union says that prices have to be maintained at a minimum of U.S. $3.10 per quintal if the industry is not to run at a loss. In 1961 President López Mateos reduced export duties in order to help farmers, but in spite of a saving of about $11 million a year in production costs the situation remains critical. The policy now is to transfer poor-yield coffee lands (about 20 per cent of the total) to rubber, spices, and fruit. Rubber cultivation particularly would help Mexico's balance of payments, since Mexico spends about $21 million a year on rubber imports. When the projected plantations are in production the country should produce about 25,000 tons a year, or half the present internal needs. A synthetic rubber factory will also soon be producing 30,000 tons yearly.

Cattle and Other Livestock and Poultry. Mexico has not the rich grazing lands of Argentina, and in many parts of the country cattle graze, lean and hungry, on the meager highland grasses. Efforts are being made to improve breeds. Herefords, Shorthorn, Holstein (from Canada), and Zebu cattle have been introduced. Fodder is being varied. Fattening and slaughtering methods are being improved. There are about 24 million head of cattle in the country, 6 million horses, 6 million pigs, 11 million sheep (new breeds are being introduced from Australia), and over 10 million goats. Chicken and egg production rise steadily, though table fowl are apt to be lean and eggs have thin, brittle shells. There are estimated to be about 166 million farmyard birds including turkeys, geese, and ducks.

Sugar. Since Cuban sugar no longer goes to the United States, the latter has been buying about half a million of the 1.8 million tons produced yearly by Mexico. The National Sugar Producers' Union plans a growth rate of 100,000 tons a year, to reach 2 million by 1967. Home consumption is growing and is now 1.3 million tons.

Henequén (Sisal). *Henequén* provides a cautionary tale of the disasters that can befall an area when social reforms are hurried forward regardless of local conditions. Yucatecans nowadays watch the world market for hard fibers with some bitterness. In articles on sisal, Yucatán is often ignored, yet the peninsula is sisal's native land and was for a long time its only producer.

A thin crust of soil saves this flat limestone plain from being swallowed by the sea. Even the undemanding *henequén* cactus can grow only if bagasse is continually plowed back. "When mushrooms appear in the bagasse mulch, *henequén* can grow," say the farmers. The suckers are then planted in neat rows to give the landscape its spiky austerity and its strangely contradictory, romantic, blue-green mist. For generations this "camel of the plant world" has given Yucatecans a marginal livelihood. A legend dating from before the Spanish conquest tells how the discovery was first made that the tough cactus leaves could be stripped for fiber. A prince was pricked one day by the thorn and his followers punished the plant by slapping it against a stone until, to their surprise, a fibrous cord emerged.

There are two varieties of *henequén*, the green kind properly called sisal, and the white variety that came to supply the binder twine upon which the United States wheat crops depended. Monopoly of the world market led to complacency, and Yucatecan landed families refused to see the signs of impending disaster. During the First World War production soared. Never again were the landowners to know such prosperity; but even as they were building massive mansions, importing marble sculptures, and sending their children to schools and universities in Europe, the green *henequén* of the south was being transplanted to Cuba, Haiti, and East Africa. In 1921 non-Yucatecan production was 14,000 tons. By 1925 it had risen to 260,000 and Yucatán was producing only 137,000. Reformers earnestly trying to improve the peninsula's economy parceled out land to the peasants, confiscated machinery from the estates, and left the peasants at the mercy of bureaucrats and loan banks. By 1951, after two decades of "reform," the situation was as bad as it had been in the record low year of 1931. Today, efforts are being made to diversify the economy, but since the staple product is likely to remain *henequén* the more farsighted farmers are calling for experiments to industrialize by-products and to improve the quality of the plant and the efficiency of decorticating processes. In 1962 production was 158,000 tons, still 11,000 below the record year of 1920 but slightly up on figures in the fifties.

Fishing. In spite of Mexico's long coastlines the average Mexican eats less than four and a half pounds of fish per year. Ex-President Abelardo Rodríguez has been put in charge of an integration program to give fishermen better working conditions, to establish a research bureau, and to prevent pollution such as has occurred at the mouth of the Coatzalcoalcos River on the Gulf, where waste products from oil refineries and textile factories are endangering the survival of many species of fish. Production of oysters in the lagoons of Veracruz and in the Gulf of California is being considered, and there are possibilities of harvesting over 1300 pounds per hectare of oyster beds yearly. A pilot fishing port has been built at Puerto Alvarado south of Veracruz on the Gulf, and it is recommended that the Pacific sardine industry be boosted by modernizing the trawler fleet, which could also make a tuna catch of perhaps 20,000 tons a year.

Forestry. One-tenth of Mexico's population are unintegrated Indians living in forest-covered mountains which they cannot exploit because they have neither roads, capital, nor adequate technology. In 1958 Dr. Alfonso Caso, Director of the Indigenous Institute, told Senate: "If we do not give the indigenous Indian the means to exploit the forests, he will destroy them." This, he said, would not be because the Indians are ignorant of the problem, but from sheer need to survive: "They fell the woods, burn the trees, uproot the stumps, and then sow. A few pounds of corn are obtained in exchange for acres of valuable trees."

Anyone who has traveled in the mountains has seen the evidence of what Dr. Caso described: range upon range of bare, parched hillside that ought to be thick with forest. In defense of the Indians Dr. Caso cited the experience of his own Institute when the necessary elements for forestry exploitation were given to Tarahumaras working one Chihuahua holding. Within four years the holding had yielded $103,000 of timber and had been kept reforested.

Unfortunately, there is no adequate inventory of forestry resources. The properties of many species are unknown, and tannin-producing trees such as the *quiebrahacha* or wild crab, the holm-oak, and the native acacias are in danger of extinction. Only the more common building woods—pine, cedar, mahogany—are exploited fully. Every now and then there is a press campaign to stop illegal exploitation and to make full use of the potential forest wealth, but patrolling is difficult in this vast land, and nearly $17 million is needed to pay forest guards and to make a full study of resources.

INDUSTRY Mexico has laid the foundations for most of the basic industries required in the modern world: for steel, cement, aluminum, and glass; for chemicals and fertilizers; for motorcars and trucks; for zinc refining; for textiles (including natural and artificial fibers, though the whole industry is in need of modernizing); for the packing and refining of foodstuffs; for production of alcoholic drinks and cigarettes (Sir Walter Raleigh is honored in a brand-name); for the design and manufacture of office and home furniture; for clothing and shoes (shoe manufacture was first developed by Spanish refugees); and, not least, for handicrafts.

Although heavy industry depends on capital equipment, technical help, and patents from more industrialized countries, Mexico's long handicraft tradition has helped to make training of semi-skilled labor relatively easy. Due to the speed with which industrialization has taken place there is a shortage of skilled workmen, but there is talent enough waiting to be disciplined. Some original and functional designs in office and kitchen furniture have already been produced.

The government and the private business sector differ about the degree of participation that the government should allow itself in the manufacturing industries. Although government manufacture may sometimes have proved inefficient, there is no doubt that many key industries would never have been set up without the help of public funds—especially in a country where the private sector has tended to seek quick profits or alternatively to export capital to "safer" areas of the world. In the years from 1955 to 1962, private investment rose only from $608 million to $1 billion, whereas public investment jumped from about $339 to $826 million and represented nearly half the total investment in the country.

"When is the government going to stop making sewing machines?" asks the private business sector. Mexicans are backed in their complaints by Americans who rail against government participation in industry as if this were necessarily and irrevocably a Communist trend. The government, on the other hand, recognizes no quarrel between the public and private sectors and believes that they have complementary roles to play. It maintains that much of its promotion of industrial activity is in infrastructure which will in the long run benefit the private sector. The more public-spirited and responsible Mexican private businessmen agree on the whole with the government's views and differ only in questions of detail.

Of the total public investment in Mexico in 1962, somewhere around $568 million went to the *organismos decentralizados,* which include public welfare organizations as well as government-aided companies. There are 393 of these in many respects self-administered bodies; but by far the greater number are concerned with social security, education, and culture, with regional assistance, and with distributing heavily subsidized food and clothing to the poor. The organizations that are particularly criticized and feared by the private sector fall into two groups: public utility institutions such as railways, electricity supply companies and the like, of which there are about seventy; and a handful of companies taken over by the government from private enterprise when they were in a condition of near bankruptcy. These will soon be approaching solvency—or so the government's bright young economists hope. The government claims to have put companies like Siderúrgica Nacional (previously Toyoda de México and formed with Japanese capital to make textile machinery) and Diesel Nacional (making trucks and Renault compact cars) on their feet. Diesel Nacional and the government railway-car factory together raised their production by 67.1 per cent in 1961 over the previous year and continue to do well.

Some private companies receive government financial help because they supply essential goods. These include the successful Altos Hornos de México (steel) and its subsidiary La Consolidada: Tubos de Acero de México S.A. (tubing for oil and gas ducts and the like); Guanos y Fertilizantes de México (fertilizer); Fábricas de Papel Tuxtepec (newsprint—a suspect government interest, since there is always the fear that censorship can be exercised indirectly by withholding supplies from newspapers that are too outspoken); and some government-supported sugar usines. The fact that the partly government-financed Tubos de Acero is closely allied to the totally private Aluminio S.A. shows that there is no irreparable enmity between the two sectors of the economy.

Breakdown of the total Mexican public investment shows that about 18.6 per cent of the funds allocated to *organismos decentralizados* go to communications and transport, subsidized in most industrial countries as Mexico points out: 32 per cent to electric energy; 28.5 per cent to petroleum for expansion and to help maintain low price of fuel; and lesser amounts to the industries that might be thought to compete with the private sector.

The government claims high performance for its organizations. In 1958 a selected fifty-three government-aided companies had $960 million capital, roughly the equivalent of the federal budget, and increased their output by 11 per cent. On the other hand it has to be remembered that a large amount of Mexico's growing foreign debt is incurred on behalf of government-aided industry, 41.6 of whose finances came from abroad in 1962 (most of it for the acquisition of capital machinery or for financing projects that will pay their own way in a short time).

Mexican financiers continue, of course, to hold the view that nobody can run a business better than a businessman. Some leading politicians, too, allege that the *organismos decentralizados* are, in the words of one Senator, "so tangled that nobody really knows anything about them." The impression is that each of them is a sovereign state, managing its funds as it pleases and with insufficient government vigilance. It is difficult to verify such allegations, although it is easy to show that institutions like Petroleos Mexicanos and the national railways could be less wastefully managed. But without such bodies as the Federal Electricity Commission, Pemex, Altos Hornos, and the government financing agency Nacional Financiera, modern Mexico would scarcely exist. In any case the government has fully acknowledged that its *organismos* have ramified to such an extent that administratively they need a complete overhaul. A warning is being taken from British failed nationalization just after the war, and more positive lessons are being learned from successful Italian government-aided industry.

The Motor Industry. The Mexican motor industry deserves study if the government's industrializing policy is to be understood, for this industry has set the pattern for the home manufacture of typewriters and other machinery. In order to reduce imports and the drain on dollar reserves by gradual home manufacture, prohibition of the importation of luxury cars was followed in 1960 by regulations insisting on assembly of all cars within the country. The aim was to achieve first 60 and then, more remotely, 100 per cent home manufacture. The number of makes allowed in Mexico was cut down until the only companies continuing were General Motors; Ford; Automex (making Dodge, Plymouth, Valiant, and Fiat cars); Willys; Diesel Nacional; Promexa (Volkswagen); Borgward; and the Japanese Toyota and Nissan. British cars are out, probably due to the extreme skepticism shown by British manufacturers when Mexico first began to lay plans for this industry. U.S., French, German, and Japanese companies were willing to collaborate with Mexican groups in setting up mixed-capital factories, with the result that by 1963 one British firm was fighting a hopeless rearguard action to be allowed in. Its excellent proposals to the Mexican government could not overcome the prejudice that had by that time hardened against British makers.

It is estimated that when fully Mexicanized the motor industry will save the government somewhere between $78 and $100 million in imports and that by 1970 over 320,000 cars and trucks will be turned out yearly. At present the demand in Mexico is calculated at 60,000 units yearly including buses and trucks, but this figure has risen steeply from less than 40,000 in 1961. It is uneconomic for a Mexican firm to produce less than 15,000 units yearly; and even as it is a foreign car in Mexico costs about $560 more than in its country of origin. Prospects of reducing prices depend not only on the growing home market but also on whether Mexico can capture a fair share of the Latin American market in competition against Brazil and Argentina. In other words, we have here an example of the dangers of nationalism and excessive national pride which has in many basic industries prevented over-all areas planning and seems to be creating serious overproduction.

Investments in the Mexican motor industry are around $59 million and will at least treble if present plans are carried out; but here again the disadvantages seem to outweigh the advantages since a large proportion of this figure is necessarily represented by direct foreign investments. National pride depends, for the moment at least, on international know-how.

Nevertheless one should not be too hasty in criticizing the plans of the motor and other industries. A very long-term view is being taken, both by Mexicans themselves and by the foreign companies whose plans for Mexican manufacture have been accepted. The same forward-looking nationalistic outlook is prevailing in other and smaller industries and can be expected to increase.

Alcoholic and Soft Drinks. The two national drinks, *tequila* and *pulque,* are made from the maguey cactus. The first is a short distilled drink of the schnapps or vodka variety; the second a milky-gray fermentation of the cactus milk, fundamentally the poor man's liquor, although a commission has been set up to insure sanitary methods of collecting and bottling and to counteract the erroneous view that this drink is unhealthy. The vitamin content is said to be high and its ill effects no worse than those of any other alcoholic drink consumed in excess. Neither *pulque* nor *tequila,* however, compete with beer and with American-style bottled soft drinks. The latter are so popular that, absurdly, in a fruit-growing country it is difficult to buy natural fruit juices in provincial restaurants.

Mexican beer is mostly of the lager type, the modern industry having been founded by Swiss, Bavarian, and Alsatian brewers toward the end of the last century when Cervecería Cuauhtémoc was founded in Monterrey. Today this company is the largest beer manufacturer in the country, its strongest competitor being Cervecería Moctezuma of Orizaba, Veracruz. The Federal District did not have a modern beer plant until the opening of Cervecería Modelo in 1925. Today the country has nineteen breweries distributed in eighteen States and the capital. Production reached a peak in 1960 with 852.5 million litres, but brewers have been worried by a fall-off in consumption since. They are trying to cut costs by using more home-produced raw materials, and the Rockefeller Institute and the Mexican National Institute have undertaken experiments on the high central plateau with various types of barley. Imports of malt have been reduced to less than 2 per cent of total consumption. Hop cultivation has been tried in Baja California. At present over 2 million pounds a year are imported from the United States and smaller quantities from Europe.

Natural Hormones. World production of raw materials for hormones in the pharmaceutical industry is not known, but it is estimated that nearly 70 per cent comes from Mexico which earns from this source about $11 million yearly. At one time Syntex S.A. could claim about 40 per cent of national production and most of the credit for the original development of the industry; but this firm has sold its interests to Schering, and is now concentrating on sales of finished hormone-containing drugs.

Years ago Dr. Russell Marker of Pennsylvania State College, vacationing in Mexico, began to investigate the properties of native roots of the Dioscorea genus. He found that they contained a glycoside which by hydrolysis produces diosgenin. Diosgenin soon became the most important source of hormones for the pharmaceutical industry, replacing animal sources which were exceedingly expensive. From diosgenin Dr. Marker produced progesterone, which he commercialized with a Mexican firm, Laboratorios Hormona. Out of these beginnings, Syntex was born in 1944. It produced diosgenin first from a root called Cabeza de Negro and later from another root, Barbasco, found in the forests of Veracruz. Roots are harvested by peasants who sell them via contractors to collection stations where they are processed into diosgenin.

Although Syntex Corporation is now an international organization based in the United States, much research continues to be done in Mexico. The Mexican Government has recognized the value of this work by awarding the vice-president of the Mexican firm—a young Englishman, Dr. Albert Bowers—the first national science prize to go to a foreigner.

TOURISM Tourism is one of Mexico's most important if erratic dollar-earners. This industry, with all its ramifications, is particularly vulnerable to "scares" (earthquakes, hurricanes, and the left-wing tendencies of governments included). However, it usually nets enough money (around $785 million) to compensate for the deficit in Mexico's trade balance.

Mexico can offer tourists an excellent climate (though heart sufferers need to be careful on the high plateau); coral beaches; mineral springs; pre-Columbian and viceregal art and architecture; folklore; and modern hotels in the chief population centers especially in the capital and Acapulco. The tourist who ventures off the beaten track may find that close contact with rural Mexico amply compensates for the hardships of long hours on muleback, meals of black beans, and a bed of straw.

The decision to hold the Olympic Games in Mexico in 1968 has been welcomed as much by the tourist industry as by the athletes, and hotels are already preparing for a boom. An athlete's suburb is to be erected southeast of Mexico City beneath the ancient Hill of the Star where fires were once lighted to keep the Sun alive. Not more than three athletes will share a single room, and all modern facilities will be available, including international cuisine, laundry, barber shop, information and press offices, public relations facilities, medical services, lecture halls, and shops. The authorities say the site is just eight minutes from the university stadium and the other main sports centers, though they may not be reckoning with traffic jams.

Mexico's university stadium is one of the finest in the world to perform in, according to a woman who was once a champion sprinter. The university has also a prettily designed Olympic pool. A new football stadium is being built on an ingenious scheme—copied from Monterrey's Technological Institute—of selling boxes and seats on life tenure in advance of construction.

Athletics are not the only sporting attraction for tourists, for whom the bull rings are a regular port of call. A border-to-border motor race had to be suspended because of its dangers on the mountain roads, but international dirt-track events have replaced it. On the tennis courts, the Mexicans Rafael Osuna and Antonio Palafox are in the top class. The main *frontón* (Basque *pelota*) court is a gambling center rivaled only by the National Lottery, but if spectators can bring themselves to take their eyes off the bookies they will find some exciting play. *Frontón* is also among the favorite amateur sports, together with Association football, baseball, and cycling.

NATIONAL CONFLICTS AND INTERNATIONAL HOPES Mexico was one of the first countries to ratify the Montevideo Treaty for a Latin-American Free Trade Association (Lafta). Together with Argentina, Uruguay, Paraguay, Chile, Peru, Brazil, Colombia, and Ecuador, Mexico is thus working for the integration of the economy of Latin America's 200 million people. Mexico and Brazil may be said to be the prime movers in an Association which has been regarded with extreme skepticism by European and particularly British observers, but which is already perceptibly altering the trading patterns of the area. Inter-zone trade, almost non-existent before Lafta's formation, has been creeping up. Communications, traditionally bad, have improved and there are shipping lines running regularly on the Atlantic coast. Technical experience in the petroleum and other key industries is being exchanged.

Lafta's agreement calls for gradual elimination of tariffs and other trade barriers over twelve years. The low standard of living of some countries, their extremely variable currencies, and their political instability make such an agreement difficult to put into effect;

but it is more likely that political unity will follow from economic integration than *vice versa*. It is also possible that a genuinely Latin American effort toward economic integration and improvement in living standards will succeed where the much richer and more powerful Alliance for Progress will fail: partly through ignorance of Latin American psychology and of the varying problems in individual countries, partly through the dominant part played in it by a country suspect of "imperialist" methods, but mainly through its innate inability to correct fundamental weaknesses in the economic structure of the area (so that it may justly be accused of acting as a panacea rather than a permanent corrective).

Recently, however, the Alliance for Progress has done much to alter its earlier and suspect image. An Interamerican Committee has been formed to bridge the gap between the magnanimous donors of dollars and the Latin American people. It met for the first time in Mexico City in July 1964, bringing together a distinguished group of economists including Dr. Carlos Sanz de Santa-María (President of the Committee) and Dr. Walt Rostow representing the U.S. government. The most important result of the meeting was the decision to make a precise inventory of Latin American needs. One of the difficulties that the Alliance has had to face has been the lack of adequate knowledge within each country of its own aims and resources. This lack may now be repaired, and the Alliance looks as if it may finally get down to such practical tasks as promoting internal markets and international roads and communications.

This Committee has no formal contact with Lafta but realizes that development of the free trade area would be one of the strongest single forces to lift Latin America out of its doldrums. Businessmen—especially the younger ones—are also interested in seeing Lafta prosper and have formed an "Association of Latin American Impresarios Participating in Lafta," which has branches in each of the member countries and which is studying ways and means to achieve faster economic integration.

Latin Americans are watching African territories—growers of the same raw products as themselves—being assimilated into the European economy. They see industrial countries beginning to encourage production of raw materials. They note trade falling off with European Common Market countries. They have lived for centuries upon incomes that have fluctuated arbitrarily with the rise and fall of world prices of their basic products. And they believe that the only barrier against recession will be their Free Trade Association. The greatest obstacle in their way is the lack of a sufficiently large market for consumer goods. The market exists potentially, but narrow nationalism and unshod, illiterate millions prevent it from being tapped.

One of the most cogent champions of Lafta is the Mexican economist, Victor Urquidi,[20] who points out that the consumption within the area of cars, copper, steel, basic chemicals, and other necessities is increasing at a rate that will mean economic disaster if these continue to be imported from abroad. But, adds Urquidi, Lafta is not aggressive, since the future growth of Latin America will depend on equipment and techniques offered by the rest of the world, and every available financial resource will have to be mobilized to buy them. The Mexican Urquidi together with the Argentine Raúl Prebisch, the Chilean Felipe Herrera, and other economists who have ceased to think nationally and are Latin Americans before they are whatever they were born to, are beginning to make their counsels heard in governments; so that the bodies created by the Prebisch school of economists—the Economic Commission for Latin America, the Latin American Monetary Studies Center, Lafta itself, and the Interamerican Development Bank—are far more important for the future than the ups and downs of politics in these so frequently and so sadly unstable countries.

[20] Urquidi, Victor. *Trayectoria del Mercado Común Latinoamericano*. Latin American Monetary Studies Center, Mexico City, 1960. Published later in an American edition by the University of California Press (see bibliography). There is also an excellent section on Lafta in *Integración de América Latina: Experiencias y Perspectivas*, edited by Miguel S. Wionczek for the *Fondo de Cultura Económica* in 1964.

[21] For the chapter on economics the following valuable publications have been consulted: *50 Años de Revolución Mexicana en Cifras*, published by the Mexican Presidency and *Nacional Financiera* in 1963; *México 1963, Hechos, Cifras, Tendencias*, published by the National Foreign Trade Bank; *Principles Exportaciones de México, 1960*, also from the National Foreign Trade Bank; *A Guide to Mexican Markets* by Marynka Olizar, 1960–61 (privately printed in Mexico); and *México: 50 Años de Revolución*, 1963, *Fondo de Culturas Económica.*

7 The Arts

Mexico is not going to make the elementary mistake of supposing that economic improvement will solve all problems. At the round-table discussion on economic growth which has already been quoted, the Under-Secretary for Industry and Commerce, Hugo Margain, reminded participants of the ancient Nahua definition of a sage:

. . . like a torch or a great flame, a mirror with two faces polished and shining, a good example for others, understanding and well-read; he is like a path or a guide to the rest. The good sage, like the good physician, heals, and gives advice and instruction with which he guides and lights others, because he is a man of trust and repute, and because he is reliable and faithful in all; and so that things shall be done well, he provides a plan and a scheme with which he satisfies and pleases everyone, fulfilling the desire and the hope of those who come to him; he looks favorably on all men, and helps them with his wisdom.[1]

There is in the Mexican heritage a dual pull that reaches back to a time when ancient poets were singing of another world, to which man goes after a brief sojourn in this land of ephemeral flowering, sadness, and death. The struggle between opposites was deeply rooted in the native past. In Aztec times the dilemma created by it was solved by violence, but the dichotomy has never been overcome. Either materialism has won, and we get the concentration on man's stomach and on his physical needs as manifest in the powerful, uncompassionate frescoes of Siqueiros and Rivera; or all is spirit, and the Mexican no longer troubles to put his aspirations to practical test, but sits in a soporific dream, nibbling narcotic

[1] *Codice Matrinense de la Real Academia.* Facsimile edition of Paso y Troncoso, Vol. VIII, p. 118.

mushrooms, flirting with death, ready to inflict it on others and to welcome it for himself—since all that is matter is unreal.

Once, in the remoter preconquest times, the two sides of the Mexican nature must have fused, for the great god-king Quetzalcóatl never made the mistake of supposing that material creation was despicable. He loved flowers, would not have tolerated human sacrifice, and crowded jewels, birds, and butterflies into the iconography of the old Mexican religion. True, there are also skulls, but these are the obverse of life and not a denial of it.

LITERATURE Though the mystical Nahua poets may have sung of a paradise hereafter, their feet were never really off the ground. They may seem to turn from the harsh material fact when they sing:

> We have come only to sleep,
> we have come only to dream.
> It is not true, it is not true
> we have come to live on the earth.

In another and not contradictory aspect of their song they asserted the need for the most exquisite control over the physical body and all its potentialities:

> A heart firm as stone,
> a wise countenance,
> master of his face, and a heart that is able and understanding.[2]

The dichotomy was resolved by the voluntary discipline of the seeker after truth. Then, with the coming of the Spaniards, another tension was created. Two bloods, two lines of culture jointly reinforced the struggle between the outer and the inner man. Although the pure literature of the indigenous peoples soon died out, the best of the post-conquest writers were acutely conscious of their American-Creole origins and were thus permeated, whether they wished it or not, with the Indian past.

[2] There is not space here to do justice to preconquest literature and its immediate post-conquest sequel of Christian-influenced works still written by the indigenous peoples in their old traditions. A previous study, *Firefly in the Night, a Study of Ancient Mexican Poetry and Symbolism* (Faber and Faber, 1959) deals with this poetry in more detail.

The first genuinely Creole writer in Mexico was a hunchback whom Lope de Vega sneeringly called "the poet with a trunk on his shoulders." Because of his physical defect he took a gloomy view of the material world: "Thou shalt not seek beauty and grace in man's physique. His beauty lies in nobility of soul, his grace in wisdom." These words are perfectly in the spirit of ancient Mexican art and sculpture, and worlds apart from Greek-influenced Europe.

Juan Ruíz de Alarcón was born in Taxco in about 1581 and entered the legal profession, but was soon writing poetry tinged with pessimism. Receiving no recognition in Mexico, he went to Spain but fared there even worse, although some of his plays are worthy to stand with all but the greatest Spanish drama of the time. He was scorned not only because of his deformity but also for his Creole birth, and he died in introspective bitterness in Madrid in 1639.

The second great figure in viceregal letters was Juana Inés de Asbaje y Ramírez Santillana (1651–95), better known as Sor Juana Inés de la Cruz. Although essentially feminine, she buried her nose in books at a time when women were expected to ask no more of life than that their delicate features should be admired. Although Spanish in her outlook, Juana evidently inherited from her Creole mother a keen interest in ancient Mexican lore. Her assertion in a miracle play, *The Divine Narcissus*, that pagan symbology was not altogether devoid of truth and not unlike the Christian symbolism of communion, antagonized the Church against her. Her life and work deserve to be studied at some length, not only because her poetry is unique in its combination of colloquial ease and sophisticated formalism, but also because her life synthesized the problems of the intellectual Creoles of the seventeenth century.

Juana Inés was born in a village high in the Mexican plateau between the two snow volcanoes. At the age of three, she tells us, she became a precocious pupil, refusing to eat cheese because it was supposed to dull the brain, and cutting off her hair as self-punishment for stupidity. Her beauty, and her skill in answering questions put to her by university doctors, brought her to the attention of the Viceroy, to whose wife she became lady-in-waiting, but she remained unmoved by her success at court and decided to enter the cloister. She joined first the Barefoot Carmelites; but, the rule being too rigorous for her delicate health, she transferred to the more lenient Convent of San Jerónimo, which still stands in Mexico City and is now a night club.

Several portraits of Sor Juana show an oval face with fine eyes, long, dark brows, and delicate, mobile lips. Because of a series of love poems it has been supposed that she entered the convent after having been crossed in love. Some of her verse does have the ring of authentic suffering; but in one well-known poem written while she was still at Court she seems to have seen the limits of what love could bring, and her censure is that of one who takes affairs of the heart lightly, having more serious things upon which to turn her mind:

Stupid men, who accuse
Women without reason:
You've never noticed, I suppose,
It's you who *taught* the lesson.

If, with an upsurge of desire,
You storm her disapproval,
Why would you have her be so good?
Inciting her to evil?

You wear her last defenses down,
And then you gravely tell her
She's frivolous, though it was *you*
Who caused harm to befall her.

. . . . . .

Why do you look so shock'd, when you
So well deserve the blame?
Love the girls as you'd make them be,
Or make them as you'd love 'em.

Stop asking them for favors, and
You'll have a right to rant
Against the one who asks of you
To sin and not repent.

The arrogance of men, it seems,
Comes full equipp'd with evil,

In promise and insistency,
The world, the flesh, the Devil.[3]

Of course Juana must have fallen in love, and her warm nature no doubt suffered; but her first love, her love of letters, was to prove more powerful. Her values were always mature, and even in her teens she could write with disillusion about Hope:

Lunatic hope, and frenzy all of gold,
Of human life the ravisher most green,
Dream of our waking selves, and we all nettled
In our dreams, and trapped by treasures vain;
Soul of the world, old age, so falsely gay,
Decrepit and imaginary green,
For whom the unfortunate must always yearn,
And whom the fortunate possess today:
Rose-colored spectacles the hopeful wear
As they pursue your name and your predestined
Time, and paint things as they'd have them be:
But I, more apt my appointed fate to bear,
Hold my two eyes within my either hand,
And nothing else but what I touch, I see.[4]

[3] Hombres necios, que acusáis
A la mujer sin razón,
Sin ver que sois la ocasión
De lo mismo que culpáis.

Si con ansia sin igual
Solicitáis su desdén,
¿Por qué queréis que obren bien
Si las incitáis al mal?

Combatís su resistencia
Y luego con gravedad
Decís que fué liviandad
Lo que hizo la diligencia.

¿Pues para qué os espantáis
De la culpa que tenéis?
Queredlas cual las hacéis
O hacedlas cual las buscáis.

Dejad de solicitar
Y después con más razón
Acusaréis la afición
De la que os fuere a rogar.

Bien con muchas armas fundo
Que lidia vuestra arrogancia,
Pues en promesa e instancia
Juntáis diablo, carne y mundo.

[4] Verde embeleso de la vida humana,
Loca esperanza, frenesí dorado,
Sueño de los despiertos, intrincado,
Como de sueños, de tesoros vana;

Alma del mundo, senectud lozana,
decrépito verdor imaginado;
El hoy de los dichosos esperado
Y de los desdichados el mañana.

Sigan tu nombre en busca de tu día
Los que, con verdes vidrios por anteojos,
Todo lo ven pintado a su deseo;

Juana entered convent life hoping for peace, but the world would not leave her alone in her retirement. She received callers, carried on correspondence with important people, and filled her study with books, scientific apparatus, and musical instruments. The convent must at times have seemed more like a salon than a cloister; but Sor Juana's devotion to books was serious, and popularity came to her spontaneously—she did not seek it out. Intellectual she may have been, but she was not cold; and her talents kept her much in demand. Requests would frequently arrive for her to write verses for special occasions, and soon she was also composing *autos,* or miracle plays to be performed in churches. After her plea in favor of the ancient Mexican religion in *The Divine Narcissus,* books were forbidden her. Separation from them was so unbearable that she fell seriously ill and the ban had to be lifted. Later she wrote to the Bishop of Puebla arguing against the tenets of a Jesuit, Antonio de Vieira, confessor to the King of Portugal, and resenting the need for women to submit unquestioningly to the decisions of men. The Bishop published her letter and a reply suggesting somewhat curtly that she devote herself to her duties as a nun. The charge of heresy was brought against her, and her own confessor, Father Nuñez de Miranda, withdrew his support which had previously stood her in good stead.

She continued to fight for her rights. The saints, she reminded her critics, had cultivated literature, and she had a volume of Santa Teresa in front of her as she wrote. But the Archbishop ordered her once more to renounce her books. All seemed lost, and she appears to have genuinely repented, making a confession lasting several days, writing out two protestations of faith, and signing them with her blood. In 1695, nursing her fellow nuns through plague, she contracted the disease and died.

Sor Juana lived out of her time, but the conflicts within her were those inherent in the Mexican-Creole-Spanish environment. The two mingling cultures, though essentially opposed, had a number of characteristics in common; and the admixture tended to fortify and exaggerate the dichotomy between matter and spirit already

---

Que yo, más cuerda en la fortuna mía,
Tengo en entrambas manos ambos ojos
Y solamente lo que toco veo.

present in the old cultures. Sor Juana's acute mind helped her to come to terms with herself. For many of her contemporaries it was more difficult.

In a poem attributed to her—and one would be hard put to it to find any other author of the time who could have written it—she seems to sign her own death warrant. It is called *To a Linnet:*

> Crimson cithern, as the daylight broke,
> Trilled a song for his beloved spouse,
> Fed her the sweet amber of the rose,
> Splashed and coral-stained her golden beak.
>
> Sweetest linnet, mournful little wing:
> Scarcely had he seen the enchanted dawn
> Than, at the first full throttle of a tune,
> He discovered death, and lost his song.
>
> There is in life no moment fixed for death;
> His very voice beckoned the marksman on,
> Who, when he struck, was thus full sure of aim.
> O fortune sought for, yet we fear thy wrath!
> Who could foretell the song that hailed the sun
> Would be the accomplice of the singer's doom?[5]

Such a thoroughly Mexican poet as Sor Juana—Mexican, that is, in the sense of Creole, with both native and Spanish traditions strongly operating—was not to appear again until the period of in-

[5] Cítara de carmín que amaneciste
Trinando endechas a tu amada esposa
Y, paciéndole el ámbar de la rosa,
El pico de oro, de coral teñiste;
Dulce jilguero, pajarito triste,
Que apenas el aurora viste hermosa
Cuando el tono primero de una glosa
La muerte hallaste y el compás perdiste;
No hay en la vida, no, segura suerte;
Tu misma voz al cazador convida
Para que el golpe cuando tire acierte.
¡Oh fortuna buscada aunque temida!
¿Quién pensara que cómplice en tu muerte
Fuera, por no callar, tu propia vida?

The poems of Sor Juana here reproduced in translation were broadcast on the BBC Third Program in July 1957, with Prunella Scales, Anthony White, and Guillermo Beltrán as readers. A more complete study of her work than is possible here was printed in *The Mexico City Quarterly Review*, Vol. I, No. 3, 1962.

dependence, although viceregal times did produce at least one eulogy of the Mexican landscape (*Grandeza Mexicana* by Bernardo de Balbuena, *c.* 1561–1627). But the eighteenth century was more prosaic, its most important literary figure being José Joaquín Fernández de Lizardi (1771–1817). His picaresque novel, *El Periquillo Sarmiento,* has been called a Mexican *Gil Blas.* It gives a sardonic picture of pre-independence Mexico which was later balanced by *El Pensador Mexicano,* a work in which the peccadilloes of the insurgent revolutionaries are treated only slightly more mercifully than those of the viceregal rich. ("Most of our misfortunes have been caused by the insurgents; but . . . there are those who help them and join in increasing our misery . . . the monopolists.")

Fernández Lizardi draws up a will in which he leaves his body to earth, to become part of a rose, of an evil-smelling vine, of a philosopher, or an old shrew. To his fatherland he leaves independence from Spain though it is "not very free from the latter's laws and the despotic red tape of its government." He leaves "a multitude of churches, chapels, retreats and convents for monks and nuns, but very little religion." To the Indians he leaves "the same state of civilization, freedom, and happiness to which the conquest reduced them," and to the President of the Republic good advice such as that he should walk about publicly among the common citizens.

The nineteenth century was more romantic, more hopeful, more nature-loving, and we find poets like Ignacio Rodríguez Galván (1816–42) writing on Cuauhtémoc, and Ignacio Manuel Altamirano (1834–93) extolling the beauties of the river Atoyac. Principally it was Altamirano, a full-blooded Indian who could not speak Spanish until he had reached adolescence, who headed a patriotic Mexican literary revival. He was fourteen years older than the educationalist and philosopher Justo Sierra (1848–1912), and influenced the latter profoundly in his liberal tendencies.

Two streams of thought now mingled in Mexican poetry, European positivism and a Rosicrucian-influenced mysticism such as we find in the tragic Manuel Acuña (1843–73). Contemporary with Acuña was Salvador Díaz Mirón (1853–1928), a Byronically romantic figure, equally gloomy in his mysticism, jailed for having killed a man in self-defense, a Congress deputy, a journalist who lived long enough to take part in the revolution. He, with Justo Sierra and Gutiérrez Nájera (1859–95), became the moving spirits of a group of writers who drew on European sources for their style but who were authentically Mexican in their thought. They were the forerunners of a talented younger generation which included Amado Nervo (1870–1919), Enrique González Martínez (1871–1952), Francisco A. de Icaza (1863–1925), and José Juan Tablada (1871–1945) who specialized in Japanese Haikku. González Martínez particularly expressed in an original way the deep mistrust of Mexicans for surface prettiness and the longing to get under the skin of organic life and see it in that sinewy form so natural to the ancient sculptors:

Twist the swan's neck with its plumage deceiving,
Scrawling a white word on the fountain's blue;
He struts with vain conceit, who never knew
The deep voice of nature, nor the soul of things.

Flee from every shape and every language
That does not beat in time with the latent
Rhythm in life's depths . . . Be thou most ardent
Lover of life, that life accept thy homage.

See how the wise owl with wings outspread
Dives down from Olympus and the lap of Pallas
To rest on yonder tree his quiet flight.
He may lack the swan's grace, but his eye's sharp bead
Prods the shadow with its restlessness
And reads the muted riddle of the night.[6]

[6] Tuércele el cuello al cisne de engañoso plumaje
Que da su nota blanca al azul de la fuente;
Él pasea en su gracia no más, pero no siente
El alma de las cosas ni la voz del paisaje.

Huye de toda forma y de todo lenguaje
Que no vayan acordes con el ritmo latente
De la vida profunda . . . y adora intensamente
La vida, y que la vida comprenda tu homenaje.

Mira al sapiente buho cómo tiende las alas
Desde el Olimpo, deja el regazo de Palas
Y posa en aquel árbol el vuelo taciturno . . .
Él no tiene la gracia del cisne, mas su inquieta
Pupila, que se clava en la sombra, interpreta
El misterioso libro del silencio nocturno.

Here we find the ancient Mexican view of life and art, so at variance with the Greek ideal of formal perfection and physical beauty, pervading the thought of the most powerful Mexican poet of his generation. From the philosophy of González Martínez, it is easy to slip into that acceptance of death which has so characterized Mexican thought and which permeates the work of such writers as the dramatist Xavier Villaurrutia (1903–50) and the poet José Gorostiza whose poem *Muerte sin Fin* is regarded as one of the finest of this century.

González Martínez was not a pessimist, however, nor was he devoid of gentleness; and he sought to perceive holiness in dust and stone. When it is given you, he said, to find a smile in mist and sun and bird and wind, then with St. Francis you may call all things brother.

We hear the same voice in Justo Sierra who, though he was a leader among the group known as "scientific thinkers," regarded science as a means and not an end. Ironically he, who was constantly questioning the validity of positivist thought, was the involuntary instrument perpetuating that thought in Mexico down to the present day. The group who followed him, especially Antonio Caso (elder brother of the anthropologist Alfonso Caso) and Pedro Henríquez Ureña, well understood Sierra's mistrust of positivism. Their contemporary, José Vasconcelos, although vociferously Roman Catholic, in his deeper nature did not; and this led him to sympathize with Nazi Germany during the war. As to younger men like Leopoldo Zea and Ricardo Guerra, they have interpreted Caso's interest in science as an indication that positivist thinking can be perpetuated exactly at a time when science has been forced by the disintegration of matter into rejecting it.[7]

The nineteenth century was essentially one of philosophy and of poetry. The spirit of the independence fighters was romantic and idealistic, more appropriate to verse and thoughtfulness than to the novel of action which some writers of the time tried to create, filling their pages with bandits and duels and swooning heroines suffering fates worse than death.

[7] Nineteenth-century poetry has not been dealt with as fully as it deserves because it is very completely represented in Samuel Beckett's *Anthology of Mexican Poetry* published by Thames and Hudson and by the Indiana University Press in 1958.

The revolution reversed all that. A strong school of realistic novelists arose; and poetry, except for the folk poetry known as the *corrido* with which we shall deal presently, became of minor importance.

First of the revolution novelists was a physician, Mariano Azuela (1873–1952), who, after a few efforts in the old style, abandoned the flowery romanticism of the nineteenth century to develop a clipped, colloquial prose well suited to his tales of the underdog. This style was further developed by younger men like Agustín Yañez (though his essential romanticism breaks through) and Martín Luís Guzmán, who was a close friend of Pancho Villa. He edited and filled out the latter's autobiography and he used Villa as a model for the hero of *El Aguila y la Serpiente*. Typical of this new, terse prose is a scene in which a soldier, Fierro, shoots 300 prisoners with the same callousness as he had just idly shot a bird. As he sleeps among the corpses he is wakened by a cry. Prodding his adjutant, Fierro says, "One of the dead's asking for water. Get up and shoot that son of a . . . See then if he'll let us sleep!" The adjutant gropes among the dead, fires twice, and the whining stops.

An extract from this same scene will show Guzmán's method of contrasting the cruelty of war with the anxieties of living men to ease their minor bodily discomforts:

The last condemned platoon was made up not of ten victims but twelve. The twelve stumbled over one another as they went out to the firing squad, each trying to cover himself behind the rest while attempting to shove the grizzly procession forward. They skipped as they advanced over the stacked corpses, but the bullets aimed true: with diabolical precision they struck one man after another and left them with their legs and arms spread-eagled, lying halfway to the stockade, clinging to the heaps of their motionless comrades. Only one, the last to remain alive, managed to reach the fence and vault it. . . . The firing stopped, and suddenly the group of soldiers crowded into the angle of the next corral to watch the runaway.

The afternoon turned gray. It was some time before the soldiers grew used to the interfering flicker of double light. At first they could see nothing. Then far off, in the vast plain now in shadow, they could distinguish a silhouetted blob, motionless at the beginning, then moving, then running. The man's body was so bent as he scurried that at times one might have thought he was some creeping thing on the ground.

A soldier raised his rifle and aimed.

"One can hardly see," he said, and fired.

The detonation was lost on the evening wind. The blob ran on.

Fierro had not moved from his place. For a while he let his tired arm hang limp to the ground. Then he discovered that his index finger was hurting and raised his hand to his eyes: in the half dark he confirmed his suspicion that the finger was slightly swollen; he squeezed it gently between the palm and fingers of his other hand. And there he stayed: surrendering himself for a while to the pleasure of slow massage. Then he bent to pick up the *sarape* which he had thrown to the ground when the executions began. He put it over his shoulder and moved to the lee side of the shed for shelter.

Stopping in his track he said to his aide:

"See to the horses when you've done."

And walked on.[8]

With the passing of the active phase of revolution the creative impulse of such writers as Guzmán dried up, and he nowadays edits a left-wing journal. In contrast to his irony is the prose of Alfonso Reyes, for long the doyen of Mexican literature: he died in December 1959. His interests were wide and extended from Greek civilization to Goethe; but his finest prose is to be found in that concentrated précis of a nation's history, *Visión de Anáhuac,* through which the typical cacti of Mexico run like unifying symbols. "The desiccation of the valley of Mexico," Reyes tells us, "extends from 1449 to 1900," from the Nahua poet-king Nezahualcoyotl through the viceroyship to Porfirian days. "Three races, three civilizations, three monarchies with anarchic parentheses between" made the valley as near desert as its stubborn succulence allows. The present century, says Don Alfonso, is doing no better. Yet his descriptions of the land are green and glittering with onion, watercress, garlic, plums, honey, and corn. He quotes the ancient poet who picked flowers for the nobles that they might be glorified before the face of the Lord of All. Through his limpid prose, ancient Mexico

[8] Extract from *El Aguila y la Serpiente* spoken by Martín Luís Guzmán on a phonograph record in the series *Voz Viva de México* published by the Mexican National University. An unabridged version of *The Eagle and the Serpent* was published by Dolphin Books in early 1965 (see bibliography).

reaches forward to the modern, and the typical vegetation of the high plateau receives more enthusiastic treatment than the tropical forest:

The European always asks his American visitors whether there are any trees in America. They would be surprised if we were to tell them of an American Castile, loftier and more harmonious than theirs, probably less acrid (though it is split by vast mountains instead of hills), where the air shines like a looking-glass and there is perpetual autumn. The plains of Castile encourage thoughts of asceticism: the valley of Mexico, by contrast, thoughts that are restful and temperate. The one gains in tragedy, the other in plastic contours.

With us, Nature has two contrasting aspects. One, the more frequently praised virgin forests of America, scarcely deserves mention. In the Old World it is an essential subject for praise and it inspired Chateaubriand's verbal hyperboles. This fertile oven is spendthrift of energy and our souls become stranded on a tide of intoxication. Here we see both the ecstasy of life and the image of life's anarchy: showers of green over the ramparts of the mountains; blind, laced creepers; awnings of banana orchards; the deceitful shade of trees that rock one to sleep and steal away one's power for thought; sulky vegetation; endless, voluptuous stupor as insects buzz. Parrot cries, thundering waterfalls, eyes of wild beasts, *le dard empoisonné du sauvage!* There must certainly be other tropical regions that surpass ours in their squandering of fire and dream—in their poetry of fan and hammock.

Our own Anáhuac is better and more bracing, at any rate for those who like to keep the will constantly sharpened and the thought clear. It is the scenery of the high plateau that suits our nature best: the shy, heraldic vegetation, the tidy landscape, the limpid atmosphere in which even colors are drowned—their disappearance is compensated by the penciled harmony of the whole; the luminous air in which every object stands out separately. . . .[9]

In the same international tradition yet with equal love of the Mexican scene is Jaime Torres Bodet, once Director General of UNESCO and more recently Mexican Minister of Education. Torres Bodet describes his slow discovery of Proust, in whose works "Rouen or Chartres weigh no heavier than Monet's waterlilies."

[9] Spoken by Alfonso Reyes in *Voz Viva de México.*

Beethoven's Seventh Symphony reveals to him that his own childhood had "hereditary wounds"—wounds inflicted no doubt by the need to reconcile two warring psychologies in the Mexican nature.

Alfonso Reyes and Jaime Torres Bodet on the one hand, and Martín Luís Guzmán and Agustín Yañez on the other, represent a bifurcation in modern Mexican writing—the first line being international in trend, the second concentrating on specifically Mexican themes. The more nationalist writers can also be subdivided into those who are primarily anthropologists, finding their material among the Indians who are outside the stream of Western culture; and those who turn rather to the *Mestizo* villages and the provincial towns or the more characteristically Mexican aspects of the big city. In many authors these trends mingle to create a specifically Mexican pattern, but the threads are distinct nevertheless. From the European point of view the Creole-*Mestizo* literature is the most interesting—the anthropological tending to lack style, and the cosmopolitan-Western to have been done better elsewhere. It would, however, be wholly artificial for Mexican intellectuals to turn to "indigenous" themes when they themselves are living sophisticated lives in a city that is—in all aspects that concern them directly—among the most modern in the world.

Of the younger generation of writers, the most successful are Carlos Fuentes, Juan Rulfo, Juan José Arreola, and Rosario Castellanos.[10] Carlos Fuentes, son of a Mexican ambassador and himself a typical member of the cosmopolitan intelligentsia, does his best—or so it would seem from the internal evidence of his novels—to prop up his assumed left-wing-Marxist attitude against the protests of his own common sense. Artemio Cruz, his hero-villain, is a revolutionary turned successful businessman who is by no means unsympathetic in the latter role. He is a many-faceted char-

[10] It is impossible in the space available to do justice to the whole range of contemporary Mexican literature, which is here merely sampled. Many important names have been omitted, including the delightful short-story writer Efrén Hernández; Jorge López Paez who has some sensitive reminiscences of childhood; poets such as Marco Antonio Montes de Oca, Alí Chumacero, Gilberto Owen, and Jaime García Terrés; the versatile Carmen Toscano; and Rubén Bonifaz Nuño; or more straightforward writers of good tales like Roberto Casellas. Their omission in the general discussion implies no adverse criticism of their work, the authors selected for comment being those who seem most representative and most easily synthesized.

acter, capable of deep love and appreciation of beauty, and one feels that but for the odd chance he might almost have been redeemed to saintliness.

Juan Rulfo, who in his youth studied for the priesthood, has no interest in politics, and his compassion for the Mexican underdog is thus more directly emotional and less wrapped in theory. Pedro Páramo, the hero of his short novel by that name, is a landowner upon whom a whole village depends for its livelihood. He has loved one girl since childhood, but the girl goes mad and dies. When the church bells are rung for her funeral, people of the neighboring villages think this is the signal for a *fiesta,* and they come in their crowds to the village of Pedro Páramo. Pedro can never forgive this insult to the girl he so much loved, and vows not to help the village any more. He sits and folds his hands, the village decays, and people die one by one. The crazy, utterly Mexican scene of the ringing bells and the people crowding to the *fiesta* occurs close to the end of the novel, which begins with Pedro Páramo's illegitimate son returning to the village to meet his father for the first time. But the village is dead. The boy talks to the corpses who walk the streets or creak rheumatically in their mildewed coffins. In broken snatches they tell him their stories. Who is alive? Who is dead? Where are we in time? There is a deliberate haziness, a macabre, acrid humor and compassion that make one long for more by the same hand. Apart from this novel and a crop of fine short stories, however, Rulfo has remained silent.

Rosario Castellanos, in *Balún Canán,* describes her own childhood during the agrarian reforms of President Cárdenas, and the persecution of the clergy at that time. Like Rulfo she is too sensitive an artist to take a political line, but she notes the virtues and stupidities of the Spanish-Creole landowners and the Indians alike. The beauty and skill with which an old Indian nurse tells folk-tales to the estate-house children is authentic, and the provincial Mexican scene is poetically evoked:

The balconies are forever staring into the street, watching it go uphill and down and the way it turns the corners. Watching the gentlemen pass with their mahogany canes; the ranchers dragging their spurs as they walk; the Indians running under their heavy burdens. And at all times the diligent trotting donkeys loaded with water in wooden tubs. It must be nice to be like the balconies, always idle, absent-minded, just looking on. When I'm grown up . . .

Now we begin climbing down Market Hill. The butchers' hatchets are ringing inside, and the stupid, sated flies are buzzing. We trip over the Indian women sitting on the ground weaving palm. They are talking together in their odd language, panting like hunted deer. And suddenly they let their sobs fly into the air, high-pitched, without tears. They always frighten me though I've heard them so often.

We skirt past the puddles. Last night came the first shower, the one that brings out the little ants with wings that go *tzisim*. We pass in front of the shops smelling of freshly dyed cloth. Behind the counter the assistant is measuring with a yardstick. We can hear the grains of rice pattering against the metal scales. Someone is crumbling a handful of cocoa. And through the open street doors goes a girl with a basket on her head, and she screams, afraid that either the dogs or the owner will let fly at her:

"Dumplings—come buy!"[11]

In many of her views Rosario Castellanos is at one with her contemporaries; but talking to her, one has the impression of a life proceeding on two levels, the one extrovert, the other so precious that she hides it from all but her most intimate friends. As a student, during a grave religious crisis, she was exalted by reading Bergson on memory, and has since believed in God but not in the clergy. Like her literary forebears, the ancient Mexicans, she is convinced that the language of poetry is the language of permanence. Her concept of love is characteristic: "Its mission is to expose one to be wounded, to break the cradle of 'I' in which we are bound, and in this way to allow us to communicate with others." Since we are egoists, this rupture is painful. Therefore she sees solitude—a very Mexican preoccupation—as the other face of love. Continually she returns to the questions that intrude disquietingly upon her *jolie-laide* vivacity: "What is death? What is fate? Why do we live? How can we fulfill ourselves?" She holds in tension the two yearnings of modern Mexico: forward to material progress, and back to

[11] Castellanos, Rosario. *The Nine Guardians*. Faber and Faber, London, 1959. (Translated from the original, *Balún Canán,* published by the *Fondo de Cultura Económica,* Mexico, 1957.)

speculation on life and death. Her poetry contains more of her religious preoccupations than her prose:

> A trapped bird
> and a throat on loan.
> I come to offer obedience.
> Lord of the open hand
> and the omnipotent house . . .

Listening to her, we recall how the Mexican preconquest poet sang:

> I? Who am I?
> I live as a fugitive, singer of flowers.
> Songs I make, and butterflies of song . . .

But for her preoccupation with style, Rosario Castellanos might belong to the "anthropologist" group of writers, who are stronger in content than in presentation; but in their best stories the force and originality of their subject matter carries the reader along. Ramón Rubín, for instance, who makes and sells shoes and who travels into many primitive districts, has tales based on hard, unhappy fact. In one, an Indian boy and girl marry and decide to go to a big town in search of work; but they find they are a burden to their relatives, so they wander out into the barren countryside. They find a donkey straying by the road, and since it seems to have no owner, they take it along. They are far too innocent to think of this act as theft. The boy takes the beautiful white-painted stones from the edge of the highway to build a shanty. Then he needs wire to fence in the donkey, and he sees an electric pylon with cables strung temptingly from it. He climbs to get them and is carbonized. His wife realizes that something is wrong, climbs to his aid, and suffers the same fate. This is the tragedy of the Indian who can neither read nor write, who hopes for betterment and finds only an alien world. The tragedy is muted and deepened with pathos. Good and evil, right and wrong, seem to have no meaning in this world innocent of knowledge.

Two writers who are in the European satirical tradition, Guadalupe Dueñas and Juan José Arreola, have nevertheless a very Mexican characteristic: they love small insects and forest creatures, and one can imagine that in ancient times they might have modeled toads and birds in clay and not in words.

"Throughout the steady hours," says Guadalupe Dueñas in a story called *Lice*, "the Indians went searching their clothes devotedly for lice, like pearls, and sprinkled them on the ground. . . . They moved slowly like newborn camels." The little Indian Camila burns them over a flame until only one is left alive. This leftover louse is so still, Camila thinks him dead. But he is only pretending, and suddenly he pricks Camila with his incurable sting.

Juan José Arreola enjoys ironical fables, such as one about a scientist who discovers how to dehydrate a camel, pass it through the eye of a needle, and reassemble it again on the other side: thus finally making it possible for the rich to enter the Kingdom of Heaven.

An ironical vignette shows a girl going to draw water at the village pump. Rival suitors approach by converging paths and fight for her to the death, like cocks. The girl has run away at the first sign of trouble, breaking her jug and spilling the water; but she is forever afterward ostracized as a troublemaker and bad woman.

A writer who has something of the same concise irony is Carmen Baez. A cowardly soldier suddenly became brave and, with fifty men, put 2000 to flight. He had merely remembered his own childhood in the revolution, and how he had walked with his sister through streets that sang with bullets like birds, and how the sister had been killed and lay among the cypress trees and crosses.

"Where do you rake up your tales?" begins one of Carmen Baez's stories, and the taleteller answers, "From the well. They're stirred in with the water and frogs and stars. . . ."

Except for Carlos Pellicer, a poet preoccupied with ancient Mexican themes of death and flowers, and Rosario Castellanos who has caught the haunting nostalgia of her native Maya soil, most poets living today are less adept than the short-story writers at fishing inspiration out of the well. The poet with the highest reputation, Octavio Paz, has remained tied to the whispering sadness of Eliot, translating Eliot's dryness across the Atlantic to a landscape of *pirú* trees and cacti and a marihuana dream. It is good derivative poetry with single passages of great beauty and depth, but it has not the originality of Paz's analysis of the Mexican character, *Labyrinth of Solitude,* quoted in earlier chapters.

Twentieth-century Mexican literature has suffered (in spite of noteworthy exceptions) from degeneration in style and vocabulary due to too close a contact with Americanized English. Ermilo Abreu Gómez, Angel María Garibay, and other Mexican writers have attacked a hybridism that prevails more among the cultured than the unlettered classes. Not only is the quality of translation into Spanish poor (it is complained of by language experts such as some United Nations officials), but many young Mexican writers are actually reading and absorbing more English than Spanish literature, with the result that their ears become accustomed to the passive voice where Spanish would more naturally use the reflexive, to idiomatic phrases literally translated, and to coined words like *rentar, reportar* (to rent, to report), or even the hideous *parquear* (to park) replacing honest Spanish: and this in a country where the peasant has a talent for enriching the language with nouns converted into adjectives or verbs, cumulative superlatives, and the like (a peasant wanting to describe a thickly wooded region called it *palísimo* ["very much stick"], for example, and a servant girl who did not take readily to lipstick and high heels said she was not one of those *taconeras,* high-heeled ones).

Clumsy, upper-class malformations of language do not exist in folk literature such as the ballad form known as *corrido,* whose rough, peasant phrasing is the very stuff to strengthen a language. The *corrido* has some characteristics in common with the West Indian calypso. It is colorful and expressive; it often deals with political or social problems; and it treats the rules of rhyme and scansion like minor government regulations—to be broken *"porque sí"* (just for the hell of it). But the *corrido* is sadder and reflects the difference in character between the introspective Indian and the Negro who is always ready to sweat pain away in uninhibited carousal.

Even the *corrido's* jokes have a tinge of pessimism. These ballads, which can be traced back to the religious contentions of the mid-nineteenth century, are born of war and revolution. From 1880 to 1930 the form flourished, its themes being first rebellion against Porfirio Díaz and later the Mexican revolution itself. Sometimes it was a dead man's relatives or his soldier comrades who mourned him in song, and they had little inclination for humor. But sometimes the musicians were professionals, wandering with their guitars from fair to fair so that their song became permeated with a happy-go-lucky philosophy of vagrancy.

When the active period of revolution had passed the *corrido* slid into what its most loving student, the late Vicente T. Mendoza, calls a false form, studied, classified, and imitated by the intellectuals. Nowadays—if they are determined enough in their Mexicanism—good families publish *corrido* broadsheets for birthdays or other festive occasions. Nevertheless, though in some aspects the form has become as middle-class and respectable as the revolution itself, basically it remains of the people.

The *corrido* derived from Spanish romances, and just as the old romances created heroic myths, so the *corridos* build Madero, Zapata, Obregón, and Pancho Villa into outsize figures greatly endowed with *machismo* or male toughness. But at their elbows stand bitterly humorous realists ready to prick the bubble of heroism: "Obregón told the Yaquis: 'Boys, fear not to die, you'll be reborn later in your homeland.' One of the soldiers answered, 'General, that's a lie. I wrote to a dead brother. He never answered.'"

On the whole, war brings more boredom than glory, and even that modern Robin Hood, Pancho Villa, is said to have surrendered so that he might return to the pleasanter occupation of sowing cotton. A full belly is better than wealth: "I'd like to be a great man, full of wisdom; but I'd like still more to have lots to eat. Yes, sirs, it's worth more than hard cash."

The *corrido* is the cry of the underdog, and the underdog remains in his lowly place, revolution or no. He complains that he is nowhere wanted, that at the inn he is not served but ordered to wait. Even in hunger he turns to the everlasting theme of fickle woman: "Between a woman and a cat, you'll never guess whether the cat is more Indian or the woman more ungrateful. A sparrow among the carnations told me once: 'Don't believe in women, for they are bottled honey and lovers of treachery.'" But the singers can recognize male fickleness too, "for there's no meal more appetizing than another man's wife."

The *corrido* at its best is a poignant self-portrait of the down-at-heel Mexican, loving, working, and dying in resignation at life's injustices. One wonders just how much the revolution myth has been kept alive by its occasional heroics, and how much of the patriotism is tongue-in-cheek. "In 1910," says one, "prophecies began, and the nation rose against Porfirio Díaz. Fly, fly, little dove, fly and perch on the hill, and go and greet Don Francisco I. Madero. For I'm going with Madero with a good heart. Long live effective suffrage, which allows no re-election." The two sacred slogans of revolution sound prosaic after the doves. If this were a calypso singer, one would suspect irony. In the *corrido,* the intention is more ambiguous. All that can be said is that these folk poets anchor their ideals firmly to the ground, that their warnings are as true today, in industrializing Mexico, as they were in the high days of revolution. "The Constitution takes us along a path to joy. . . . Forget quarrels, go back and work the earth, let no more blood be spilled on the plains or in the hills. Love one another, as the Redeemer commanded. The people are tired of revolution and want peace." This is the common man's philosophy, which causes sporadic uprisings to die nowadays like damp squibs. But the final lines of the *corrido* revive the theme of eternal discontent: "The fields are waste and the peons without food, they are going to the cities in search of life and ease. If only they would busy themselves on the ranches or in the mines, another cock would sing and our ruin would end."[12]

ARCHITECTURE The *hacienda* chapel, gold-encrusted, seemed cool in contrast to the glaring sunshine that struck the whitewashed walls of farm buildings and peasant huts. The massed villagers formed a rhythmic pattern as their cartwheel hats twisted nervously in their hands. The women's *rebozos,* once gaudy, had faded under hard scouring on river stones. Old and young bobbed continually as they crossed themselves, making a kind of syncopation to the slower movements of priest and acolyte and to the murmuring voices of the Mass. The chapel portico was packed with late arrivals who

[12] The *corrido* quotations are all taken from the collection *El Corrido Mexicano, Antología, Introducción, y Notas,* by Vicente T. Mendoza, which also contains the basic musical themes. The collection was published by the *Fondo de Cultura Económica* in 1954.

shoved forward to get a glimpse of the effigies with their curling artificial hair and their tawdry satin garments. Above the congregation, like a marigold in the desert, the tiled dome winked at a cloudless sky.

Scenes such as this, repeated all over Mexico, give the clue to the success of Mexican baroque, and indeed to all Mexican architecture from ancient pyramids to modern shell vaulting. Each style has been molded to a particular context from which it cannot be torn without loss. Walls, massive or fantastic in their tracery of gesso, form the backdrop to a year-long liturgical rhythm, to the ebb and flow of agriculture, to the explosive punctuation of *fiestas* with their fireworks and masquerade. If the generous catholicism of Mexican architectural design did not spill over beyond its enclosing walls, to embrace the whole community and its activities, it would lose a dimension and appear either too stark or ridiculously ornate.

It is because the surrounding movement has been cut away that the ancient archaeological sites seem cold when compared to the poetry or the sculpture. The life has gone from them and cannot be returned. Nobody knows what went on inside; and though there are intelligent guesses in plenty, they are made from a distance, from the point of view of an alien culture. Teotihuacán, with its royal road from the temple of plumed serpent to the Pyramid of the Moon, and with its pillars of butterfly and Quetzal motifs and its paintings in glowing earths, is majestic but remote and, in reconstruction, just a little cold. Tajín conceals its secrets in the jungles of Veracruz; but since its forms echo the jungle, it is warmer. In the shadows of the massed masonry of Chichén and Uxmal the tourists look diminutive, like beetles; and even when, out of the thousands, one discerning visitor may stop to grasp the total meaning of the sites, the stones have a way of closing on their secret. Only Mitla sometimes offers a flicker of life, when the Zapotec peasants chatter together like birds; and Monte Albán under the moon may be glossed by a passing donkey and its rider, as if the little ephemeral figure were being weighed against the gigantic temple.

Modern imitations of pre-Hispanic architecture—such as Diego Rivera's Anahuacalli museum or the appalling Monument to the Race on the northern artery out of Mexico City—are stone dead;

9. Rosario Castellanos, author of *The Nine Guardians,* surrounded by folk pottery.

10. Zapotec children of Oaxaca.

11. A Zapotec-speaking Indian woman of Yalalag in her traditional costume. She could speak no Spanish but asked through an interpreter to be photographed.

12. Typical provincial woman of Oaxaca.

13. Dressed for an annual festival of *charro* horsemanship, in an old colonial suburb of Mexico City.

14. Display of folk costumes in an old colonial suburb of Mexico City.

15. An old-fashioned village market, contrasted with . . . (see following photograph)

16. . . . a modern market in Mexico City.

whereas colonial Christian architecture—even when much restored—still stuns us with its vitality.

Mexican colonial architecture is neither European nor indigenous but a blending of both. The friars quickly perceived that talent abounded which could be put to Christian use. Spain itself, at the time of the conquest of Mexico, was riddled with architectural styles, but it had molded this variety into a native idiom that deferred very little to its models: Gothic, Islamic Arabic, Renaissance European. The mixture of Moorish and Gothic which created the style known as plateresque, for example, would seem a monstrous hybrid in any European country but Spain. In Mexico the specifically Gothic element has always seemed for some reason out of place. And yet when the open-air plateresque atrium at Tlalmanalco was used to stage Calderón de la Barca's *La Vida es Sueño* (not the early and more famous version but a later miracle drama), it came to life as it must have done when the friars first preached Christianity in the New World. Acolman, on the way to Teotihuacán and easily accessible to tourists, is classified as plateresque but is so much more massive than the slender Tlalmanalco that it looks like first cousin to Norman. It is the total simplicity that is effective here. A single bird flying through its nave is like a calligraphic flourish by contrast. Actopan, too, in the State of Hidalgo, would give the impression rather of a Norman fortress than a sixteenth-century church were it not for the frescoes filled with arabesques and depicting ecclesiastical life in some complexity. The barrel arches on the façade and in the walled niche of a well in Tepoztlán (where the high plateau drops in Valkyrie-like cliffs to the Cuernavaca plain below) have a delicacy that is more truly plateresque; and Cuernavaca cathedral itself has been coaxed from its original severity by the upkeep of its gardens and its constant use of the town around it through centuries as a subtropical haven.

Such is sixteenth-century church architecture. Simultaneously the conquerors were building administrative palaces and homes worthy of their newly acquired opulence. They had no temptation to flaunt their wealth before the natives, and the domestic architecture of the time has a severity that makes it in some ways extraordinarily modern. It was heavy on the ground, and turned inward toward shady patios; but the unblinking walls with which it faced the street, its sparsely placed and well-proportioned grille windows, and its plain rectangles of white or weathered pink, are more honestly functional than a good deal that has gone by that name since. The best of the modern blends very well with sixteenth-century walls, and this is a test for both. Bought for a song as old shells and rebuilt inside, the main structures of the old buildings perfectly fit the mood of today, whether in town or village. Plain walls are a constant theme of Mexican architecture, and their presence in the landscape has engendered an awareness of good proportions which was submerged only in the worst follies of Porfirianism. It even survived through the fashion for chinoiserie when trade routes opened from the Orient through Mexico to Europe.

It was this unerring sense of proportion that saved Mexican baroque and turned its craziest exaggerations into masterpieces. By the end of the sixteenth century native labor, which had quickly grasped the essentials of the new spatial order brought from Spain, was capable of showing the whole range of its skills. Santo Domingo in Oaxaca, enclosing a rosary chapel, seems to hold an exotic flower inside the simple calyx of late sixteenth-century structure. The Tree of Jesse in the stuccoed vault beneath the choir is one of the earliest suggestions that Mexican plateresque was giving way (about 1625) to true baroque. Still more important, the freedom of modeling and unexpected naturalism suggest that local workmen had at last found a way to marry ancient ingenuity with Christian themes. Of all Mexican churches, Oaxaca is the most pagan; and when it is crammed with Indians who have come from the mountains around for the Good Friday Stations of the Cross, it gives the impression of a great sun, veiled in purple but restless for the moment of resurrection. Only Tonanzintla equals it in being basically Indian; and only Tonanzintla together with the rosary chapel of Santo Domingo in Puebla, can rival it in baroque fantasy.

Tonanzintla's façade and tower are classically austere. If its red and blue and white tiles did not hint of a richer baroque within, we should be taken completely by surprise when confronted with the chubby angels and cherubs, the saints so primitively expressive, the dove, the fruit—a whole storehouse of nature spilling shyly out from tangles of gold leaf.

Tonanzintla in the Nahua language means "place of the little mother"; and here beneath the mountains of Popocatépetl and Ixtaccíhuatl there may have been a shrine to an ancient goddess, perhaps to Coatlicue "with the petticoat of serpents." Pedro Rojas[13] points out that the Christian church perpetuates the ancient love of flowers, which tumble in gesso from dome to floor.

Equally prolific in its inventiveness is the tiny rosary chapel tucked into Santo Domingo of Puebla, where Mexican baroque reaches its peak of splendor. The balance between exuberance and bad taste is here so fine that only the classic structure has saved this little jewel from dissolving into foam. One of the most sober scholars of Mexican architecture, Joseph Armstrong Baird,[14] exclaims that it is ". . . alive with an ecstasy of heavenly joy in the midst of a fantastic ornamental jungle of beige and gold strapwork and foliation. . . . Saints, angelic children, and insignia are engulfed in a waving Sargossa Sea of Mannerist-inspired interlaces. . . . The Pueblan stucco tradition, carried by its itinerant workers to Oaxaca, reached a pitch of fervor and craftsmanship here, to be attained later only in the small churches near San Francisco Acatepec."

While Mexican baroque was thus exploding into catherine-wheels of color and movement, José Benito Churriguera was perfecting his retable techniques which gave the name to a new style—though, as Armstrong Baird suggests, the modern use of the word Churrigueresque applies to Andalusian excess rather than to José Benito's Catalán austerity. It was the former style, rather than Churriguera's own, that was imported to Mexico in the eighteenth century by Lorenzo Rodríguez, a Spaniard from Córdoba. His first work in Mexico was the carpentry at the central Mint, but he later developed his "*estípite*" pilasters, a hybrid order with Corinthian topping which can be seen at its finest on the façade and tower of Tepozotlan just outside Mexico City (although these columns may not be by Lorenzo Rodríguez himself). Churrigueresque, for lack of a better definition, might be thought of as the baroque spirit translated from surface decoration into three-dimensional archi-

[13] Rojas, Pedro. *Tonanzintla.* National Autonomous University, Mexico City, 1956, p. 40.

[14] Baird, Joseph Armstrong, Jr. *The Churches of Mexico, 1530–1810.* University of California Press, 1962, p. 106.

tectural space. A characteristic Rodríguez work, for instance, is the south façade of the Sagrario jammed side by side with Mexico City cathedral; and some Mexican Churrigueresque can also be seen in Taxco. But the term is generally very loosely used to denote the tail end of baroque which was already moving gently into neoclassicism.

Manuel Tolsá (1757–1816) represents the bridge between these styles. Like Lorenzo Rodríguez, he was a Spaniard and was imported to Mexico to become director of the official art academy of San Carlos. By his day the fervor of church architecture had given way to a demand for civic buildings befitting a rich colony, and his most famous works, were the Palace of Mines and also the bronze equestrian statue of Charles IV which stands at the junction of Avenida Juárez and the Paseo de la Reforma in Mexico City.

It was the slightly younger and Mexican-born Francisco Eduardo de Tresguerras (1795–1833) who brought Mexican neoclassical architecture to perfection, although he too, like Tolsá, remained influenced by late baroque. Tresguerras' finest works are in his native Celaya, especially in the Church of Carmen; but he also built the imposing Degollado theatre in Guadalajara, and other civic buildings of the same type.

The neoclassic period was one of individual architects, and by this time the folk-like exuberance of church decoration had given way to a more sophisticated and deliberately developed formalism. As Pedro Rojas points out,[15] churches such as Tonanzintla are much more than the sum of their walls, and are rather the creation of countless artisans. This corporate quality did not endure, and neoclassical architecture initiated a trend toward greater dependence on individual talent. With the death of Tresguerras it very quickly declined—first into Porfirian showiness (though Porfirian architecture still retained a semblance of dignity), and later into a hotch-potch of imitative styles that make English Victorian architecture look pure by comparison. We have to move forward to the twentieth century and to the doyen of contemporary Mexican architecture—José Villagrán García—before we find any glimmer of the old genius emerging once again.

The mid-nineteenth-century architectural eclipse did more, un-

[15] Rojas, Pedro. *Op. cit.*, p. 24.

fortunately, than throw up bad buildings. It was responsible for the neglect and destruction of much earlier work, especially of domestic architecture by Manuel Tolsá and other masters. Those works that still stand are crumbling, their ground floors used for small printing establishments and the like, their future existence threatened because new highways are being driven through the cities. Public awareness of the value of colonial architecture has been slow to catch up with enthusiasm for the modern. Protests from connoisseurs, however, are at last making the government have occasional second thoughts about some casual plans for demolition in the name of progress.

It is close on forty years since Villagrán García put an end to the *nouveau-riche*-and-Moorish-gingerbread period. Many of his clean, functional hospitals, dispensaries, and administrative buildings seem to have some semblance to the work of the Dutch Willem Marinus Dudok, who was born in 1884 and was one of the first Europeans to break into modernism. Like Dudok's, Villagrán's structures look already a little old-fashioned; but he takes the credit for having swept away the bric-à-brac. He has been the teacher of almost every outstanding Mexican architect working today, and he is still able to use his tongue to good effect, mocking the new "academism"—all façade, all glass, regardless of the comfort of those inside the sun-traps. He is badgering the young to take account of man as a complete creature, both animal and spirit.

Since Villagrán's early revolution, modern Mexican architecture has earned a reputation for daring; yet the visitor to Mexico looking for proof that this reputation is deserved may be disappointed unless he has time to explore the byways. Along the main streets of Mexico City much of the architecture is of the international grand-hotel variety that can be seen in any capital in the world, and the jewels of the modern movement hide shyly behind walls or in outer suburbs. Provincial towns are cluttered with bourgeois homes that have been copied haphazard from the world's architectural journals. The working-class housing estates are more neatly planned and quite as comfortable, with their pumice brick walls, good plain flooring, labor-saving kitchens, and space for expansion as the family grows. In a country where the architects cannot keep up with the rising population, prefabrication is all the rage, for rural schools as well as homes. The need to pare down the budget is doing what utility clothing did to the middle-class English wardrobe during the war: ridding design of fripperies and revealing virtue in simplicity. Even the *multifamiliares*—the large housing blocks that suffer from too scant a provision for decent human privacy—have an elemental severity that makes up for many defects.

But where, asks the visitor, is the vaunted originality? There is the National University of course, anything but shy, and photogenic as a film star. The buildings rise like mountain chimneys from their lava rock foundations. The campus has rough outcrops with wild plants growing in the cracks, or is smoothed into quadrangles of lawn and hedged with the yellow bole and waxy red flower of the *colorín*. From upper floors the sweeping views of purple-black, glowering Ajusco and the two delicate snow-capped volcanoes increase the sensation that these towers are natural outcrops in a broken landscape. Some of the detail is questionable, particularly the poster-crude murals in plastic relief, but the total effect is a fitting modern solution to the problem of housing what may be the largest and is certainly one of the most nationally representative universities in the world (for no Mexican who makes a minimum effort to get there is denied access, though the buildings split at the seams).

Individually, the best structures in the university complex are Juan O'Gorman's four-square library block, almost without windows except in the ground-floor reading-rooms from which bookstacks rise inside their mosaic walls; and Félix Candela's cosmic ray laboratory on stilts, with a shell-vaulted roof three-quarters of an inch thick.

Candela has produced so many utilitarian gems that it is difficult to pick any one out for special praise: the Mexico City customs shed; the British Council's auditorium and the stock exchange interior (both in collaboration with Enrique de la Mora); modest structures such as a small factory for making fruit juice cartons (with Fernando Barbará Zetina—a model of plainness with comfort, and it was built in four months); the immense span of the aluminum factory potshed in the State of Veracruz.

There is a myth that Candela does not calculate mathematically, which is, of course, nonsense; nevertheless, he is not much in favor of detailed calculations and at a certain moment he seems to rely on the unknown faculty vaguely termed intuition. For Candela it may be that intuition arises from muscular memory, from a fine sense of balance developed through years of athletic activity. He began mountaineering when he was six, and was later the best amateur on skis in Spain. He also played first-class Rugby football and squash. These facts may help to explain the unerring sense of balance we find throughout his work.

Candela's arrival in Mexico in 1939 as a Spanish republican refugee seems to have been due to a series of lucky accidents. He was not to begin evolving his shell structures for another decade, but he had come, as it happened, to a country ideally suited for the development of his special talents: a country prepared to experiment, and with a labor force of unskilled but artistically sensitive workmen.

Candela's structures are extremely strong, not because they are massive and buttressed, but on the contrary because they are light like the strong structures in nature. This is particularly true of his "free-edge" buildings, in which the weight and stress are taken not at the rim of the cover but along one or more inner ribs. Among these is a restaurant in Xochimilco which Candela seems to regard as his most significant work. Structurally it is perfect; it rests on eight buttresses and waves in the air like a poised leaf. Nevertheless, there is something a little embarrassing about its prettiness, about the regularity of its gentle curves reflected in the water. The epitome of structure pared down to the barest essence is rather the Jacaranda night club in Acapulco, built with Juan Sordo Madaleno. Colin Faber,[16] student and commentator on Candela's work, says of the free-edge structures:

> It was aesthetics, a desire to take the essence of a shell and express it visually, that prompted Candela to develop the free edge. In his free-edged masterpieces, in Acapulco's Jacaranda and in the restaurant at Xochimilco, nothing further could be subtracted. There is no compromise to their thinness, no ribs or props or stabilizers. Only the taut shell membranes are there. Only their shape *can* be their strength. . . . The shell suggests a form smoothed

[16] Faber, Colin. *Candela: the Shell Builder,* Reinhold, New York, and Architectural Press, London, 1963, p. 188.

by constant sea action. From the hotel's roof, it has the look of a turtle flung up by the tide; from the sea, close up, of a full-blown sail in tension.

Many of Candela's smaller buildings are difficult to find in the big city. They are as unnoticed and impudent as urchins poking fun at architectural officialdom. There is plenty of the latter, of course: the main block of the Social Security Institute; the crazy mosaic-covered units that house the Ministries of Transport and Public Works (the mosaic here has none of the subtle coloring that makes the University library change mood according to the light); the Medical Center with its uncouth sculptural friezes showing surgeons at work through the centuries.

At another extreme there is Television Center, shocking pink with a frieze of wedding-cake figures, trying hard to be folksy and ending by being mere folly. For playful, fantastic architecture this building cannot compete with the museums designed by Pedro Ramírez Vázquez and Rafael Mijares for the frontier towns of the north. One, in Tijuana, looks like an iced teacake with its flat concrete roof and its plastic dome that might well be the maraschino cherry. Another basically circular design, in Ciudad Juárez, slopes inward like one of those protective paper cuffs that used to be worn by office clerks. The entrance remains wide open so that a choice exhibit may be placed in full view of the passers-by to lure them in. A third frontier museum, at Matamoros, has a rectangular main building with a long annex reminding one of a folded-paper game, in which cones of concrete break up the space for small exhibitions.

The great work of the Ramírez Vázquez-Mijares team is the new museum of archaeology and anthropology in Chapultepec Park. This must be one of the largest modern museums in the world (over 430,000 square feet in area). It is built with plain outer walls whose large windows overlooking woodland allow exhibits to be seen in their natural setting while yet remaining protected indoors. The galleries also have windows protected by aluminum fretting, which face on to an inner courtyard shaded by a great "umbrella" that spreads from a single central concrete column. Iron cantilever girders and tensor cables hold the aluminum fabric. The umbrella measures 269 by 177 feet and is said to be the largest construction of its kind in the world. Critics say that it is an architect's rather than a museographer's building, and it certainly has not catered to the pernickety scholar who wants to make ancient history a toil among potsherds and bones. The layout is bright, gay, and imaginative, with wall patterns that are like the simplest modern abstract painting (a Ben Nicolson, perhaps). Against these are placed the old carvings and pottery, and the visitor can reconstruct the ancient environment with the help of occasional mural paintings done in sufficient detail to show us that in remote parts of Mexico life has changed not at all since old Tlaloc ruled. The Aztec calendar stone looks reduced in scale in its place of honor at the end of a long gallery. The plain modern walls dwarf it until we see people passing by and realize that one standing on another's shoulders would not be the measure of its diameter.

Among other important public buildings are social security centers by Alejandro Prieto, with their neatly ranged medical consulting-rooms, libraries, workshops for teaching skills to poor Mexicans, sports grounds, marble halls, and scented wood-paneled walls (nothing is too good for the poor, but it has to be given them in lumps and not spread so thinly over the country that nobody will notice). Architecturally, Prieto has a tendency to run wild and throw all styles together: honeycomb ceilings, buttressed walls, and Candela's umbrella sheds over connecting passageways.

Some new office blocks exploit techniques that are unique in the world. A lunatic was painting a ceiling and his mate told him to hang tight to the brush while he removed the ladder; and that, says Enrique de la Mora, is about the stage his own workmen have reached. In co-operation with Alberto González Pozo, and with Leonardo Zeevaert, as consulting engineer, de la Mora has built a "hanging structure" for the Monterrey Insurance Company's Mexico City offices. As the two hollow square supporting nuclei began to sprout out branches from above downward, passers-by wondered whether they were on their heads or their heels. Seven floors up these nuclei support two longitudinal concrete beams, which in turn support transverse armatures from which the building is hung. The advantage of the construction is that space is used to its maximum. The nuclei are just over nineteen feet square, with walls only slightly over a foot thick. Within the hollows are lift shafts, stairs, and services. Above the seventh floor is a lookout terrace, and above that a restaurant, also without pillars and with a "hanging" roof. The finished building seems disappointing in comparison with the boldness of its conceptions, but this is rather the fault of the cramped site, which does not allow the total effect to be seen. The main bulk of the building seems to crowd heavily above the parking space that undercuts it at street level, so that it is like a tree left behind and fighting for breath in an overgrown city. One would have liked to see gardens around it.

Another method of avoiding unnecessary columns has been evolved by Juan Sordo Madaleno and José Villagrán García, again in collaboration with Leonardo Zeevaert. In the María Isabel Hotel (one of the most satisfactory glass-façade luxury buildings in Mexico), two basement and three lower floors are supported by pillars. At this point a transition floor allows each pillar to split, crow-footed, into three walls that continue upward for another fifteen floors.

The early classical form of skyscraper, in which rectangular blocks of diminishing size are placed on one another like children's blocks, is giving way in Mexico to designs that allow greater flow to the façade. An example is Edificio Símbolo by Mario Pani. It is the central administrative unit for a workers' housing estate in Nonoalco, one of the poorest districts of Mexico City. Its front and rear elevations form all-glass isosceles triangles, the sides being plain sloping concrete rectangles. The upper tip of the triangle contains a carillon of bells cast in Belgium.

Auónoma de Arquitectos (a youthful team composed of Oscar Urrutia, Pascual Broid, Benjamín Méndez, and Carlos Ortega, who have since gone separate ways) designed a tall building with upward-flowing façades for the Mexican National Railways. The ground plan was an equilateral triangle whose three walls sloped inward at varying angles of steepness (no slope at the triangle points and maximum slope at the midpoint of each side) to give the plan of the upper floors the form of a Y. The façades were to be of glass placed like jalousies, the jambs forming drains. Each floor was a slight variation of the one below, so that the occupants should not have the sensation common in modern buildings of being cooped in identical cells. The weakness of this design was the need for every unit of the façades, including window frames, to be separately cast and measured. It was this defect that caused the interesting project to be shelved. Even Mexican daring was unable quite to accept such an ingenious but eccentric plan.

In some tall buildings, the twin problems of adjusting a heavy structure to Mexico City's sinking foundations, and of resistance against seismic shock, have been solved by various means. In Edificio Símbolo and in the railway building project the triangular-pyramidal shapes are designed to withstand shock by a kind of massed assault on the ground. Conversely, in de la Mora's insurance block it is the slender hollow nuclei that provide elasticity.

Leonardo Zeevaert believes that to date his Latin American tower (forty-three floors high and slender as a eucalyptus tree) is the most flexible building in the world. In defiance of accepted practice at least until fairly recently, he calculated its periods of vibration so that they are higher than those of the soil foundations; but this innovation tallies with the construction of classical Japanese pagodas, which seem rarely to suffer earthquake damage and have also been found to have a higher vibration period than their soil foundations.

The necessity to move industries out from the overcrowded capital is, however, encouraging architects to design low buildings such as those for the new car factories outside Toluca. The first to be finished, and the most beautiful factory in Mexico today, is the Automex plant designed by Ricardo Legorreta with two distinctive decorative towers by Matías Goeritz, an Austrian sculptor who also designed the brightly colored towers at the entrance to the modern housing estate, Ciudad Satélite. The Automex exterior is severely plain, its long walls depending for their effect on subtle gradations of coloring in the new white stone. The assembly plant itself is gaily painted in primary colors and lighted from above, making a pleasant environment for the workers.

Among all the wealth of modern buildings it is oddly enough the churches that offer the most exciting possibilities for a genuinely national style. More than half a dozen chapels with soaring lines, and an engineering structure so sound that one feels they are the true descendants of medieval Gothic, have been built by de la Mora and his group of young apprentice-architects, with Candela providing the vaulting.

The earliest of these chapels, set in a garden behind high walls, was completed in 1957 for the Missionaries of the Holy Spirit. The French Father Félix Rougier, founder of the order which extends throughout Latin America, has encouraged simple modern design not only in buildings but also in vestments and in the furniture of the mission houses.

De la Mora's building of gray lava stone harmonizes with an old monastery wall against which it is set. Placed on the edge of a lava bed which breaks off into a gully—now filled to form a gentle incline—the chapel has foundations concentrated at one point, from which the building wings outward toward the altar at one end and the spacious open porch at the other. The porch carries a simple cross which is incorporated structurally into the building. Its task is to act as tensor counterbalancing the weight of the larger side of the asymmetrical rhombus that forms the roof. The rhombus is a series of those now fashionable ruled hyperbolic-paraboloid surfaces whose versatility Candela was the first to exploit, and which have never been used by anyone else so fittingly or so diversely.

Not far from the missionaries live the Sisters of St. Vincent de Paul, and here the need for a central altar with three converging naves (one for the sisters, one for convalescent patients from the hospital built in the grounds by the same architects, and a third for visitors) has produced a shape that echoes the sisters' winged hoods. Three hyperbolic-paraboloid surfaces meet to receive the balancing thrusts. The glass is clear, and bougainvillaea is planted along the walks so that the chapel draws the garden into itself: though once again de la Mora has been unlucky in his site, which is too small and cramped to allow a full, free view of this small masterpiece.

Other churches have been designed for provincial towns, among them a lovely free-edge structure on a lonely hill above Cuernavaca. In appearance it is almost as light as the Xochimilco restaurant, though its lip is strengthened to resist high winds. Its gentle curves are balanced by a severe, plain cross standing free from the church itself.[17]

In a suburb of Acapulco a sanctuary to the Virgin of Guadalupe is to be an octagon with four covers supported at four points. To suit the tropical climate this will be an open construction built on sloping ground with a presbytery and altar overlooking the Pacific and with gardens intruding into the church. The design is a preliminary essay for the most important work commissioned by a foreign country from a Mexican architect, a sanctuary to Guadalupe in Madrid. This is an exceptional tribute from a country which four centuries ago taught the indigenous Mexicans how to build European baroque.

Today, as one watches Mexican laborers in their frayed straw hats, measuring up with crooked sticks, one has a sense of the medieval—of an architecture sophisticated in its engineering but so simple in execution that unskilled armies can trace out mathematical curves as casual and perfect as a bird's flight. Here one seems to be witnessing the birth of a genuine new style, a welding of geometry and fitness to the job in hand, whether it be saying Mass or turning out cartons for industry.

PAINTING AND SCULPTURE In the bewildering plastic variety of ancient Mexican art, there is little that can be regarded as personal or subjective. The total cosmic view remains constantly in mind if not in sight. The same rhythm runs like the ebb and flow of tides, like the seasons on earth or the procession of the galaxies: from the massive statue of Coatlicue in which life and death are interwoven as two strands of a single design, to the tiny modeled figures of marketeers and pilgrims.

Cosmic preoccupation excludes characteristics of gentleness that we in the West have come to regard as legitimate and indeed as a necessary cushioning to the uncompromising artistic view: characteristics such as beauty for beauty's sake, sweetness, coziness, a fond lingering on the particular and the intimate to the exclusion of the universal and the aloof. Take such characteristics away, and the result appears cruel, but only if we forget the motive force in

[17] On this church Candela collaborated not with de le Mora but with Guillermo Rosell and Manuel Larrosa.

ancient Mexican art, which was functional to a degree unknown in modern times. The function was not materialistic but religious. Every clay pot and every mural decoration served a religious end; and religion meant that all life was bound into a single unity. The stelae, the sculptures, the wall paintings, were an extension of people's inner lives.

The sympathetic arrangement of exhibits in the Diego Rivera Anahuacalli by the poet Carlos Pellicer does much to cancel out the heaviness of the building. Here, if it were still needed, is proof of the humor and plastic inventiveness of early Mexicans. The 55,481 pieces Rivera left to the nation span twenty centuries from about 500 B.C. to close upon the conquest. They represent the cultures of Teotihuacán and the Valley of Mexico, the Totonac, Zapotec, Mixtec, Olmec, and the pre-classical sculpture of Colima and Nayarit. The only important culture omitted is the Maya, which for some reason Rivera did not collect and which—in its Oriental intricacy imposed on its plain classical line—is the most purely joyous of all.

In the Anahuacalli, diminutive figures have been grouped by Pellicer in scenes that are of today or yesterday. People doze and dance and tumble and gossip as they do in villages still. Larger pieces, majestic in their niches, are evidence that the ancient sculptors were highly sophisticated. They were not, says Pellicer, so inept as to depict a man thinking. They were interested in thought, and they built it, freely and untrammeled by naturalism, out of bent shoulders and pillowed head cunningly simplified. Women with child, men laden with market wares, plump birds, sly and watchful animals: all express the inner depths of the creature rather than the anatomy we see. Even the pottery seems to round and burst with emotion and gentle laughter.

The same effect is achieved in the National Anthropological Museum with its larger monumental works—Coatlicue herself; Chalchiuhtlicue, goddess of rivers; Xochipilli, Lord of Flowers, the flayed god Xipe; Coyolxanuhque, Huitzilopochtli's sister; the Knight Eagle with his European features; and the monolith of formal beauty, the Huastec standing adolescent boy.

In Xalapa, Veracruz, we can see the bewildering range of coastal sculpture, from the massive negroid-featured Olmec heads, through the low-relief carvings of decapitated ballplayers, to the laughing figurines of Los Cerros. In Oaxaca the geometry of Mitla and the golden and earthen complexities of rain gods from Monte Albán stand side by side with strangely primitive bas-reliefs of animal-like figures known as dancers. But it is in the Maya lands that we reach the deepest serenity, in the almost Egyptian relief figures with their long profiles extending in an arc from the headdress to the tip of the nose; and in the stelae that conserve an over-all simplicity of proportion under the intricate detail.

No attempt can be made here to discuss the wealth of styles in ancient Mexican art or even to sort out the periods. It is sufficient to note that through all the variety there runs the unity of purpose that is ancient Mexico's most startling characteristic. These ancient peoples were aware of the operation of cosmic laws in every particle of creation. They showed their all-embracing universal interests in their paintings too, from the processional friezes of Bonampak to the tantalizing fragments of another procession—beast made god, chrysalis become butterfly, footprints and gift-endowing hands of god—which we find in the palaces around Teotihuacán. In them the natural forms never congeal into immobility even when they enclose geometrical designs or are in turn enclosed by them (in border patterns symbolizing water flowing or flowers or stars). The geometry here seems to serve the same purpose as beat and rhythm in music: stressing the total pattern and creating a framework within which variety can be contained and formalized. The discovery of these frescoes has thrown much light on the oddly stiffened codices or religious picture books. The wall painters were the artists; the codex-makers (at least those whose work survives) were the imitators probably more intent on recording history than on creating a world of living symbols. In the codices, the painters "in red ink and black" pinned the living inspiration to an academic framework of pure mimicry, just as the scribes were among those who stultified the religion of Christ.

Mexicans have always needed big spaces on which to paint. They feel cramped in a small area. They think of walls as books where the illiterate may read their country's history and see its beliefs reflected. Even in colonial times this mural conception continued, for there were the inner domes of the churches and their ample walls that could be filled with the narrative of Christ's ministry and crucifixion. The colonial sculptors of wooden church effigies, and the canvas and mural painters, were mainly anonymous indigenous artists imitating European styles with extraordinary facility. One whose name survives is Miguel Cabrera, who seems to have been a Zapotec Indian born about 1768. In his work we see epitomized the sweet, Indian version of the Christian story. But Mexican baroque painting did not flourish for long and soon petered out into academic clichés emanating from the Academy of San Carlos. At its best its gently flowing lines and cloud-pink tints exemplify a happy, if minor, talent; at its worst it is stiff and mannered, concerned with accurately copying the costumes of the period and uninterested in the fantasy that gives the style wings.

An exquisite collection of Mexican baroque sculpture and painting, together with other objects of the colonial period, can be seen in the church of Tepozotlán, which has been turned into a museum with its surrounding village rebuilt in the arcaded domestic architecture of the time. Strolling about the grounds of the convent with its vistas of Indian laurel, its terraces inviting masques and miracle plays, its patios with its wells and orange trees, one is thrown back to the days when artists had time to spend on the most outrageous extravagances of Mexican *estípite,* and when no canvas was quite complete till hosts of cherubs fluttered above humankind. Here are works not only by Cabrera, but also by his contemporaries such as Juan Correa who made copies of the Virgin of Guadalupe, and of his pupil José Ibarra. There is also a gallery of colonial paintings facing the central Alameda in Mexico City, and a fuller museum in a beautiful viceregal building in Calle Pino Suárez near the National Palace. These three museums together are a tardy but splendid atonement for the neglect into which the Spanish heritage had fallen during the early days of post-revolution, and which had been nurtured both in the Jesuit college at Tepozotlán itself and —after the Jesuits were expelled from Mexico—at the Academy of San Carlos in its heyday.

The Academy of San Carlos was formed to perpetuate European skills in Mexico. It was granted a royal charter in 1785 and was led by Antonio Gil, who developed an almost military rigidity in his teaching which was contrary to the previously enlightened policy of the Spanish Crown. Gil reflected the philistine attitude of local Creoles; but luckily the Academy was supported also by such men as Tolsá, a confirmed royalist who was yet sympathetic to the native culture and who taught the first native director of the Academy, Pedro Patiño Ixtolinque. In the latter's drawings we can detect vestiges of the rigidity that characterized the painted codices, but also the stirrings of pro-Indian pity that led directly, a century later, to the rise of the revolution muralists.

The history of the Academy[18] was a perpetual seesaw between European and native trends; and the times when opinion swung heavily toward European tradition were not necessarily adverse. It was the European influence that nurtured José María Velasco (1840–1912): among the finest landscape painters of all time, as subtle as Turner, as perceptive of rural details as Constable. We can never look at the two snow volcanoes of the high plateau, at Orizaba, or at diminutive trains puffing through the Mexican hills, without gratitude to Velasco for revealing to us the subtle light-values of these highlands in the tropics. If the Academy had done no more than produce Velasco, it would have justified its existence. In fact it fixed canons of style that could be remolded at a later date to include the pre-Hispanic. It should be noticed, moreover, that much of what appears pre-Hispanic in the techniques of Rivera, Jorge González Camarena, and other modern muralists derives from academic training (compare Pedro Patiño's life drawing, *Burden Bearer*—reproduced in Charlot's book—with isolated figures on Rivera murals).

An important function of the Academy was to form a collection of representative European works. Today, under the care of a Catalan, Enrique Gual, the long-neglected pictures have been reframed and rehung. They include a *Raising of Lazarus* certified in Holland as a genuine work of Geertgen tot Sint Jans—by whom there are only two other fully authenticated paintings extant, both in Vienna. The fourteenth-century Catalan rooms include two triptych masterpieces by Luís Borrasa, one of St. George and the Dragon. In the foreground a saint with apple-red cheeks, astride a rocking-horse charger, is spearing a dragon worthy of Walt Dis-

[18] *Mexican Art and the Academy of San Carlos, 1785–1915*. By Jean Charlot. University of Texas Press, 1962.

ney; while behind, through and beneath an arch of Gothic tracery, a congregation of nobles and a demure lady look imperturbably on.

The Spanish school is, of course, well represented, with four paintings by Zurbarán and two by El Greco. There are Titians too, and a doubtful but intriguing young John the Baptist by Ingres; for the collection received new works right up to the time of the impressionists and it was only during the revolution that Mexican chauvinism drove it into neglect.

European artists were fascinated by Mexico in the early post-independence period, and they received good treatment in the country; although the greatest of them, the English D. J. Egerton, was savagely murdered together with his mistress, Agnes Edwards, while they were out walking with their dog. Egerton had been in Mexico mountaineering, painting, and making hand-colored lithographs in which villagers dance to guitars in the foreground of carefully geological mountain scenes. One is tempted to wonder whether Velasco, who was two years old when Egerton died in 1842, owed anything of his technique to the English school. Velasco saw further and more profoundly, but he must have had ample chance to study the work not only of Egerton but of such minor English artists as John Phillips and A. Rider whose hand-colored lithographs of Mexico were published by E. Atchby in 1848. In their work and that of George Ackermann, the mountains and valleys of Mexico are seen through the cool filter of English eyes.

How different are the conical, flame-blue volcanoes of Dr. Atl, the incisive vegetative tangles of Diego Rivera, the hot-and-cold, sweet-and-sour mistiness of Rufino Tamayo. The Mexican revolution threw up a school of painters (painters only, oddly enough, and not sculptors, as if the ancient potters and stonecutters had exhausted all possibilities of invention for centuries to come) that is wholly Mexican and unrivaled in sheer force in modern times. Of the "Big Four," only Tamayo has eschewed politics. His vibrant colors have no message other than the delight of awakened sense perceptions. After an epoch of shocking-pink watermelons, he has gone a quiet, ascetic way, paring down color and making it an integral part of form. He is a great artist in his own right, but stands on the outer margins of the modern Mexican school which has developed from José Clemente Orozco, Diego Rivera, and David Alfaro Siqueiros.

"We had one great artist and two fine painters," said one of Mexico's leading architects; and there is no doubt that the artist was Orozco, the first of the great moderns, who painted carelessly but with deep passion and with a conviction that walls were people's books. His message is most startlingly revealed in the vast Cabañas orphanage in Guadalajara. Here, surrounded by three figures representing man asleep, man meditating, and man creating, a man of flame rises in receding perspective out to some unknown heaven. A Mexican critic has called him "the great being of the future who will have surpassed and outstripped man as man surpasses beast."

Here was a message of hope. It was otherwise with Rivera and Siqueiros in whose works the accent came to be planted on a clamoring for material equality. Their political orthodoxy was inimical to subtleties, and Rivera's early sensitiveness to natural forms and peasant faces gradually gave way to formal and psychological flatness. His National Palace murals, intriguing as they are in detail (there are echoes of Uccello in the patterns), fail to convey that the Indians—and, one might add, the Spanish soldiers—were of flesh and blood. Siqueiros uses all kinds of tricks to create spatial illusion, but he is all fists and crying mouths. It should be added, however, that nearly four years in jail have forced him to a subtler and apparently more sincere style. He was painting in a cell only about 6 feet by 12 and with one small window. He had to improvise materials and sometimes used boot polish for black-and-white drawings. He drew his fellow-prisoners but also trees and flowers with a delicacy unknown in his art before. He attributes the change of style simply to the forced regression from murals to easel painting. He says it was like turning from cinema to still photography. Beneath the technical change, however, one seems to see a profounder alteration born of real suffering—though Siqueiros is at pains to say that his politics have not changed.

For sheer volume of production, the modern school of wall painters is unsurpassed. There are probably about 200 muralists working in Mexico today, and Virginia and Jaime Plenn[19] have drawn up

[19] Plenn, Virginia and Jaime. *A Guide to Modern Mexican Murals.* Ediciones Tolteca, Mexico City, 1963.

a formidable list of works that can be seen not only in Mexico City but throughout the republic, in the United States and Canada, in France, even as far as Israel and China. Although a mural by Rivera in Radio City, New York, was defaced because it contained a portrait of Lenin, Orozco fared better and examples of his work exist in New York at the Museum of Modern Art (a nightmare called "Dive Bomber"), and at the New School of Social Research where Gandhi and Lenin are acclaimed as world leaders together with the Yucatecan Felipe Carrillo Puerto.

Whether public or private—whether Ministry, bank, restaurant, or school—every Mexican building worthy of the name must have its mural. Artists thrive on the wide open spaces inviting their brushes, their blowlamps, their mosaics; and besides the "Big Four" there are dozens of others with almost equal fame. Among them are Gerardo Murillo, known as Dr. Atl,[20] who made a study of the snow volcanoes and of Paricutín; Juan O'Gorman specializing in mosaics and living himself in a lava-rock cave encrusted with them; Roberto Montenegro, whose "Dance of the Hours" is in the National Hemeroteca or periodicals library; Pedro Coronel, who has a mural in ceramic glass in the building of the Social Security Employees' Union; Jorge González Camarena, honored to have received a place in the Palace of Fine Arts together with the "Big Four"; Miguel Covarrubias, whose illustrated maps of Mexico overflowing with exotic flora and fauna are a cheerful change from themes of revolution; Carlos Mérida (Guatemalan by birth but Mexican in spirit), whose abstractions decorate a nursery in a workers' housing estate; José Chávez Morado whose flight of the leaders of the world's religions on a serpent raft is one of the few murals in Mexico City that can be classified as non-materialistic; Adolfo Best-Maugard, one of the veterans belonging to the first generation of modern muralists;[21] Federico Cantú; Elvira Gascón who has worked mainly in churches.

Plastic paints made of acrylic, pyroxylin, and similar materials are popular and encourage boldness rather than subtlety. An experimental studio for their study was set up in 1945 by Professor José Gutiérrez and has been frequented at one time or another by

[20] Dr. Atl died in August 1964 after these lines were written.
[21] Adolfo Best-Maugard has also since died.

most of the important wall painters. One may, however, doubt Gutiérrez's claim that "the versatility and flexibility of the politec media are such that the artist's talent is enhanced and his conceptions broadened, instead of being hindered as in the case of the older, less tractable and less pliable materials."

It may be that in retrospect the revolutionary artists—revolutionary both in content and in techniques—will look conventional and even bourgeois beside the Goya-like compassion of Orozco and the austerity of that lonely contemporary, Francisco Goitia. He stood always aloof from the "Big Four" and became the mystery figure of modern Mexican art, the bearded and shaggy poor Brother Francis pursuing his own aims with the uncompromising fanaticism of a prophet. Not that his work went unrecognized, for like Velasco's before him most of it is owned by the government. But his output was small; and this fact, together with his retreat from society to a tumbledown hut in Xochimilco, set him apart from his better-known colleagues. Recognition that he could stand as their equal came only in 1958, when the artist was seventy-five years old and when he was awarded the *grand prix* at the First Interamerican Biennial of Painting and Engraving.

As a young man, Goitia had joined Pancho Villa's forces, but not because he believed in the rebel leader's cause, for he admitted that he would have followed whichever army had first chanced his way. What he wanted was to live with the soldiers in order to know them and paint them, and he could not very well do that as a tourist. His attitude seems to have been similar to that of Orozco, who says categorically in his autobiography that an artist cannot be a politician or he is no artist.

Although Goitia drew and painted soldiers, he sought for a way of capturing what he described as "the native soul." In a small Oaxacan village he found at length what he required, an Indian woman who had seen a relative drowned in a river, a stone hung by enemies round his neck. It was this sight that led him to paint the powerful *Tata Jesucristo* (Daddy Jesus), with its two peasant women mourning—one with hair and hands veiling the face, the other with hands clenched in almost animal anguish. A single candle is the only light in this somber scene, and the outstretched foot of one of the mourners is poignant because of its very anonymity.

"In politics there is right and left," said Goitia. "I prefer the center. In the center is Christianity, reconciling the good in either, and Christianity has retained its vigor for twenty centuries. Materialism is a newborn babe that does not deserve my trust." He was never invited to paint a public mural, though he particularly wanted to do a resurrection. He was, however, too independent for either the left-wing political artists on the one hand, or the Church on the other. "Some of the young," he admonished, "say that in a work of art it is all a question of technique and that inspiration can be relegated to the era of the romantics. These young people do not know what they are saying. If there is no leavening within, the bread is no good. I see that the capacity to create a painting is as mysterious as a Greek oracle, because it depends on fate."

The inner content of art which Goitia thus stressed is absent from most of the work done by the pupils of Rivera and Siqueiros. Jorge González Camarena, for instance, has allowed his fluid draftsmanship to stiffen into doctrinaire formulae; and among the younger generation of committed painters, the two who seem to have inherited something of Orozco's fire are José Luís Cuevas, unnaturally preoccupied with deformities but at his best full of genuine pity; and Francisco Icaza. These two, together with the Mexican-trained Canadian Arnold Belkin, were brought together by Selden Rodman and formed for a time a group called "New Presence" which had a political-humanist platform. The humanism seems to be winning over the political, however, for Belkin says, "My preoccupation in art is and always has been to express the human condition. Above all, the heroism inherent in man, in spite of an inhuman social organization, in spite of anxiety, fear, and a sense of guilt."

This group was dovetailed into another composed of *artistas* who decided to become *hartistas* (in Spanish the addition of the unpronounced *h* turns them from artists into fed-ups). Under the leadership of an Austrian, Matías Goeritz, this group presented itself as a huge joke, but it was serious in believing that art must turn back to its old purpose of service to something higher than the individual. "Less intelligence and more faith," they clamored. Their weakness has been that they have never been able to point the direction in which their faith might lie.

In the meantime, while they cast about without a compass in the bewildering ocean of international styles, an abstract school has grown which is in tune with the new middle-class prosperity. The buildings being decorated today are no longer viceregal palaces to which revolutionary Mexicans were determined to add an indigenous touch; but movie houses, restaurants, factories, and banks. Though not without a fight, the old didactic note is ceding to abstractionism. Among the new names is that of Manuel Felguérez, who has done an *objet trouvé* mural for a central Mexico City movie house. Its brown-gold lunar beauty spans the width of the foyer stairs in a frieze that is modern in its machine-like shapes, and at the same time suggestive of organic flow. Other artists are experimenting in similar directions, including Herbert Hoffman-Ysenbourg, who has done sculptured screens and murals in banks, supermarket offices, and other bourgeois buildings; and Gunther Gerzo (of Hungarian origin) whose abstract canvases are essentially professional and painterly, with a strange sense of black nostalgia under their bright surfaces.

There are several British or British-affiliated artists working in Mexico, the most mature of whom is the surrealist Leonora Carrington. Her technique is so sound and careful it might belong to some early Dutch master. She builds a world of fantasy, of beasts and men that never were on land or sea; of macabre, ghoulish, half-human figures lost in a medieval bestiary. In a canvas where foetal shapes peer from behind the curtains of some black-magic shower bath, a plum with all its sensuous bloom intact hangs in the air by white-magic levitation. So masterly is the texture of such details that one can look for hours at the variety in a few square inches of paint. It is the kind of quality that makes many other modern canvases seem as if their perpetrators had done them between urgent appointments elsewhere. Only her friend and colleague Remedios Varo (a Spaniard who died in 1963) can approach her imaginative range and her craftsmanship.

At another extreme, Toby Joysmith's textures are rough, giving variety to simple pyramidal shapes; and "Valetta's" canvases glow with the warm candlelight and the bobbing, dipping paper lanterns of night processions in Mexican villages. Helen Escobedo, trained at the Royal College of Art, is setting herself difficult sculptural problems: how to convey the exhausted, hollow stare of truck drivers on the roads; how to tie together the spidery fingers of a cellist with the solid structure of the instrument; how to give physical strength to the emaciated figure of John the Baptist.

Foreign artists take their place with Mexican in the Museum of Modern Art, a group of two curtain buildings of steel and dark-tinted glass near the Museum of Anthropology and History in Chapultepec Park. These two units have been criticized by people who find that the park and the passing traffic intrude upon their contemplation of the pictures. But it is just this feature of the architecture (by Pedro Ramírez Vázquez) which helps to bring back the easel painting into a living world; and it must be admitted that some of the more pathological perpetrations of modern Mexican art are hard to take unless the eye can rest between times on an old-fashioned slice of nature.

The museum leads up to the moderns via José María Velasco and other nineteenth-century painters including Hermenegildo Bustos (1832–1907) whose small portraits of gentry and peasants show a wholly unclass-conscious love for human beings. We need these reminders of nineteenth-century craftsmanship if we are to get into perspective the international groping that we find in the galleries crowded with every modern school from political haranguing and expressionism to abstraction. The last of the old and carefully realistic school was perhaps Joaquín Clausell who died in 1936 and who painted seascapes of great clarity and subtlety. And there are early Diego Riveras, especially a seated picador, a self portrait of the artist in a floppy hat sitting drinking at a table, and one or two landscapes, that make one bitterly lament his later carelessness. For the rest, too much of it is splendid virtuoso that hides a directionless fumbling toward forms that shall be at all costs new and Mexican. There is something over-complicated in the process; what is most Mexican is revealed in the occasional glimpse of scenes that are entirely simple and playful in a way that a peasant might understand.

Such is the heterogeneous contemporary artistic scene, balanced uncertainly on its infrastructure of peasant crafts which themselves are slipping down the easy road of tourist-appeal. The man who may help to bridge the gap between the promiscuous ideologies of the art world and the techniques of the craftsmen is José Chávez Morado, director of the School of Design and Crafts (a department of the National Institute of Fine Arts). He has himself worked in many media, including mosaic and bronze, so that he has had practical experience in most of the skills taught in his school. He points out that until the end of the nineteenth century almost all domestic objects used in Mexico were locally made. Such influences as penetrated from outside were absorbed into the Mexican idiom, so that local Chippendale or Sèvres, for example, had little resemblance to the originals. But somehow the native traditions fell into disrepute, and it needed a revolution to reinstate them. The swing in the opposite sense then produced a chauvinism which Chávez Morado reminds Mexicans is only the inverse of that special Mexican-Quisling mentality—*malinchismo*. Between contempt and adoration, the peasant craft worker has been treated like the spoiled child of rich parents—half petted, half neglected.

Much of the craft work is done by families who have preserved their traditions over generations. Although in the cities up-to-date techniques have been adopted, many small workshops use incredibly primitive tools. Two plates may form a potter's wheel. Pottery is baked by stacking it and then laying over and around the heaps a charcoal fire. Looms are secured round a tree trunk and round the operator's waist. The results of both primitive and sophisticated methods can be seen in markets throughout the country: *sarapes* of pure wool with natural earth dyes in neutral colors (these, and not the gaudy horrors waved before motorists on tourist highways are the ones to buy); *rebozos* in wool, silk, or cotton; straw mats and *sombreros;* plain silver-black Oaxaca pottery or elaborate many-branched candlesticks where men and donkeys mount upon each other's shoulders and birds and fishes hang inconsequently side by side; the Puebla Talavera ware originally imported from Spain in the sixteenth century; sandals and saddlebags that make elegant accessories for women; carved furniture; lacquer work (a pre-Hispanic art that lends some support to the view that the indigenous peoples may have come from China); green or amber hand-blown glass with its bubbles and irregular thicknesses; silverwork (best seen in the town of tinkling hammers, Taxco); tin and copper ornaments for altars or dining tables; magic ritual-cult pictures done in wool, where animals and birds defy the laws of anatomy and of gravity; *exvoto* paintings on tin, by peasants giving thanks for having been saved from robbery or sudden death.

Chávez Morado believes that now is the time to plan the craftsman's future. The last twenty-five years have seen new materials ousting the village crafts and reducing the workers to near pauperism. Village wares are bought, paradoxically, by two extremes of society—the peasants, and the connoisseurs who prefer naïve beauty to the "immature Mexican industrial product" (Chávez Morado's words). Between these extremes there is no market for hand-made goods, but Chávez Morado thinks that the solution is not to reject either the hand-made object or the industrial product, but to modify both. In Mexican art, the sophisticated international traditions have always been fed and strengthened by indigenous talent, and if this give-and-take between the two worlds ceases the country's art will lose robustness.

THEATRE AND FILMS When your horizon is limited by the corn stalks in your small plot of land and the gilt angels of the church beyond it, that church becomes a Mecca and also in a genuine sense a theatrical arena. The acts in the drama are the year-round church festivals, the players are other villagers like yourself. Judas may be the blacksmith, Jesus the carpenter's son in very fact. On certain days in the year the people whom you know most intimately are suddenly translated into the huge, hierarchic figures that dominate your thoughts and imaginative life. So, when a group of bricklayers in Mexico City staged a nativity play, the crowds pressed on to the stage to kiss the hem of the Virgin's dress, cheap and tattered satin though it was. In one university town, students put on scenes from Cervantes in the plaza. People move about their business among the actors, or a stray dog wags its tail at a good line. A new dimension has entered theatre, giving it a vitality that a Broadway producer might envy.

On this existing Mexican base of peasant interest in the dramatic effects of life and history, more sophisticated stage directors have been building a superstructure of formal drama, especially in the open air. The climate is by no means always kind. It can be bitterly cold on the high plateau. It can rain and blow like a scene out of *Lear*. But the mountain backdrops, the proscenium arches provided by the colonial church architecture, the massive pyramids with their curling plumed-serpent friezes, and above all the Spartan good will of the crowd: all these make Mexico an ideal country for such experiments.

T. S. Eliot's *Murder in the Cathedral* has, for instance, been played in Spanish in the open-air atrium of Cuernavaca cathedral. Seats were sold out, and the audience spilled over on to the stage in good Elizabethan style. From there one looked through the stone arch on to the audience sitting round a fountain and among beds of hibiscus; and as the drama unfolded the stars dipped into view. The urgency of Eliot's message was keenly felt in a country where the struggle for power between two opposed sets of values as represented by Church and State is a live issue still. Though some of the words from the massed chorus were swept away on the wind, the rolling lines of Spanish verse had a grandeur that would surely have pleased their author.

Later a Spanish director, Alvaro Custodio, used open-air atria for presenting Spanish classics. Lope de Vega's *Fuenteovejuna* was so realistically produced in an old Mexico City square that one actress fractured a leg. Undaunted, Custodio continued with Seneca's *Medea* and Calderón's *El Gran Teatro del Mundo* before the stern walls of Acolman. From there he proceeded to Tlalmanalco, where he staged *La Vida es Sueño*—not the well-known play but the later masque. Anyone brought up on Shakespeare might be expected to find Calderón's cardboard abstractions dull; yet against the mountains, in the crisp air with a hint of threatening rain, the characters grew surprisingly larger than the audience. The personified four elements were part of the cosmic process. Out of a turret window Man was born, tiny against the double row of plateresque arches—a thing just out of its cocoon. The birds, the water, and the flowers that had more freedom yet less life than he, the star that "dares not yet become a rose," all were visible round the audience which shrank in shame to a size more befitting its station. When the Light of Grace called Man from the belltower of the main church, set at an angle behind the audience, it seemed some voice from the Milky Way.

For the Shakespeare anniversary year Custodio produced *Hamlet* before the whole breadth of Acolman, and with the first scene high along the battlements of this monastery that looks impregnable as a fortress. It was an interesting experiment, with the mummers, the gravedigger, and Hamlet (a very talented young actor, Enrique Rocha) carrying the show.

Such productions as these give promise that theatre may yet return in Mexico to being a rough, tough, market-place thing. Custodio did less than justice to himself alas with a Hollywood-technicolor spectacle of the fall of Moctezuma staged against the great pyramid of the Sun; but the will to good theatre is there, as it has been in some experiments conducted by the Ministry of Hydraulic Resources with its own employees; or by Juan José Gurrola adapting Dylan Thomas and Dostoevsky to the Mexican scene; or in the University Theatre group that won the International Universities Theatre Festival prize in Nancy, France, in 1964. Two productions, *L'Amour Médecin* by Molière and the prize-winning *Las Divinas Palabras* by Ramón del Valle-Inclán, have given ample demonstration why these students won. They have ability, verve, and supreme artistry in the sets and costumes (the Molière translates an Alice in Wonderland world to the seventeenth century). Both productions created their own laws that blended with considerable daring a Saint-Denis stylization and a realism born of Stanislavsky out of Brecht.

The Mexican student theatre movement began only ten years ago. The actors, undisciplined and hamming horribly, submitted themselves and the public to overdoses of the more gloom-ridden examples of anti-theatre. Happily, due to the efforts of Héctor Azar, director of theatre at the National University, this adolescent phase soon passed. It requires maturity to penetrate into the superficially realistic but actually deeply symbolic world of Valle-Inclán, who anticipated Brecht in many ways though he died in 1936. In the Mexican student version of *Las Divinas Palabras* the successful blend of naturalism and stylization, and the fact that young actors were concealed beneath the rags of the demented and the maimed, created an almost unbearable tension. One felt all the pity of the mute cripple in the cart, grunting like the pigs who deface his corpse; for the half prostitute; for the child wailing incoherently out of her innocence. No future director of Valle-Inclán can ignore what the robust young actor-director Juan Ibáñez did with this difficult play, so Spanish in essence, so often misunderstood by Spaniards, and now reinterpreted for them by students who had drifted into acting apparently by chance, having come to the stage —via medicine, dancing, or teaching—in the hope of "finding themselves" (so they say).

Gurrola has designed a model "fluid" theatre with sixty-two different space arrangements which he hopes one day may help to break the artificial and deadening awe for the "divine ghosts" of great dramatists. He is not aiming at theatre in the round, but at a type of building that would achieve perfect equilibrium between audience and play, so that the two elements would act and react dynamically on one another. His model is designed on two levels, with crescent-shaped extensions to a central and circular stage. These extensions allow the play to move outward or close in according to the director's needs, and the plastic translucent dome and circular drops are also movable, giving scope for scenic projection. True theatre, says Gurrola, should not have to depend on currents and cross-currents flowing between an aggressive drama and a complacent public. In his building the audience would have to abandon its habitual role of passive observer and would have to make up its mind to take an active part in the play, as if it were a grand chorus.

Drama techniques have lagged far behind these experiments in stage direction. There is Rodolfo Usigli, whose *Crown of Shadows* (it has been translated into English) presents an ingenious explanation of the tragedy of Maximilian—that he voluntarily allowed himself to be martyred in order to show Europe and the world that Mexico would have no more of foreign intervention. But Usigli, thoughtful writer though he is (his *Gesticulador* is a sardonic parody of Mexican politics), bases his techniques on Shaw and is out of tune with the younger generation. Other dramatists, such as José Gorostiza, Salvador Novo, and Luisa Josefina Hernández, have concentrated on problems of the Mexican social scene: class prejudice, women's battle for recognition. Outside Mexico they seem worn-out stuff. Emilio Carballido has some neat pieces on problems of time but does not get beneath the skin of his subject. Sergio Magaña's *Los Signos del Zodiaco* is an ambitious effort to do for

Mexican tenement life what *Street Scene* once did for the American. And Elena Garro has some one-act sketches of the little Mexican with his spiced vocabulary and sweet-sour philosophy.

But writers are needed both for stage and film. In spite of prizes at international festivals, Mexican films have not come up to the expectations they roused with such early successes as Luís Buñuel's *Los Olvidados* (*The Forgotten*). Sergei Eisenstein went berserk in this photogenic country and then left his spools of skull-dancing and peasant anguish to be cut by others; since when Mexico has been struggling to establish both an *avant-garde* art worthy of such propitious beginnings, and an industry that might exploit the country's romantic history commercially. Failure to distinguish between the two genres with sufficient clarity has caused near-disaster.

The present output is one hundred features a year, the largest in any Spanish-speaking country. About $4 million is invested yearly, and tens of thousands of people are employed. Leaving Hollywood out of it, Mexican films have captured the market in Latin America and in Spain, and many are successful in the United States, especially along the border where there is a large Mexican population. If the total world market is to be stormed, however, strategy will have to be changed. It is not sufficient to hold an annual festival in Acapulco and to attract foreign groups to Mexico for filming such high-powered productions as *The Night of the Iguana* (with Richard Burton and an all-star cast).

Mexican films began three decades before Eisenstein when a young engineer, Salvador Toscano, sold his stamp collection in order to buy one of the first movie cameras and projectors made by the brothers Lumèire. He traveled the country and even crossed the border into Texas, but wrote home that people there were uninterested and tight-fisted. When the revolution broke out, Toscano was able to record history. He photographed a vast footage which his daughter, Señora Carmen Toscano de Moreno Sánchez, later edited into a film built loosely round the story of a boy growing up during those disturbed times: *Memorias de un Mexicano*. Toscano had journalistic sense and an eye for composition, and his orthochromatic document is a classic of its kind. Through dust and smoke we see the trains that carried Madero to triumph, the rough peasant armies of Zapata and Pancho Villa, touching and almost toylike in retrospect; the smiles and betrayals of leaders; the women camp followers.

By 1936 Mexico was producing twenty-five films a year. Singers such as the tenor José Mujica, who has since become a Franciscan monk, made their reputations. Then came Eisenstein with his stimulus to the *avant-garde*. In true Russian tradition, *Redes* (*Nets*), made under the patronage of the Ministry of Education, used no actors but authentic Gulf fishermen. The Mexican composer Silvestre Revueltas wrote the score, and the photography was by Paul Strand. Unfortunately, the promising *avant-garde* directors of this period, together with excellent cameramen such as Gabriel Figueroa, were tempted into commercial films and the impulse from Eisenstein died.

Soon a younger crop of popular stars arose, including Jorge Negrete, Pedro Infante, and Pedro Armendáriz. Among women, there was no one to rival Dolores del Río (who still acts sometimes on the legitimate stage); though María Félix and Silvia Pinal have also been popular. The greatest of all the commercial successes, however, was Mario Moreno, better known as Cantinflas, who acquired world fame in *Around the World in Eighty Days*. His best films have been too local for export, with a patter only very slightly caricaturing the Mexican down-and-out. He has been compared to Chaplin, and Chaplin is said to have praised him highly; but the comparison is unfortunate for Cantinflas is a genuine Mexican product, garrulous, shiftless, battling at moments for the rights of Man, his trousers low on his hips and a cigarette stub hanging forgotten from the corner of his mouth—a clown with a hatred of hypocrisy and a longing for suburban comforts.

Mexican comedies and musicals have on the whole been more successful than dramas; though the director Emilio Fernández, known as El Indio, has made some creditable attempts at melodrama, notably in a version of John Steinbeck's *The Pearl*.

Since the formation of the Mexican movie workers' union in 1945 there has been an unhappy tendency to adopt the "star" system and to measure success in terms of box office. Luís Buñuel has continued to pursue his lonely, embittered *avant-garde* ideals; and Manuel Barbachano Ponce (noted for high-quality shorts) has made one excellent feature, *Raíces* (*Roots*) based on stories by the late Francisco Rojas González. In one of these a boy blind in one eye is taken on a pilgrimage to a saint who will cure him. At the church he loses his mother, joins a crowd of boys sending off fireworks, and is blinded in his second eye when a cracker bursts in his face. The miracle has been done, says his mother, for now that he is blind in both eyes he will no longer be a laughing stock, but people will pity him.

Until recently one of the virtues of the Mexican movie has been its candor, but in 1962 three films making a passionate effort to convey truth, however unpalatable, seem to have so upset cozy consciences that passage to the public screen was barred. It was particularly odd that *La Sombra del Caudillo* (*The Chief's Shadow*) was not allowed public release. This is a mature film showing that Mexicans can take self-criticism. The novel is by Martín Luís Guzmán and deals with the corruption that comes with power. There are no direct portraits from life, although the *Caudillo* himself is probably an amalgam of three real-life presidents; and the ambushing and shooting in 1927 of a presidential candidate, Francisco Serrano, and his aides seems to have served as a model for the climax of the story.

The film follows the novel truthfully. It does not denigrate, but is a sober, dignified, biting condemnation of practices which, as its director Julio Bracho says, need to be understood if the whole Latin-American political scene is to be assessed, and before it is too late.

A second banned film, *The Strong Arm,* deals also with *caciquismo* but in a small *Mestizo* village. It was made by an American, Norman Thomas, and by a Dutch-Italian, Giovanni Korparaal. The script is by a Mexican, Juan de la Cabada, and the cameraman was Walter Reuter, known for his photography in *Raíces*. The villagers are the actors. Although uneven, with a necromantic sequence that seems to have little connection with the main theme, it has the rough texture, the detail, and the spontaneity of true documentary. The method of production infringed union regulations, and this was the pretext for banning the film. It is about a roadmaker who is fired by the government for incompetence and fraud, but when the letter arrives with its official envelope the rumor circulates that it comes from the President of the Republic. Believed to be a man of importance, the roadmaker is feasted in a sequence that is pure René Clair. He stays in the village, marries the daughter of the local shopkeeper, builds the road at his father-in-law's expense, and becomes the key figure in a political clique with loose morals. Charnel-house drawings after the greatest of Mexican cartoonists, José Guadalupe Posada (1851–1913), are superimposed on village scenes. The fierce satire occasionally infringes good taste, but judicious cutting would put this right. For the most part the fun of Mexican village life is interlaced with apt comment on universal human weaknesses.

A third film, at first banned but later shown in central theatres, is Luís Buñuel's *Viridiana*. Obviously this vast, Brueghelesque panorama with its allegedly blasphemous "Last Supper" offends Roman Catholic sensibilities, although Buñuel denies that it is an anti-religious satire and calls it rather an attack on all hypocrisy. Indeed, as the English movie critic Penelope Houston has pointed out, the most forceful scene in the film is not the controversial "Last Supper" but that in which a man frees a dog trotting behind a peasant's cart, and another dog is promptly tied up to replace the first victim.

MUSIC AND DANCE Musically in Mexico one must begin with the popular and work up, if only because it is the bands of Mariachi serenaders that awaken one of a morning.

"These are the morning songs King David sang. . . ."

Or, to a favored lady who remains coyly behind her bedroom curtains, "The day you were born, all the flowers were born too. . . ."

Delightful sentiments if you are the recipient; hardly so if you are robbed of precious sleep before a working day.

The Mariachis are not the only noisy songsters. Of a Sunday in the oyster houses about Veracruz, where shells pile on the tables under the thatch beside the lagoons, toothless minstrels will compose songs for each client in turn, inventing the rhymes as they go along and charging ten pesos (under a dollar) per composition. It is surprising on these occasions how freely Mexicans will part with hard-earned money. In the evenings in the central square the *marimba*—an outsize xylophone played by three people—will strike up the latest international song hit or the old Mexican favorites: *La Llorona, La Zandunga, Cielito Lindo*. There is an honored roll of composers of popular songs, including Agustín Lara, Guty Cárdenas, and the grand old man Ignacio Fernández Esperón (Tata Nacho), who dresses as an authentic rancher.

Popular music is a hybrid, only distantly if at all related to the native idiom. In Indian villages there are feather dancers pounding the earth to monotonous rhythms, dancing the dances of Tezcatlipoca or the Four Suns. In Papantla a man will be piping reedily from the top of the sixty-foot pole of the *Voladores* as four companions throw themselves backward and upside-down, unwinding slowly on their ropes in a maypole dance of planets circling the Sun. In Teotihuacán one threefold clay flute has been discovered (the Mexicans do not seem to have used shinbones as Indians do in the Andes). On the roof of the church in Tepoztlán one may discover a knot of Indians beating a heavy hollowed wooden drum inherited from the preconquest.

The spontaneous self-expression of the folk musicians is poles apart from the deliberate cult of the Indian adopted by the modern nationalist composers. The father of Mexican concert music was Manuel M. Ponce, who died in 1948 and whose work is little more than a competent reflection of French impressionism, though he used folk music at times. His main achievement was to provide a basis on which younger Mexicans could work. His contemporary, Candelario Huízar, was more closely identified with what has come to be regarded as a specifically Mexican idiom, and Huízar did much to form the style of a succeeding generation of whom the most representative is Carlos Chávez. *The Indian Symphony, The Four Suns* (a ballet based on the ancient legend), and *Toccata for Percussion* have earned Chávez an international reputation although his style bears about the same relationship to Indian music as Longfellow's *Hiawatha* to Indian poetry. A younger composer, José Pablo Moncayo, takes the Veracruz dance *huapango* almost unadulterated, and Blas Galindo does the same with Mariachi music. Many composers have written for ballet, an impulse having been given to classical ballet and modern dance by José Limón (who has worked mainly abroad), Anna Mérida, and the two excellent dance-choreographers Guillermo Keys and Guillermo Arriaga. The success of the Institute of Fine Arts' folk ballet is based rather on its gaiety, bright colors, and quick pace than on serious dancing; it is first-class light entertainment and is one of the few really carefree achievements of the Fine Arts' Institute which, though it has done very much in many fields, is bedeviled by politics and works at times, one suspects, under a cloud of gloom.

Cinema has provided material for musical experiment, and the greatest of the older generation of composers may well turn out in retrospect to be Silvestre Revueltas, who died in 1940. Besides putting six of García Lorca's poems to music, Revueltas wrote for ballet and especially for the American Martha Graham. His scores for films such as *Redes* and *Los de Abajo* form strong counterpoint to the visual drama.

Two contemporary composers who have remained more closely in the European tradition are Carlos Jiménez Mabarak, trained in Belgium; and Miguel Bernal Jiménez who studied in Rome and has written mainly church music. He established an important musical school in Morelia and trained a children's choir there. Jiménez Mabarak has moved with the times into electronic music and has given a lead to the younger and less nationalistic generation: Leonardo Velázquez, Raúl Cosío, Joaquín Gutiérrez, Rafael Elizondo, Guillermo Noriega, José Antonio Alcaraz, and Eduardo Mata. Some of them are scarcely out of their teens, and when they have had their fun and played havoc with classical canons they may well settle down to something more original.

Sadly, not one of these Mexican composers, old or young, has had the courage to follow the revolution of the grand old man of Mexican music, Julián Carrillo, who has spent a lifetime peering into an unsuspected microtonic world of sound. In 1895, fifteen years before Walton and Cockcroft split the physical atom in Cambridge, Carrillo was probing into the units of our twelve-note scale. He was then twenty years old, a violin student whose teacher had just explained to him that between one C and the next vibrations double. Experimenting secretly, he found that he could not produce more than twelve clearly separated sounds in the octave. Then he hit upon the idea of tamping the string with a sharp-edged blade. The first new sound that emerged he dubbed "Sound Thirteen," and the name became attached to his new system. The title does it little justice, because between each note and the next Julián Carrillo had isolated sixteen tones, thus splitting the atom on which

Western music had been based since the eleventh century. Between note and note he had found two full octaves of sounds that he could repeat at will and with perfect precision. This was a more startling revolution than when Terpander, twenty-six centuries before, had added two notes to the Chinese five-tone scale; but the young musician had little idea of the potentialities of his findings and it was not until 1922 that he began composing. Instruments for the new tones were expensive to make. Young musicians were reluctant to write in the new modes; and although Carrillo is known to connoisseurs and has been decorated by various governments, his discovery remained dormant until in 1962 the Philips recording company, with the Orchestre Lamoureux and the France and Villers quartets playing instruments that had been assembled in Paris, produced an album of twelve stereophonic long-playing records.

Many people listening to the new sounds for the first time report that they seem to penetrate through the coarse emotions that generally satisfy us in life, to a finer and deeper emotional world. Carrillo's compositions, especially *Prelude to Columbus* and *Horizons*, show him to be working, like all real innovators, essentially within the tradition that formed him. What is new in his work is not any desire to smash the old composers' reputations or achievements, but quite simply this extraordinary technical revolution. His latest work, a mass dedicated to Pope John, is strangely instinctive, like a cry to Heaven from man's very entrails.

Carrillo has made a gift to the Mexican nation of fifteen pianos tuned for quarters, fifths, and other fractions of a Western note up to sixteenths of a tone. They wait for other pianists besides his daughter, Dolores, and for other composers to continue the experiment begun by this grand old man so shamefully almost unrecognized in his own (revolutionary!) country.

8 The Social Scene

Mexico is today a welfare state in which, in theory at least, every citizen is cared for in all essentials from the moment of conception to the day of his burial. This growing country, with access to international loans, can afford to be lavish in its spending on education, social security, community housing, and free meals to school children, where richer countries of the world must think twice and maybe lay on an extra tax before ends can be made to meet. The splendid surface of social opulence is spread unevenly, and there are vast shoddy areas between the marble halls; but at least a beginning has been made.

SOCIAL SECURITY Among the slums of Mexico City rise modern buildings decorated with sculptures of ancient heroes, surrounded by flower gardens and equipped with swimming pools and football fields. They are the new social security centers, built on the principle that nothing is too good for the poor, that out of the slums will rise the new generations upon which Mexico will depend for her technologists.

The centers range from housing estates for families who have paid social security contributions, through simple clinics, to complexes that include hospital and out-patient facilities combined with men's and women's clubs and workshops for training in skills required by local industries.

Due to its youth (relatively few pensions have been paid yet though the number is rising and is now about 73,000) the Social Security Institute is one of the richest organizations in Mexico. It was founded in 1944 and worked first in the capital, gradually spreading to other large towns and thence to the country. Its income from insurance contributions in 1963 was $241 million, its expenditure $185 million. Its active capital is around $361 million. It pays doctors' fees ranging around $476 a month, plus benefits including two and a half months' extra pay at Christmas, help with rent, and a month's holiday with pay. Its nurses receive about $104 a month.

Services extend today to 6,250,000 people (17 per cent of the total population) of whom 2.1 million are insured workers. The rest are dependents of the insured who are also automatically entitled to benefits. One million of these benefiting are peasants, and gradually more farmworkers, such as cane cutters, are being brought into the scheme. (To the above figures must also be added government employees, who have a social security fund of their own and their own clinics.)

Obligatory social security covers salaried workers in industry, commerce, and transport; members of cooperatives; salaried farm workers, *ejido* landstrip farmers and settlers on new lands; and small-property owners. It is hoped soon to bring in domestic workers, artisans, and people with small family industries. Wives, whether legal or not, children under sixteen, and dependent parents have a right to benefits, which include insurance for accidents at work and all illnesses, occupational or otherwise, maternity care, and insurance for incapacity, old age, dismissal from work, and death.

Contributions are split between the employer, the worker and the government in the proportion of 50, 25, and 25 per cent, the total contribution amounting to between 6 and 9 per cent of the insured person's wages.

The Institute owns throughout the country 167 hospitals with 11,636 beds, 425 clinics; 228 medical posts in important industrial plants; and 90 auxiliary clinics in small rural communities. The rural help needs to be extended but this is slowly being done. There are also 86 youth centers; 34 industrial training centers; and 13 housing estates with a total of 10,885 apartments or cottages.

Of the simple residential centers, the most important is Unidad Independencia, built to the south of Mexico City on what was once a wooded estate of Japanese landscape gardeners. It cost about $9.5 million and consists of 2500 apartments and self-contained cottages capable of housing 12,500 people. It was designed by the Institute's architects, Alejandro Prieto and José María Gutiérrez, to hold a cross-section of the Mexican lower and middle classes, the idea being that income groups should not live separately but should mingle in a balanced social life. For not much over $300, unit-dwellers can furnish a three-bedroom house with government utility furniture, and their rents will range from about $9 a month upwards. Even in the most expensive apartments, about $65 a month rent, there are no living quarters for servants. Mexico, said one of the architects, wants to do away with the feudal servant system. Records of health, schooling, diet habits, social tastes, and hobbies of each family are kept, and it is expected that these will give material for a full anthropological study. But it needs no statistics to convince the visitor that these families—many of them removed from districts where they did not see a tree and where children played hopscotch among the traffic—are appreciative of their new surroundings.

Of the complex centers, one of the finest is Unidad Cuauhtémoc in San Bartolo Naucalpan, a factory district in the State of Mexico. A survey of the labor needs of the area was made before the center was planned, and training workshops have been equipped for such skills as mechanical drawing, lathe work, soldering, and enameling.

The clinic-hospital consists of general and specialist consulting rooms, laboratories, and emergency and observation hospital beds for adults and children. Family doctors in this clinic and others of the same type work an eight-hour day and receive about $560 monthly (specialists' salaries are higher).

The club includes a cafeteria, libraries, lecture halls equipped with projectors, theatres, and children's nurseries. Here women can learn dressmaking, machine embroidery, and cooking to supplement their husbands' earnings. The attractive interior decorations are designed to stimulate in the poor Mexican a pride in his surroundings. Few middle-class children have access to such equipment as these centers provide. The cost of Unidad Cuauhtémoc was a little over $5 million including the land, but this is capital investment to improve an area of 60,000 inhabitants, many of whom live in conditions of outright misery.

These people, and the other insured in Mexico City, have access to the Medical Center built first with funds from the National

Lottery but bought by the Social Security Institute at cost price—nearly $32 million, and then improved with an additional $25 million spent on it. The center with its tall modern buildings and its auditorium for international congresses is a landmark from the air. Departments include pneumology, cancerology, gynecology and obstetrics, general medicine and surgery, nutritional diseases, psychiatry, acute neurology, and emergency. There are living and teaching quarters, pathological and biochemical laboratories, and a central library with twenty-six classrooms that can hold 1170 students.

There is a separate State Employees' Social Security Institute which has been responsible for the enormous popular housing project in the poor Mexico City district of Nonoalco-Tlaltelolco, and which has small clinics throughout the country.

In Mexico City there is also an Interamerican Center of Social Security Studies whose handsome lecture halls were inaugurated in 1963. Here come post-graduate students from all over Latin America and the United States to train in social security methods. There has never previously been such a full-scale effort systematically to plan social security throughout the hemisphere and to train personnel; and it was only by the efforts of the Director of the Mexican Social Security Institute, Señor Benito Coquet, that a certain skepticism was overcome, this ambitious center was founded, and lecturers were brought from all over the world, including Britain. Students are keen and include even intellectuals and poets who want to base their more lofty pursuits firmly on work for their fellows.

CHILD CARE Nearly half Mexico's population—45.7 per cent in 1963—are children under fifteen years old; but public organizations for child care scarcely existed until Doña Eva Sámano de López Mateos, wife of the President from 1958–64, began to interest herself actively in this aspect of public welfare. Before that time there had been a small Association for the Protection of Infants which had no legal status but which distributed 30,000 breakfasts a day in the Federal District alone. Under the López Mateos administration a modern plant for packing and distributing breakfasts was built in a center which also includes model nurseries for its own workers. About 1.6 million breakfasts are distributed daily throughout the country.

Next door to the National Institute for Infant Protection's building, which cost over $1.4 million to build, is a poliomyelitis rehabilitation center where selected children are given modern physiotherapy and are taught crafts which will help them recover the use of damaged limbs.

EDUCATION Throughout Mexico the State schools have the same *texto gratuito,* the free textbooks which have been complained of in Catholic strongholds but which contain nothing more noxious than a call to serve the *patria.* Love of family, love of country, loyalty to the rest of Latin America, civic virtues: all are inculcated in phrases that are a little mass-made perhaps; but the thirst for knowledge is nevertheless great and touching. Though prefabricated classrooms are being built at high speed, and though a rota system fills them several times in the day, there are neither enough schools nor enough teachers. Of 280,989 children passing through primary grades in 1960, only 36.7 per cent found places in secondary schools. The situation is critical not only in elementary grades but even in high schools and universities, although it is calculated that for every 1000 children being educated only seventeen reach higher educational levels and only one actually graduates professionally. In 1961 over $252 million was spent on education, of which the central government provided about $165 million, the State governments and municipalities $56 million, and private enterprise the rest. The total amount budgeted was less than 2.4 per cent of the gross national product instead of the 4 per cent which has been recommended as a minimum in Latin America as a whole. Yet the government is doing more than its share. In 1963 the federal budget for education was over $239 million, or 21.7 per cent of the total national expenditure, as against 10.8 per cent allocated for defense (in 1920 it was 62 per cent for defense and only 0.9 for education).[1]

Obviously if the country is to continue investing such high sums in the potential talents of its youth, it must make reasonably cer-

[1] *Cincuenta Años de Revolución Mexicana en Cifras. Op. cit.*

tain of adequate returns; yet any process of student selection is a negation of the revolutionary principle that even higher education should be free for all—a principle, incidentally, which even the Soviet Union does not attempt to uphold. After decades of expensive trial and error this indiscriminate enrollment of unprepared students to the universities has been admitted unworkable. The cost in defaulting students, who incidentally, swell the army of political discontents, has proved too high. Of 1000 students entering the National University, half fail at the end of the first year and only 200 graduate. In the architectural faculty only 2 per cent of entrants finally pass, and in engineering 18 per cent. Many students abandon their careers between the third and fourth years. Others change faculty and continue to clutter the classrooms, harassing the overworked staff.

University professors put the blame on the inadequate pre-university training, especially on the fact that only two years' schooling is required in order to matriculate from the *preparatoria* to the university proper. The *preparatoria* teachers in turn blame the secondary schools, and the secondary schools the primary. Very few people will yet admit that the real fault is in the indiscriminate attempt to make professional men and women out of young people with no capacity for shouldering professional responsibilities. However, both the Minister of Education, Agustín Yañez, and the National University Rector, Dr. Ignacio Chávez, are well aware that most of the 60,000 students at the University (including the *preparatoria*) would have been more suitably accommodated in technical or agricultural colleges; but both of them have had to fight for their reforms. They have been blocked by the long-standing prejudice against honest manual labor, and by protests from students that university entrance examinations are undemocratic and unfair.

Dr. Torres Bodet, previously Education Minister, instituted a program of practical training for the thousands of young people who never reach the secondary or higher school levels. Training courses of eighteen months or two years are immediately useful to industry and agriculture, especially to the mechanical and electrical industries, to animal husbandry, and to administration. To help this drive a special 1 per cent income tax was levied for education.

It was expected to bring in approximately $2.8 million a year but was at first bitterly contested as unconstitutional by right-wing businessmen who would themselves benefit from a skilled labor force. In contrast a suggestion from the Mexican Workers' Confederation that every laborer should set aside a day's salary for educational needs has been received with approval. (In the national budget for 1965 the 1 per cent tax has been included in general taxation and controversy has been avoided.)

It is interesting that during 1962 the two areas where private sources contributed most per head to education were the very poor Province of Quintana Roo (where each individual gave an average of $1.40) and the agricultural-petroleum State of Tamaulipas (which gave about 90 cents a head).

The planning of university education is hampered by three interconnected factors: the strong attraction of the National University which is draining off students from provincial colleges; the tradition of student-political involvement; and the autonomous status of University City.

Although one of the oldest centers of learning in the New World —its Charter was granted by Charles I of Spain in 1539—the National University is today more proletarian than royal. The pressure on teachers and lecture halls comes from the new middle classes, young people who serve behind counters or work in factories in their out-of-class hours. These are for the most part orthodox in their politics and their religion; and it is rather the vociferous professional agitators and student leaders who make this center of learning a potential source of left-wing, Marxist-impelled, and Cuban-Soviet-financed rebellion.

Since immediate post-revolution days, when the various university faculties were scattered in old colonial buildings in the center of Mexico City, the government has been afraid of the students, believing them to be an easily organized and easily influenced group. This view suited the student leaders who blackmailed rector after rector into quieting them with substantial bribes. In more recent years, massed together in their new skyscrapers on the lava-rock bed south of the capital, the students have held sovereign sway over a small but legally impregnable area. Only by breaking the sacred decree of autonomy could federal police enter to restore order if students should chance to set fire to buildings, break windows, slash paintings, or assault professors. The myth of the bold, bad, but bribable student was further strengthened, and it required a fearless rector like Dr. Chávez to shatter it.

When this small but dauntless man—an internationally respected heart specialist—was appointed to the rectorship in 1961 there was open rebellion from students who had made merry over the years with the lowered educational standard and what had come to be known as "student gangsterism." By the time Chávez had moved into his new offices he had called the rioters' bluff and the serious students and their parents were on his side. He refused to continue the system of bribes. He cut the long vacations. He experimented with a system of vigilance by professors, psychologists, and senior students. And he instituted his controversial entrance examination which—though its standard is low—is at least a first step to restoring the prestige of this once-royal university.

The financing of this colossus must remain a burden for the government so long as students pay $16 a year for tuition. In 1963 the budget was over $18.2 million, of which the federal government provided about $15.7 million. The government has also to support the National Polytechnic Institute with an approximately similar sum; and the latter bids fair to repay the country in more reliable interest. Its new buildings to the north of the capital could hardly present a greater contrast to University City. The "*Poli's*" buildings are low and strictly utilitarian. They lie on the edge of the old dry lake that blows grit across them just to remind the students that Mexico needs their technical skill if it is to put an end to the land waste of centuries.

Although it has an excellent new fundamental research unit, the *Poli* is almost wholly concerned with applied sciences. Its historical background dates from the opening of the College of Mines in 1792. After independence the need for technical skills became acute, and a "school of arts and crafts" was founded in 1843, followed by a commercial school two years later, and an agricultural and veterinary college in 1883. In 1890 a "practical school for machine workers" was established; and in 1901 women were given the opportunity to join in the country's economic activities with the founding of a commercial school exclusively for them. The revolution was a setback, and the Polytechnic itself was not founded until 1937, its aims being to train men and women on a professional level and in semi-skilled techniques; to undertake scientific and technological investigation as required by industry; and to prepare technical teachers. Today the Polytechnic has twenty-eight faculties of applied science teaching on five different levels. Each level of training is self-contained, so that pupils can end their studies with any one of them and still be fully capacitated for jobs in industry. In 1963 there were 36,000 students, about half the number at the National University; but the *Poli* is growing fast too, for in 1958 there were only just over 22,000 pupils.

A condition of entry is that the student shall have received 80 per cent marking consistently through pre-polytechnic school years. He may then enter the lowest of the five student levels, the "technical secondary," where he can spend three years from about the age of thirteen learning elementary techniques that will fit him either for industry or for continued technical studies. From here he goes to a "preparatory technical" course of two years, specializing in engineering, physics and mathematics, in medico-biology, or in social sciences. He is then ready either for a foreman-type job, or to continue on to the professional level of training. Professional courses take from four to six years, and the pupil may specialize in any polytechnic subject. Between the "technical secondary" and the "preparatory technical" there is a course called "medium technical" into which students not apt for higher training may be shunted to qualify as links between the ordinary workman and the industrial foreman. Those who have gone through their full professional training may attend graduate courses for Master of Science degrees.

About 1800 professionals graduate yearly, and these must do a six months' social service "stint," often in remote villages. They are organized in brigades of six or more specialists—say a doctor, a nurse, an engineer, a sanitary expert, an economist, and a biologist—who together make a survey of the village, its resources, potentialities, and problems. Brigades work in parts of the country that by themselves could not afford such surveys. Many of the graduates will find suitable work in the districts where they are doing their service. Others will apply to the Professional Services Commission which helps to find them jobs.

The Polytechnic has no tuition fees, and it is run wholly on government grants and private donations. It is thought that between 60 and 70 per cent of students come from extremely poor homes, and many receive scholarships of about $22 a month, the allocation for scholarships being about $980,000. The Polytechnic's total budget runs to around $11 million, excluding any special sums for equipment and new buildings. Apart from these government grants, students and graduates are asked for voluntary donations, and students sometimes arrive with offerings of small sums gathered in piggy banks at great sacrifice to themselves and their parents. In 1961, for instance, over 2600 students donated more than $57,400.

A center for original scientific research works in collaboration with the Polytechnic but as an independent organization under the directorship of the internationally recognized neurophysiologist, Dr. Arturo Rosenblueth. It has five departments: for mathematics, physics, physiology, biochemistry, and engineering. Postgraduate students may apply for admission free of charge, to sit for Masters' and Doctors' degrees; foreign students are admitted but must pay a small laboratory fee. The research staff includes the Polish relativity expert, Dr. Jerzy Plebanski, and a Scottish physiologist, Dr. Leonard Macpherson. Research includes mapping neurone pathways, training cats to distinguish musical intervals (one at least does so unerringly), replacing pituitary function by transplanting other glands, transformation of energy in living organisms, the biosynthesis of the vitamin B complex, and the circulation of lipoproteins in the blood. There are also some applied research projects, carried out at the specific request of industry or government departments, who pay the Institute a fee for this service.

A rival to the Polytechnic is the privately financed Monterrey Technological Institute supported by the local beer, steel, and glass magnates. In 1943 it was decided that it was time to create an institution to train students in techniques needed by the northern industries, and today there are over 6000 students and over 300 professors—a ratio unique in Mexico where classes are more apt to be of 200 or more students. Students are trained for twenty-two careers and seven semi-skilled trades, and the institute represents an investment of about $7.8 million. For the original 350 students, housed at first in a private bank, $560,000 was raised by an intensive campaign among business companies which, apart from varying sums paid down in cash, agreed to donate 1.5 per cent of their profits and also to set up a mortgage plan for buildings and a scholarship fund. Today, local industries give scholarships to about 30 per cent of the students, who are helped to earn out-of-pocket expenses by being found temporary jobs in the district. Money is lent to students who could not otherwise complete their courses on condition that they pay it back after graduating. The repayment finances another needy student, and so on in a continuous chain.

The Monterrey institute has a higher reputation than most of the provincial State universities, but many of the latter are trying to develop specialties and are concentrating—according to the needs of their own areas—on either agriculture and agronomy, petrochemistry, archaeology, or other skills. These universities could well help the government in its drive to decentralize industry by establishing training courses in close collaboration with the factories in their neighborhoods.

In view of the number of technical agricultural problems that beset the Mexican countryside, the National School of Agriculture and its Postgraduate College, in Chapingo near Texcoco, must be considered one of the most important centers of higher studies in the country; although it comes under the Ministry of Agriculture and not of Education. Its delightful combination of disinterested investigation and—literally—down-to-earth application of the discoveries of the eggheads, makes it a fascinating place to visit. Indeed the same man may be egghead at one moment and farmer the next, and it is a pleasure to discover that many of the professors have come from rural and quite poor backgrounds. Here is Dr. Alfredo Campos Tierrafría studying in his laboratory the ill effects of penicillium on apples; and then driving out to his plots of stony ground to see how his chickpeas are doing, growing rapidly with scarcely any water, fixing nitrogen in the exhausted soil, producing three times more protein than corn, and thus giving hope of solving several of Mexico's problems at once. Here is Professor Efraim Hernández Xolocotzi, whose mother was a rural schoolteacher, directing investigations into Mexico's ecology and suddenly discovering that the *piru* tree can grow in desert only by spreading its roots horizontally sixteen feet or more, because they cannot penetrate the rocky layers under the sand. Why therefore not blast holes through the rock and plant fruit trees in the desert? The experiment is being tried. Here is a Polish refugee, Dr. Czeslawa Prywer, studying tripsacum, the forerunner of corn, and Professor Trinidad Vásquez González who is one of the few world experts in the relatively new science of nematology (those microscopic pests called eel-worms). As Dr. Basilio Rojas, director of the Postgraduate School says, his professors are all individualists, a characteristic which perhaps helps to produce unusual keenness in the students of both college and school.

An important postgraduate center of learning is the Colegio de México, founded twenty-two years ago by the late Alfonso Reyes to provide a suitable atmosphere in which intellectual Spanish refugees might carry on their researches. It was later taken over by Dr. Daniel Cosío Villegas, Mexico's representative on the Economic and Social Council of the United Nations, who built it up as a center for international studies.

The Colegio de México is not to be confused with the Colegio Nacional, a college of wise men elected for life and limited to twenty. It is tucked away in an austere renaissance building (once a monastery) behind Mexico Cathedral, and works almost unnoticed, its members giving obligatory lectures which are open to the public but attract only the highest brows. It was founded in 1943 by the late President Manuel Avila Camacho, who said that "it is the bounden duty of a government to foment . . . the development of scientific, philosophical, and literary culture." The articles of the new institution allowed for membership of twenty Mexicans by birth "eminent for their knowledge and virtues," who were to represent all currents of thought except those allied to militant politics. There were fifteen founder members including the revolution novelist Mariano Azuela; Dr. Antonio Caso, one of Mexico's most eminent philosophers; the biologist and biogeologist Dr. Isaac Ochoterena; the mineralogist Ezequiel Ordoñez who did important studies on the volcano of Paricutín; the humanist Alfonso Reyes; and the painters José Clemente Orozco and Diego Rivera. The latter was perhaps the only member who was ever inclined to flaunt the "no politics" rule and to indulge in periodic tub-thumping. Of the original members, only four are alive: Dr. Alfonso Caso, the archaeologist brother of Antonio; the musician Carlos Chávez; Dr. Ignacio Chávez, the university rector and cardiologist; and the internationally known physicist Dr. Manuel Sandoval Vallarta.

Over the years the college has continued to add to its roll of distinguished men, and it now counts among its members the hematologist and cytologist Dr. Ignacio González Guzmán; the neurophysiologist Dr. Arturo Rosenblueth; the historian and economist Dr. Daniel Cosío Villegas; the astronomer Dr. Guillermo Haro (co-discoverer of the so-called Herbig-Haro objects, which it is thought may give a clue to the origin of stars); Dr. Jaime Torres Bodet; Dr. Eduardo García Máynez, an authority on the philosophy of law; Dr. Victor Urquidi, the economist; and Dr. José Villagrán García, the architect.

The college forms a center for discussion among highly trained minds in many specialties. A government stipend of about $400 a month to each member is supposed to allow time for original research and for preparing papers. A portrait gallery of deceased members looks down from the council-room walls, a reminder to the young that there are standards to be maintained—standards that might, with the passage of time and the accumulation of tradition, give this young institution an honored place alongside the learned societies of the Old World.

So many foreign businessmen, technical experts, and officials of international organizations now live for extended periods in Mexico that they are anxious to know what kind of education is available for their children. Something should therefore be said about foreign preparatory and secondary schooling.

Today American and British nationals in Mexico have the choice of sending their children to one of the relatively new British schools (Greengates or Edron Academy) or of opting for the French *lycée* or the German college, which have the highest scholastic and disciplinary reputation of all foreign schools here. Another choice is the American School Foundation, which has existed since 1888 and is a vast, highly organized, but by no means austere center of up-to-college-level education. There are also the Pan-American Workshop and some smaller American schools of similar pattern.

Greengates, which is beginning to have a discipline not easy to establish in a young organization, was founded in 1951 by two British former members of the British Council staff: Frank Whitbourne and Edward Foulkes. It was started purely as a language academy, but soon grew into a school for British children which ultimately and inevitably—by sheer force of numbers—attracted more Americans than British.

Frank Whitbourne returned to England but left behind him a tradition of theatre which has continued—so that the blonde troupe of Anglo-American cherubs grace such local productions as Benjamin Britten's *Noye's Fludde,* produced with billowing waves rising to fury round an exuberantly rococo ark. Edward Foulkes, with a colleague, Henry Ronald, recently started their own small school, Edron Academy, though Mr. Foulkes still remains a member of the board of Greengates, whose headmaster is Henry Coelho. The two British schools remain thus loosely affiliated.

Neither of these British schools is accredited by the Mexican Ministry of Education, but the Mexican authorities have specifically asked that they continue their work of preparing children for schools outside Mexico. The absence of foreign schools would undoubtedly create considerable problems for the Mexican authorities. Greengates and Edron prepare children for British public schools and for the General Certificate of Education, but must keep their syllabuses broad enough to accommodate Americans who will proceed either to universities in the United States or to the University of the Americas in Mexico. At Greengates there are at present only 45 children who are technically British out of 400—though the proportion would be higher if British children born in Mexico were included.

The American School Foundation is a giant—the largest institution of its kind in the world (it is claimed) and the most important of 53 American schools in Latin America. It is run by a foundation composed of about 400 members who meet yearly to discuss general policy. Its teaching system is half Mexican, half American, with classes split between the two languages. In it, Mexican nationals roughly equal the American in a proportion of 40 per cent each, with 54 other countries making up the rest. Half the yearly $20,000 fund for scholarships go to Mexican children.

In many ways the high percentage of Mexicans helps discipline, always a problem in these coeducational day schools. The headmaster, Charles J. Patterson, says that in nine years he has had only two Mexican children up for serious bad conduct, against an uncountable number of Americans. He attributes this in part to the innate gentleness of Mexicans, in part to the fact that Americans, far from their home towns, feel free from group and family restrictions. It is also true that Mexican children are usually more conscientious students, and their presence "jacks up" the general scholastic standard—though perhaps the Mexicans could do with less learning by rote and more imaginative spark which—present in their character—tends to be suppressed by the rigid Mexican curriculum.

All foreign schools suffer from similar problems, among the chief of which is the low salary scale in Mexico. Teachers at the American School Foundation receive on an average about $250 a month, against about $425 in the United States. To raise the salaries in a country where two completely different wage scales hold between foreigners and nationals throughout all professions, would merely create further problems of adjustment.

The French and German schools receive more government help than the British and American ones, though in 1963 the American School Foundation received $50,000 from the State Department—its first direct government grant: plus about $125,000 under an arrangement whereby money paid for United States grain sold in Mexico remains in the country.

Although the British authorities would like to see both Greengates and Edron in some way incorporated into the British Council, the founders of the schools—who have kept them going through difficult years by hard work and somewhat lonely initiative—are reluctant to cede authority to any government-affiliated body even if this means living on a shoestring. The schools are paying their way but do not have money to lavish on expensive laboratory equipment or sports grounds.

The American schools think that they have a philosophical concept of teaching that is peculiar to themselves and more individual than the European. There seems to be little evidence for this view, but certainly the American School Foundation has a missionary "get-together" spirit that embraces even parents. It is arranging courses so that disoriented grown-ups may learn about the vagaries of Mexican life and may make friends. There is also much dissemination of unconcealed anti-communist, pro-United States propaganda.

Granted the relative opulence of non-British schools, however, there is something to be said for the improvised methods of Greengates and Edron. As one walks through the classrooms one feels a lively contact between teacher and pupil and a climate of cooperativeness and of thoughtfulness.

A useful foreign higher center of learning is the University of the Americas, founded in 1940 as Mexico City College by two Americans, Drs. Henry L. Cain and Paul V. Murray, as an extension of the work of the American School Foundation in Mexico —a high school mainly for the children of American residents in the country. After a prosperous period when it filled with students with GI grants, M.C.C.'s private financing slumped and in 1962 the institution was reconstituted under its new name and with a new president, Dr. D. Ray Lindley, imported from the Texas Christian University. Hoping to rid it of its previous beatnik reputation, Dr. Lindley swept the University of the Americas clean of beards and sandals. He reduced its debt by enlisting the help of private businessmen, and he remains proud that his university is not government-supported either by the United States or by Mexico. It is free of color and religious bars, and although at present its students are 80 per cent American, there is hope that it will gradually become a genuinely international university training men and women for government service, education, and business posts in Latin America. It is concentrating on Hispanic studies and also—because of Mexico's interest in these subjects—on archaeology and art.

PUBLISHING AND MASS COMMUNICATION Mexico claims the first regular printing press in the Americas, established in 1539 by Bishop Juan de Zumárraga. There was sporadic printing even earlier, mainly of Christian tracts in native languages for use in converting the Indians. Later came newspapers, periodicals, and broadsheets in which corrosive cartoons reflect the struggle for power between liberals and conservatives. But it was the need for popularizing knowledge—particularly as a result of the 1910 revolution—that gave Mexican publishing its big push forward over twenty years ago, when some intellectuals decided to make available in Spanish the world classics of economics, politics, psychology, and science. This idea took shape in the Fondo de Cultura Económica, a non-profit-making house that now has branches in Buenos Aires, Santiago, and other capitals, and a list ranging far more widely than its title suggests.

The influx of Spanish republican refugees in 1940 was another stimulus. To some extent they shifted the center of Spanish-language publishing from Madrid to the Latin American capitals. Spain still publishes more books than either Mexico City or Buenos Aires, but Spanish publishers are handicapped by censorship and cannot range as widely as their Latin American counterparts who work generally speaking in a freer climate. The Fondo de Cultura complains that many of its translations, of authors as diverse as Tom Paine and Edmund Wilson, are forbidden in Spain. There was nearly an international incident when the classical work of the Venezuelan, Marinao Picón Salas, *From Conquest to Independence,* was put on the forbidden list. The ban was later removed and the Fondo has so far made up its quarrel with Spain as to have opened a branch in Madrid. This is a significant step since in Mexico this publishing house—in spite of a nearly official status—has been under fire from the right wing for its overt and allegedly fanatical enthusiasm for Dr. Castro.

Since the Fondo set the standard of Mexican publishing, other good houses have followed its example. The National University, Veracruz University, and the Prensa Médica Mexicana are all good serious publishers, and there are a number of reputable private firms besides a host of cheap publishers living mainly on pirated translations.

Largely due to the more forward-looking Mexican publishers, the first Iberoamerican Congress of Book Associations and Chambers was held in Mexico in 1964. At this Congress the Spaniards took a leading role and obviously agreed with Mexicans and other Latin Americans that all forms of censorship, direct and indirect, must be abolished. It was agreed, too, to fight the practice of "dumping" of extra-area books printed cheaply in Spanish or Portuguese.

It was agreed that if a pocket library of the best books available from all publishers in the area could be formed (these would necessarily be mainly Spanish, Argentine, Mexican, and Chilean publications); if "co-editions" can be arranged of books in Spanish and Portuguese or between publishers in the various countries of the area; and if university and small publishers can band together to form a common distributing chain, most essential problems—including dumping—will be solved. Many speakers at this meeting, especially Mexicans, expressed their faith in a Latin American culture as such, and the Fondo delegate especially deprecated imposition on the area of Anglo-Saxon ideas which enter both through subsidized translations by foreign embassies (notably the United States) of books selected for their evident propaganda value, and through the inevitable influence of the dollar on journalists.

Apart from the small government newspaper *El Nacional,* there are four national dailies of some quality: *Excelsior*, U.S.-influenced; *Novedades,* which had once a slight bias toward the left but has since perhaps over-corrected itself; *El Universal,* with a Catholic bias; and *El Día,* the youngest of them, with pretensions to being a kind of daily Mexican *New Statesman. Excelsior, Novedades,* and *Universal* run their own evening papers; and there are two English-language newspapers (*The News,* published by *Novedades,* and the *Mexico City Times* recently started by the popular newspaper *Ovaciones*). There are many dailies of the "yellow" variety, though it might be said that, if Mexican journalism never rises to the highest international standards, it also never falls quite so low as the most scandal-mongering of British papers. The paper with the largest circulation, *La Prensa,* is by no means empty of serious reading.

On the whole the coverage of world news is excellent in the Mexican press. Its home news is ample, though it may be accused of passively accepting government handouts and reporting verbatim and uncritically the long pronouncements of ministers. Individual columnists are sometimes more concerned with attacking one another than with presenting objective facts, though good informative series of articles are often commissioned on such aspects of national life as education, agrarian reforms, and industry.

A number of weekly and fortnightly illustrated papers, including the pro-Communist *Política*, the more mildly left-wing *Tiempo*, and the frankly U.S.-influenced *Visión*, base their style and format on the United States magazine *Time*. The left-wing *Siempre* and the more moderate *Mañana* supplement the daily newspapers' ration of self-adulation with sporadic hard-hitting criticism. The Treasury has an educational journal, *Boletín Bibliográfico de Hacienda y Crédito Público*. There are some good academic journals such as *Cuadernos Americanos* (left wing) and *La Palabra y el Hombre* published by Veracruz University; and two bilingual literary magazines, The *Mexico Quarterly Review* and *El Corno Emplumado*.

The technical quality of television and radio is high, but the content is almost wholly commercial and the overcrowding of the sound radio bands makes it imperative that announcers shout if they are to be heard. There are several television channels and over 400 commercial transmitters in the country, of which 34 serve Mexico City (five on modulated frequency bands). All but two or three of these concentrate on light music and soap opera with very occasional incursions into what might be called cultural programs. Jingles advertising soft drinks, beer, hair oils, and "fly now pay later" travel schemes are sandwiched between Beethoven and soap opera, with Beethoven getting the worst of the bargain. University stations are the only ones to which the important minority of people who prefer their culture unlarded with publicity can safely turn; and of the university stations, the only one with sufficient funds to do more than put on disc-jockey programs is the National University. Yet its present director, Max Aub, far from receiving much public support, has to fight against the difficulties of a small budget and inadequate equipment. Even in the University itself the radio is a Cinderella, looked upon askance by many professors who think they are lowering their scholastic sights if they go before a microphone. Little by little, however, *Radio U.N.A.M.* has gained a loyal audience which includes all cultural ranks from cancer specialists to humble artisans. To these latter, who write touchingly appreciative letters, devoid of grammar and almost illegible, the radio is intellectual meat and drink. To appeal to the intellectual minority of all classes is the chief task of this station, and it believes that it could, with some obvious defects put right, attempt to emulate the BBC Third Program. There is youth on its side, for the average age of contributors must be well under forty.

In 1958 its personnel was squashed knee to chin in fusty studios in a colonial building in the center of town. At that time its director, Dr. Pedro Rojas (to whom the pioneering credit is due), had to fight to achieve a niche in University City where the studios are now housed. Even here, in cheerful modern cabins, the shout of a gardener or the song of a bird may make an occasional duet with the announcer; but these extempore effects, together with a view of pepper trees and squirrels, are an aid to carefree broadcasting.

A weakness of this radio is that it has not always the courage of its cultural convictions and is apt to descend to a half-hearted imitation of commercial radio, thus throwing away its great advantage, that time on its wavelengths is not money. When this has been said, the achievements are impressive: fourteen hours or more a day of well-selected music interspersed with spoken programs that cover all manner of themes, and discussions on the cultural scene in foreign countries. Jazz is solemnly assessed as an art form, and there is a children's program that is really a satire on Mexican life. Regular broadcasters are featured, and the amateur is not encouraged to step before the microphone. This is an unfortunate restriction, for the voices of *locutores* in Mexico (the professional readers of all things from news to long cultural talks) have a monotonous quality which does little to help listeners appreciate what the original writers of the scripts may have taken pains to enliven. The University Radio is trying to produce a kind of objective "newspaper of the air." It has yet to learn the old lesson that objective radio is not achieved either by shrouding voices in anonymity or by a stilted, "correct" literary style. The important thing, however, is that *Radio U.N.A.M.* is not going to accept anybody else's theory of what good broadcasting should be. By trial and error it is gradually evolving a style suited to Mexican needs.

Periodically there are witch hunts against this station because of its supposed bias toward Communism, which means no more than that it is run by privileged young people who feel some anger and much compassion when they contemplate the disparities of the

Latin scene. Contributors include Roman Catholic priests as well as left-wing intellectuals, and there is an attempt to balance views. The general taboo on political or religious broadcasting in Mexico has in any case been relaxed in recent years, especially since one ex-Cabinet Minister (Ramón Beteta, now editor of *Novedades*) popularized a program of interviews with visiting statesmen and prominent Mexicans. The legally autonomous status of the university allows it to extend its own comments fairly widely, although one political discussion program was suppressed after foreign embassies had protested at allegedly unfair criticism.

The best live musical program[2] is by an American, Joseph Hellmer, a dedicated collector of folk music of every type from the pure Indian to the *Mestizo*. His material is so good that one hopes the series of phonograph records for which *Radio U.N.A.M.* is responsible—*Voz Viva de México*—will be extended to include it.

The work of the University Radio is being slowly extended by linking it up with provincial universities. An Association of University Radio Stations has been formed, and it can safely be said that the future of good broadcasting in Mexico will be through centers of learning and not through commercial stations.

THE CHURCH From village to village drove the country priest, saying Mass, baptizing, burying, marrying. To relieve the monotony of the road his acolytes sang patriotic songs as they bumped along in their high-sprung jeep. Suddenly the priest pulled a revolver from beneath his surplice, fired three shots into the air; and then, turning apologetically to the foreigner sitting beside him, said by way of excuse for his eccentric behavior: "These, you see, are the songs of my *tierra*. I sang them when I fought the Church war from the hills, and ever since I have carried a revolver."

It was a lame excuse for carrying arms, for the *Cristeros* rebellion had ended decades past. For a long time there has been no war between Church and State, and Mexico has the first Cardinal in her history: José Garibi Rivera, from the ancient Catholic stronghold of Guadalajara. Graham Greene's picture in *The Power and the Glory* and *Lawless Roads* is happily long out of date. So too is

[2] Since these lines were written this program has unfortunately been suspended.

the village priest with his revolver, though he likes to be theatrical. His village is poor. The rachitic pigs and children, and the meager corn stalks are evidence enough. Yet on Guadalupe eve a year's savings from its 500 souls explode in fireworks, a touching tribute to Mexico's patron saint.

The Church has been to the poor of Mexico the center of their pageantry, their drama, their yearning for beauty. It was so in pre-conquest times when all poetry and music were ritual acts. It was so again after the conquest when the Indians concealed their esoteric symbols among the angels of the new churches, and when the Christian mystery was enacted for them by the friars. This pageant crystallized in the *nacimientos* and *posadas* of Christmas (the cribs and the procession of Joseph and Mary to find where they might lay their heads); the Grand Guignol of *Carnaval* and of Holy Week with the macabre burning of Judases as the British burn Guy Fawkes; the village passion plays during which for some reason the dry season invariably explodes in sympathetic thunder; the pagan mêlée of Corpus Christi in which Christian ritual still merges into ancient dances; and All Saints and All Souls when marigolds are spread so that the dead may return to eat their fill until another year is gone.

During the time of President Calles the theatre turned to tragedy and produced its martyrs, for whom there are plaques in some churches as for example in Santo Domingo in Puebla. But for many years now the anticlerical laws have gone by default. Public vehicles have their Catholic images swinging above the driver's seat together with bullfighters' costumes in miniature and baby's first shoe. Once priests and nuns, if they walked abroad at all, did so with clandestine steps, in the drab black suits of minor clerks or wretched orphans. Once the brown-robed Franciscans were no longer to be seen even in the precincts of their own ancient monasteries. Now they are back again. Dominican orators are advertised like film stars throughout the Oaxaca villages, whence peasants crowd into the State capital to listen to their puritanical reprimands which even Calvinists could not outdo. It is not unusual today, when the wife of some high-ranking government servant gives birth, for the announcement to include a commendation of the child to his patron saint. A Marxist-sympathizing intellectual novelist had his first child baptized with full display. And papal encyclicals are discussed at great length on the University Radio.

In 1964 Cardinal Tisserant was received with open acclaim when he paid an unofficial visit to Mexico, mainly to see archaeological sites; but the view of Church Mexicans was synthesized in the remark of one humble laborer: "I am Catholic, but I am also an admirer of Juárez and would not want his laws changed." In other words, reunion of Church and State would not be popular even with the faithful. At the same time General Cárdenas, supposed to be one of the strongest anticlerical influences in Mexico, appears to think that diplomatic relations could one day be resumed with the Vatican, though not quite yet. He told a *Siempre*[3] reporter, "I do not believe that the time is yet ripe for Mexico to resume diplomatic relations with the Vatican. Such a move would simply not be understood by our nation's humble classes. They are not mentally prepared to accept it, as the inhabitants of our cities perhaps are. Nevertheless such an arrangement would give the clergy greater powers to achieve their goals."

In the same interview Cárdenas admitted: "I have often found places where the authority of the priest is stronger than the civil authority, places where the State holds a position secondary to the Church."

The Roman Church is, of course, pre-eminent in Mexico though there are minority groups of all denominations including Mormons. The Summer School of Linguistics is an organization of evangelizing missionaries who combine their faith that all will somehow be provided with a very practical program of studying the indigenous languages and of printing dictionaries and school textbooks for the remote Indians. Cárdenas saw that these evangelizers could be useful to his own campaign of rehabilitating the Indians and gave them permission to enter the country when other religious denominations were still suspect. Since then welfare workers with diverse religious banners have entered the country and are building schools and clinics, distributing protein-enriched foods, and instructing the poor in assorted brands of Christianity. But the Roman Catholic Church remains supreme.

[3] *Siempre,* July 1, 1964.

The change back to religious tolerance came slowly and with no alteration in the law. As we have seen, persecution of the clergy was not an innovation of Calles, but dates back to the reforms of Juárez in 1857, including the separation of Church and State, the nationalization of Church wealth, the suppression of religious orders, and the establishment of the marriage ceremony as a civil contract. Undoubtedly, at that time many of the religious orders were rich and corrupt, but it was overlooked or ignored by the Indian Juárez that it was the Franciscans and Dominicans who had worked most sincerely during all the years of Spanish dominion for the welfare of the Indians.

Juárez preferred to forget all that, and though the anti-clerical movement went underground during the Díaz régime, it erupted again with the 1910 revolution. Article 130 of the present Constitution gives the Federal authorities power to interpret the law in religious matters, though it denies Congress the right to dictate laws establishing or prohibiting any religion whatsoever. The legislative bodies of the separate States can determine the maximum number of ministers of religion allowed "according to local needs." Only Mexicans by birth may exercise the office of clergy, and no clergy, either in public or private meetings, may criticize the fundamental laws of the country or the Government in general.

It was under one of the many sweepingly worded phrases of this Article that in 1923 President Alvaro Obregón expelled Monseñor Phillipi, the Apostolic Delegate, for holding a large open-air meeting. Several years later, during the Presidency of Calles, more serious trouble broke out after a protest had been made by the Archbishop of Mexico at the antagonistic attitude of the authorities to the Church. By a clever extension of another Article, which, if taken literally, obliges all representatives of foreign governments to register as such and secure licenses, Calles brought the clergy into subjection. Catholic clergy, Calles said, were directly dependent on the Pope, and the Pope was the head of a foreign government. Mexican clergy were thus automatically deprived of certain liberties enjoyed by Mexican citizens in general and could not fulfill their duties unless they had licenses issued by the government; these became increasingly difficult to obtain.

In 1929 Calles—retired from the Presidency—allowed his young successor Portes Gil to reach an agreement with the Church which included an amnesty to those involved in the *Cristeros* revolts; return of temples and other buildings to the Church; and permission for Church doctrine to be taught within Church confines. Religious services in Catholic churches were openly held on June 27, 1929, for the first time in three years.

Persecution was resumed in 1932 when the Apostolic Delegate, Archbishop Ruíz y Flores, was deported by President Abelardo Rodríguez as an "undesirable alien." In 1934 Calles called on all revolutionary forces to "fight religion" and to deprive all people not affiliated to the revolution of the right to educate their children as they thought fit. There was to be no teaching of religion in schools or any institution, and "socialist" education was to be the rule up to and including university standard. The press stirred up anticlerical feeling with talk of dark conspiracies by the Mexican clergy against the revolution.

As a result of the reduced number of licenses to clergy and the tightened laws, by 1935 there were certainly fewer than 500 priests in Mexico; and some authorities, including Sir Kenneth Grubb, estimate that there were even less than 200. In half the States there were no priests at all. This situation had been achieved in the name of "spiritual freedom."

With President Avila Camacho the tide turned. The laws were not amended, but the natural inclination of Mexicans of all classes, including the governing hierarchies, led to a tacit agreement that, provided people did not parade religious fervor too openly, there would be no further persecution. In later régimes the government has been tolerant of Roman Catholic activities even when these have contravened the Constitution. Persecution of clergy and nuns in Cuba led the Mexican Church to become surprisingly bold and —in 1960 and 1961—to make pronouncements that might well have been regarded as political and therefore offensive to revolutionary principles. "*Cristianismo si, comunismo no*" became the new cry. Bishops issued warnings and pastoral letters, held meetings, and distributed anti-Communist literature. Reports came from many small parishes that Communism was being openly attacked from the pulpits. These activities culminated in Puebla with an orderly and solemn anti-Communist protest by 100,000 Catholics. In an attempt to justify the re-entry of the Church into active politics, the Archbishop of Puebla, Monseñor Octaviano Márquez y Toriz, said: "This is not a political meeting. We attack no one. We want to save our country from the danger of Communism." (The contradiction was quickly noted by Church enemies.)

The left wing took advantage of the situation and accused the National Synarchists' Union of working in political collusion with the Church. It also accused the U.S. Ambassador in Mexico, Mr. Thomas C. Mann, of having promoted another large protest meeting in the capital. The accusation was denied, but there were Mexican Catholics who allowed themselves to wonder whether the Church's new outspokenness was merely coincidental with Catholic occupation of the White House.

One anonymous bishop seemed at this time to confuse God and Mammon by publishing "Ten Economic Commandments" ("You cannot create prosperity by discouraging private initiative"; "You cannot raise the wage-earner's salary by putting pressure on the wage payer," and eight more in the same tone). The left-wing organ *Politica* reminded him that many Mexican liberals have been priests and that the Curate Hidalgo had said in 1810: "Open your eyes, Americans; do not let yourselves be seduced by our enemies; they are not Catholics except politically: their God is money. . . ."

Some Anglicans feel that the activities of their own churches can provide a bridge or buffer between the anticlerical faction in Mexico and those who are believing but without a Church. When, in February 1963, the Archbishop of York headed a meeting of the Anglican Communion in Latin America, an excellent understanding was established between the minority Churches in Mexico and the Roman Catholics. There have been signs lately that the average Roman Catholic—encouraged nowadays to read the New Testament as he has scarcely done before—is surprised to discover that "all Christians worship the same Trinity." It is at least partly the threat of Communism that makes Roman Catholics anxious today to work on friendly terms with the Anglican and nonconformist groups.

Today the Roman Church in Mexico faces a dilemma. Many Catholics are convinced that the propensity of some bishops to consort mainly with high society and big business circles is scarcely helpful to their cause. The Vatican, they feel, has been shown wise in retrospect, in the appointment of Monseñor José Garibi Rivera —an unpretentious prelate—to the College of Cardinals. Cardinal Garibi directed a message to the Cuban clergy suggesting that, so long as the Cuban revolution "gave hope that it would promote social justice, true democracy, and the common weal," prayers for its success were warranted; but that, when it "put itself in the hands of Communism," events became a lesson to the area. He and his clergy have shown in clear terms that they believe this is no moment for soft words; but they must feel it an ax over their heads that Article 130 still announces that the religious groups called churches have no existence (*personalidad*). Their safety lies in the religious tolerance which was expressed by President López Mateos and which has been evident throughout the country for many years. Nobody, probably not even Mexican Communists, would want to see this tolerance suppressed.

Epilogue: Where Now?

We are back to the question implied in the dates on the University rectory tower, marking the conquest, the independence, the reform, the revolution, and ending with an enigma. Can we rightly regard 1960 as approximately the beginning of the industrial revolution? And, if so, where is that revolution to lead? Thoughtful Mexicans may be forgiven for asking whether the nationalism that accompanies the drive toward material progress is only self-deception. Every year Mexico becomes clogged with more and more international technological bric-à-brac, transistor sets and all. Some think it not unlikely that the Communist murals and the radio jingles, only apparently at opposite poles, will some day find a common meeting ground; and that the essential oneness of their materialist points of view will be evident. If such a culmination to Mexican endeavor is accepted and welcomed, it will be the end of the way of life that inspired the ancient Nahua poets, the builders of baroque, the modern architects with their churches and their efforts to create housing estates in which flowers and theatres and old symbols are as prominent as the supermarkets. It will be the end of the principles of Morelos and the reforms of Juárez.

On the whole, though, the prognosis both economically and on deeper levels is bright. The silence (strangely moving when it occurred amid the grit and rubble of a new dam site in the hinterlands) with which a group of Mexicans received the news of President Kennedy's assassination on November 22, 1963, was not merely a tribute to a friend of their country, to a liberal thinker who was fighting against opposition for more aid to Latin America. It reflected also the profound horror that such a thing could happen *there*, not in the countries so often accused of instability, of trigger-happy murder, of graft and corruption and violence, but in the United States, surely one of the guardians of the democratic way of thought. Mexicans up and down the country were shocked that day into a new seriousness and a new realization that the adventure upon which the Western Hemisphere embarked a century and more ago when the countries achieved their several independences is but just beginning; that they are all—the "developed" no less than the "developing"—in it together and must take responsibility for whatever breeds violence and hatred in the area. Mexicans, by nature gentle people, have perpetrated their share of horror and they know it, and they seek now by debate and by international give-and-take to correct their past excesses.

Not with bloodshed as in some Latin American countries still, but calmly in July 1964 the country elected a new President: the former Minister of the Interior Gustavo Díaz Ordaz. He received the overwhelming majority usually given to the PRI candidate, but the voting does not mean that there will be no need during the next six years for tolerance between opposed factions on the home front. Señor Díaz Ordaz was disliked at first by the extreme left and was an easy butt for cartoonists because of his protruding upper teeth and his horn-rimmed spectacles. (He is not photogenic but face to face has a charm of manner that does not appear in his poster image. He took jibes against his person in good part, however, and told foreign correspondents he had invented many himself.)

He is a native of the State of Puebla, a notorious Roman Catholic stronghold. In the cabinet of President López Mateos he was responsible for jailing Communist agitators. Nevertheless—and this shows his own desire to remain at peace wherever possible—he was the only Minister at the time of the Cuban rocket-base crisis to support his President's view that relations with Cuba should not be broken (as they were not). During his election campaign he pronounced in favor of traditional revolutionary principles, especially in favor of helping the workers and farmers to a better life; though he reiterated that it would be deception to make promises that cannot be fulfilled.

Soon he began to gain the confidence of many who had at first been against him; and he received official support from the Communist-affiliated Partido Popular Socialista, which had no candidate of its own and certainly had no desire to support the candidate of the right-wing Partido Acción Nacional. During election speeches, Señor Díaz Ordaz said that he would insist upon public servants behaving in a responsible manner, that he would continue educational reforms, and that he would uphold the principles of self-determination and non-intervention. Answering those rumor-mongers who suggested that the first thing he would do on taking office would be to renew relations with Spain, he said, "Mexico feels that it cannot establish diplomatic relations with a régime resulting from Nazi-Fascist intervention." He also said that he was anxious to strengthen the opposition parties; and in fact the Congress formed a few weeks after his election (though all fifty-eight senators were PRI members) contained twenty PAN deputies, ten from PPS, and five from the small Partido de la Auténtica Revolución Mexicana. Although the PRI, with 175 seats, had still an overwhelming majority, the minority voice was actually stepped up artificially. Only two PAN and one PPS members won regular seats. The rest of the opposition entered Congress under the new law of proportional representation which was stretched to include PPS and PARM even though neither party gained the 2.5 per cent of total votes needed by law. This magnanimity shows PRI's shrewdness for it allowed the PAN leader Adolfo Cristlieb and the PPS Vicente Lombardo Toledano to be included in Congress. Their voices can thus be heard from the legitimate rostrum, and extra-Congressional tub-thumping may become superfluous.

Señor Díaz Ordaz clearly, by tacit agreement, supported the last flourishes of reform given to Mexican law by President López Mateos as a send-off to his final year of office. In December 1963 a new minimum wage was fixed which varies in different parts of the country but raises the basic wage by about 20 per cent. Simultaneously the projected reforms were endorsed whereby workers, entitled under the Constitution to share in the profits of industry, are now effectively to receive a fixed proportion of such profits. After reasonable rates of interest and sums for reinvestment (about 30 per cent of gross profits) have been set aside, and after a deduction has been made varying between 10 and 80 per cent according to the proportion of invested capital per employee, each worker will be entitled to his share of the residue. This was itself a compromise agreement with which neither side was overjoyed; and, with self-employed workers such as taxi-drivers immediately pressing for higher tariffs, the atmosphere in the first days of 1964 was disgruntled to say the least. Evidently care will be needed if the theoretically enlightened reforms are not to cause inflation and a recession in the economy just at a time when Mexico is more favorably placed economically than ever before. The next years will be crucial; but the very careful balance of the profits-participation law is in itself a sign that the government intends to pursue what has by now become its traditional middle-of-the-way course.

The question remains though: Will Mexico's progress graphs continue upward, or will they slip back, as has happened too often in other countries of Latin America? Much will depend upon how old principles continue to be interpreted. What can certainly be said is that President López Mateos ended his régime with full popular support and with a series of impressive statistics detailed in his final State-of-the-Nation report in September 1964. For example the total public investments during his term of office were over $5 billion and the gross national product (which had increased by the alarmingly small amount of 3.5 per cent in 1961) had registered a 6.3 per cent rise in 1963 and looks healthy for the future. There had been a time when the President's globetrotting was a stock joke, but by 1964 people were noting how physically worn he was after six years' unsparing labor. His last rendering of accounts was strangely moving, for he was touched by the people's evident affection for him, sincerely mindful of the deficiencies of the régime, but proud of Mexico's self-confidence and place of dignity among nations. It is certainly no sinecure to be president of a country so large, so varied, with so many problems, and which has grown and changed more rapidly in twenty years than most countries do in a century. What is more, these changes are undertaken with the *élan* and originality of youth but with the support of tradition, both ancient and European.

It behooves the United States to encourage and not to stifle Mexico's independence of spirit, but there are signs that some sectors of American opinion do not take this view. At the end of 1963

U.S. Ambassador Thomas C. Mann was recalled to Washington to be appointed Assistant Secretary of State for Latin American Affairs and Special Presidential Assistant at the White House under his old friend President Lyndon Johnson. These appointments show the importance the United States attaches to Mexico as a leader in the turbulent Latin American area, for Mann is a Texan born very close to the border, who has often said he considers Mexico his second home. Whether the appointments are altogether appropriate in the delicate circumstances holding throughout Latin America will have to be proved, however. As we have seen, Mr. Mann began his term as Ambassador in Mexico with the unfortunate statement, deprecated by Mexico's Foreign Minister, that the Monroe Doctrine is identical with Mexico's policy of non-intervention. It is true that later he scored something of a personal triumph in finally negotiating the return to Mexico of the disputed border area of Chamizal; but during his period of office only a temporary solution was found to the other and far more urgent border problem—the salting of water in the Mexicali Valley from tributaries of the Colorado River. The left wing does not forget, either, that during Mann's ambassadorship the novelist Carlos Fuentes, who had been invited to discuss Latin American affairs on the National Broadcasting Company's network, was refused a visa into the United States. Airing of left-wing views, they felt, might have done away with a number of misconceptions.

Rightly or wrongly, then, Latin Americans suspect Thomas Mann of representing conservative opinion in the United States—opinion that is not very favorably disposed toward full sharing of planning and responsibility for the Alliance for Progress among all the American countries.

If Washington makes the mistake in the next decade of trying to swing Mexico strongly over to supporting U.S. policies, the results may be unfortunate. Cuba has to be recognized as a friend of the Communist bloc; the governments of Venezuela, Brazil, Peru, and one or two other countries are continually harried by left-wing agitators. At the other extreme there are still dictatorships in the area suspected of being propped up by U.S. business interests. Mexico stands at the pivot point between these extremes, neither of which can be considered desirable, and both of which could lead to internal revolutions or worse.

An example of Mexico's independent thinking was her refusal to apply sanctions to Cuba or to break relations with Dr. Castro's government even after the O.A.S. vote in the summer of 1964 that such measures should be taken by all member States. Mexico's view was that the vote went beyond the powers of the O.A.S., and that Venezuela's accusation that Cuba had intervened in her internal affairs had not in any case been satisfactorily proven. It was felt to be particularly unfortunate that the vote gave the right to use armed force against Cuba even if a hypothetical Cuban aggression against a member State proved in the event not to be an armed attack. This was a moment when left, right and center in Mexico seemed to agree unanimously, and it was generally felt that the O.A.S. vote was a clumsy forcing of the U.S.A's will on the smaller or more chicken-hearted Latin countries. Mexico felt proud of standing firm; and could see no reason for the fear that the very existence of the O.A.S. was endangered by her refusal to conform to what she regarded as only apparent majority opinion. She expressed herself ready to abide by the decision of the World Court should any member country decide that her refusal to comply needed to be referred there.

Mexico is not an appendage of the United States and should not be forced to become one. When José Vasconcelos designed the emblem for the reconstituted National University, he understood long before the Alliance for Progress the need for a Latin American brotherhood; therefore he placed the Mexican eagle beside the South American condor, and the whole map of South America below a somewhat cramped Mexico. The shield was bounded below by mountains and by the nopal cactus; and circling the map was the motto: "Through my race the spirit shall speak." The university emblem could well stand for the aspirations of Latin America as a whole; but the villains of one nation will too easily infect the unscrupulous elements in all the others unless the ancient philosophies are revived and given a reformulation suited to modern times. There is, after all, nothing dated about the aim of the old Nahua poet to create a

> Man made man:
> a heart firm as stone,
> a wise countenance,
> master of his face,
> and a heart that is able and understanding.

Today the X in Mexico, with its archaic appearance, represents more importantly than ever the re-volution which seems to have taken place at all critical moments in the country's history. Mexicans have tried to assimilate the material benefits of modern industry while re-inquiring into the old beliefs. There are skeptics today who like to suggest that Mexico is advancing and prospering merely because she happens to be next-door neighbor to the United States. This is a great deal less than fair and discounts many qualities of dignity and seriousness from which other countries—not excluding the United States—could profit. Mexico's problems are the problems of a region that has had its ideals and its heroes, but has been frustrated at every turn by selfishness and villainy from certain sections of the community. In a sense they are the problems of a country that has set its sights too high.

The future must depend upon whether the whole Latin American area can devise means to curb its predatory citizens so that the idealists can at last establish the basis for welfare states that take into account the whole man. In this task, Mexico must be among the leaders; for, as Alberto Lleras Camargo, once President of Colombia, says:[1]

> Here is a country which, in contrast to the rest of Latin America, shows no symptoms of exhaustion, paralysis, or regression. The stability of the political régime, strongly supported by complex party machinery, has precluded any faltering in the will to do, to build, and to create. . . . This does not mean that there is no misery, squalor, despair and ignorance as in the rest of Latin America, but these forms of backwardness do not seem to be static, nor do they seem to be increasing and destroying the rest of the Mexican social scene. On the contrary there is an active battle to eliminate them. . . . Mexico—and perhaps this is the difference—knows what it wants, and if it does not get it in one régime it goes on searching in the next with equal enthusiasm . . . Spanish America

[1] *Visión*, June 12, 1964.

is in the throes of a profound spiritual crisis, in which the faith of its peoples—and worse still, that of future generations—has been lost. But . . . Mexico seems to have come through her revolution and to have grown in knowledge from this great experience.

President López Mateos left office confident of the future. His successor, Gustavo Díaz Ordaz, entered with a legacy of stability and high principles that cannot easily be upset. The next step is to close the gap between principles and fact—and this not on a high government or international level but in the day-to-day behavior of small officials in whom the psychology of "each man for himself and the devil take the hindmost" anachronistically lingers. The historical process of establishing a climate of responsibility continues. Mexico's friends—and she has earned many—have faith that she will solve her problems and overcome her difficulties in her own sometimes unorthodox, often paradoxical, always individual way.

APPENDIX I

Politico-Administrative Divisions of Mexico

Division	*Capital*	*Area (Sq. miles)*	*Population (1960 census)*
Federal District	Mexico City	600	4,870,876
States			
Aguascalientes	Aguascalientes	2,500	243,363
Baja California (Norte)	Ensenada	27,800	520,165
Campeche	Campeche	19,700	168,219
Chiapas	Tuxtla Gutiérrez	28,700	1,210,870
Chihuahua	Chihuahua	94,800	1,226,793
Coahuila	Saltillo	58,100	907,734
Colima	Colima	2,000	164,450
Durango	Durango	47,000	760,836
Guanajuato	Guanajuato	11,800	1,735,490
Guerrero	Chilpancingo	24,900	1,186,716
Hidalgo	Pachuca	8,100	994,598
Jalisco	Guadalajara	31,100	2,443,261
México	Toluca	8,300	1,897,851
Michoacán	Morelia	23,200	1,851,876
Morelos	Cuernavaca	1,900	386,264
Nayarit	Tepic	10,400	389,929
Nuevo León	Monterrey	25,100	1,078,848
Oaxaca	Oaxaca	36,400	1,727,266
Puebla	Puebla	13,100	1,973,837
Querétaro	Querétaro	4,400	355,045
San Luís Potosí	San Luís Potosí	24,400	1,048,297
Sinaloa	Culiacán	22,600	838,404
Sonora	Hermosillo	70,500	783,378
Tabasco	Villahermosa	9,800	496,340
Tamaulipas	Ciudad Victoria	30,700	1,024,182
Tlaxcala	Tlaxcala	1,600	346,699
Veracruz	Xalapa	27,700	2,727,899
Yucatán	Mérida	14,900	614,049
Zacatecas	Zacatecas	28,100	817,813
Territories			
Baja California (Sur)	La Paz	27,800	81,594
Quintana Roo	Chetumal	19,400	50,169

APPENDIX II

Rulers of Mexico

Pre-conquest	
Tenoch	?
Queen Ilancueitl alone	1349–1375
Acamapichtli jointly with his Queen, Ilancueitl	1375–1383
Acamapichtli alone	1383–1395
Huitzilihuitl	1395–1414
Chimalpopoca	1414–1428
Itzcóatl	1428–1440
Moctezuma Ilhuicamina	1440–1469
Axayácatl	1469–1481
Tizoc	1481–1486
Ahuitzotl	1486–1503
Moctezuma Xocoyotzin	1503 to June 1520
Cuitláhuac	June to October 1520
Cuauhtémoc	October 1520 to August 1521
Immediate post-conquest	
Hernán Cortés	1521–1524
Oficiales Reales	1524–1526
Jueces de Residencia	1526–1528
First *Audiencia*	1528–1531
Second *Audiencia*	1531–1535
Viceroys	
Antonio de Mendoza	1535–1550
Luís de Velasco (father)	1550–1564
Gastón de Peralta	1566–1568
Martín Enríquez de Almanza	1568–1580
Lorenzo Suárez de Mendoza	1580–1583
Pedro Moya y Contreras	1584–1585
Alvaro Manrique de Zúñiga	1585–1590
Luís de Velasco (son)	1590–1595
Gaspar de Zúñiga y Acevedo	1595–1603
Juan de Mendoza y Luna	1603–1607
Luís de Velasco (son)	1607–1611
Fray García Guerra	1611–1612
Diego Fernández de Córdoba	1612–1621
Diego Carrillo de Mendoza y Pimentel	1621–1624

Rodrigo Pacheco y Osorio	1624–1635
Lope Díaz de Armendáriz	1635–1640
Diego López Pacheco Cabrera y Bobadilla	1640–1642
Juan Palafox y Mendoza	1642–1648
Marcos de Torres y Rueda	1648–1649
Luís Enríquez de Guzmán	1650–1653
Francisco Fernández de la Cueva	1653–1660
Juan de Leyva y de la Cerda	1660–1664
Diego Osorio de Escobar y Llamas	1664
Antonio Sebastián de Toledo	1664–1673
Pedro Nuño Colón de Portugal	1673
Fray Payo Enríquez de Rivera	1673–1680
Tomás Antonio de la Cerda y Aragón	1680–1686
Melchor Portocarrero Lasso de la Vega	1686–1688
Gaspar de Sandoval Silva y Mendoza	1688–1696
Juan de Ortega y Montañez	1696
José Sarmiento Valladares	1696–1701
Juan de Ortega y Montañez	1701
Francisco Fernández de la Cueva Enríquez	1701–1711
Fernando de Alencastre Noroña y Silva	1711–1716
Baltasar de Zúñiga y Guzmán	1716–1722
Juan de Acuña	1722–1734
Juan Antonio Vizarrón y Aguiarreta	1734–1740
Pedro de Castro y Figueroa	1740–1741
Pedro Cebrián y Augstín	1742–1746
Francisco de Güemes y Horcasitas (later first Count Revillagigedo)	1746–1755
Agustín Ahumada y Villalón	1755–1760
Francisco Cagigal de la Vega	1760
Joaquín de Monserrat	1760–1766
Carlos Francisco de Croix	1766–1771
Antonio María de Bucareli	1771–1779
Martín de Mayorga	1779–1783
Matías de Gálvez	1783–1784
Bernardo de Gálvez	1785–1786
Alonso Núñez de Haro y Peralta	1787
Manuel Antonio Flores	1787–1789
Juan Vicente de Güemes Pacheco y Padilla (second Count Revillagigedo)	1789–1794
Miguel de la Grúa Talamanca y Branciforte	1794–1798
Miguel José de Azanza	1798–1800
Félix Berenguer de Marquina	1800–1803
José de Iturrigaray	1803–1808
Pedro Garibay	1808–1809
Francisco Javier de Lizana y Beaumont	1809–1810
Francisco Javier Venegas	1810–1813
Félix María Calleja del Rey	1813–1816
Juan Ruíz de Apodaca	1816–1821
Francisco Novella	1821
Juan O'Donojú	(Appointed but did not take office)

Independence

Guadalupe Victoria	1824–1829
Vicente Guerrero	1829
José María Bocanegra (interim)	1829
Vélez-Alamán-Quintana triumverate	1829
Anastasio Bustamante	1830–32, 1837–39, and 1842
Melchor Múzquiz (interim)	1832
Manuel Gómez Pedraza	1833
Valentín Gómez Farías	1833, 1834, and 1847
Antonio López de Santa Ana	on and off from 1833 to 1855
Miguel Barragán	1835–1836
José Justo Corro	1836–1837
Nicolás Bravo	variously from 1839 to 1846
Javier Echeverría (interim)	1841
Valentín Canalizo	1844
José Joaquín Herrera (interim)	1844, 1845, and from 1848–1851
Mariano Paredes Arrillaga	1846
Mariano Salas	1846
Pedro María Anaya (interim)	1847 and 1848
Manuel de la Peña y Peña (interim)	1847 and 1848
Mariano Arista	1851–1853
Juan Bautista Ceballos (interim)	1853
Manuel María Lombardini	1853
Martín Carrera (interim)	1855
Rómulo Díaz de la Vega	1855
Juan Alvarez	1855
Ignacio Comonfort	1855–1858

Liberal government

Benito Juárez	1858–1872

Conservative government

Félix Zuloaga	1858 and 1859
Manuel Robles Pezuela	1858
Miguel Miramón	1859 and 1860
Ignacio Pavón	1860
Conservative *Junta*	1860–1864
Emperor Maximilian	1864–1867

Post-reform

Sebastián Lerdo de Tejada	1872–1876
Porfirio Díaz	on and off from 1876 to 1911
Juan N. Méndez	1876
Manuel González	1880
Francisco León de la Barra	1911
Francisco I. Madero	1911–1913
Pedro Lascurain (interim)	1913 (in office for 55 minutes)
Victoriano Huerta (interim)	1913–1914
Francisco S. Carvajal (interim)	1914
Venustiano Carranza	1914 and 1915–1920
Eulalio Gutiérrez (interim)	1914

Roque González Garza	1914
Francisco Lagos Cházaro	1915
Adolfo de la Huerta	1920
Alvaro Obregón	1920–1924
Plutarco Elías Calles	1924–1928
Emilio Portes Gil (interim)	1928–1930
Pascual Ortiz Rubio	1930–1932
Abelardo L. Rodríguez (interim)	1932–1934
Lázaro Cárdenas	1934–1940
Manuel Avila Camacho	1940–1946
Miguel Alemán Valdés	1946–1952
Adolfo Ruíz Cortines	1952–1958
Adolfo López Mateos	1958–1964
Gustavo Díaz Ordaz	1964–

Select Bibliography

A complete bibliography of works on Mexico would be unwieldy and unhelpful. The following list includes works in English only, and has been compiled so that the general reader can follow up subjects of particular interest.

GENERAL

COVARRUBIAS, MIGUEL *Mexico South,* Cassell, London, 1947.

FERGUSSON, ERNA *Mexican Cookbook,* Dolphin Books, New York, 1961.

HUTTON, GRAHAM *Mexican Images,* Faber and Faber, London, 1963.

MONTES, DE OCA, RAFAEL *Humming Birds and Orchids of Mexico,* drawings by the author done in the nineteenth century, with descriptive texts revised by Rafael Martín del Campo and Norman Pelham Wright. Edited by Carolina de Fournier, Mexico City, 1963.

O'GORMAN, HELEN *Mexican Flowering Trees and Plants,* Ammex Asociados, Mexico City, 1961.

PARKES, H. B. *A History of Mexico,* Eyre and Spottiswoode, London, 1960.

ROMERO, PEPE *My Mexico City and Yours.* Dolphin Books, New York, 1962.

SIMON, KATE *Mexico: Places and Pleasures.* Dolphin Books, New York, 1962.

SIMPSON, LESLEY BYRD *Many Mexicos,* University of California Press, 1959.

Terry's Guide to Mexico, Doubleday, New York, 1963.

Travel Guide–Mexico, Nagel Publishers, Geneva, Paris, London, and New York, 1961.

WILHELM, JOHN *Guide to Mexico City,* Ediciones Tolteca, Mexico City, 1964.

WOODCOCK, GEORGE *To the City of the Dead: An Account of Travels in Mexico,* Faber and Faber, London, 1957.

WRIGHT, NORMAN PELHAM *Mexican Kaleidoscope,* Heinemann, London, 1947.
Mexican Medley for the Curious, Ediciones Tolteca, Mexico City, 1961.

PREHISPANIC CULTURES

BERNAL, IGNACIO *Mexico Before Cortez: Art, History and Legend,* Dolphin Books, New York, 1963.

BURLAND, COTTIE *Magic Books of Mexico,* Penguin Books, London, 1953.
The Aztecs (Young Historians Series), Weidenfeld and Nicolson, London, 1961.

COE, MICHAEL D. *Mexico,* Thames and Hudson, London, 1962.

COLLIS, MAURICE *Cortés and Montezuma,* Faber and Faber, London, 1954.

GILMOUR, FRANCES *Flute of the Smoking Mirror (a portrait of Nezahualcóyotl),* University of New Mexico Press, 1949.

KINGSBOROUGH, LORD *Antiquities of Mexico*, London, 1831–48 (privately printed).

MORLEY, SYLVANUS G. *The Ancient Maya*, Stanford University Press, 1946.

NICHOLSON, IRENE *Firefly in the Night, a Study of Ancient Mexican Poetry and Symbolism*, Faber and Faber, London, 1959.

PETERSON, F. *Ancient Mexico*, Putnam, London, 1959.

Popol Vuh, The Sacred Book of the Ancient Quiché Maya, University of Oklahoma Press, 1950.

PRESCOTT, W. H. *History of the Conquest of Mexico*, George Allen and Unwin, London, 1957.

RIVET, PAUL *Maya Cities*, Elek Books, London, 1957.

SÉJOURNÉ, LAURETTE *Burning Water: Thought and Religion in Ancient Mexico*, Thames and Hudson, London, 1957.

SOUSTELLE, J. *Daily Life of the Aztecs*, Weidenfeld and Nicolson, London, 1961.

THOMPSON, J. ERIC S. *The Rise and Fall of Maya Civilization*, University of Oklahoma Press, 1954.

VAILLANT, G. C. *Aztecs of Mexico*, Penguin Books, London, 1950.

THE CONQUEST AND THE COLONIAL PERIOD

CALDERÓN DE LA BARCA, FRANCES INGLIS *Life in Mexico*, J. and M. Dent, London, 1954.

CORTÉS, HERNÁN *Five Letters, 1519–26*, Norton, New York, 1962.

DÍAZ DEL CASTILLO, BERNAL *The Discovery and Conquest of Mexico*, Grove Press, New York, 1956.

MAYER, WILLIAM *Early Travellers in Mexico (1534 to 1816)*, Mexico City, 1961, published privately.

STEPHENS, J. L. *Incidents of Travel in Central America, Chiapas, and Yucatán*, Rutgers University Press, 1949.

MODERN TIMES

BENHAM, F., and HOLLEY, H. A. *A Short Introduction to the Economy of Latin America*, Oxford University Press, London, 1960.

BERMÚDEZ, ANTONIO J. *The Mexican National Petroleum Industry: a Case Study in Nationalization*, Stanford University Press, 1963.

BRENNER, ANITA *The Wind that Swept Mexico: the History of the Mexican Revolution, 1910–42*, Harper, New York, 1943.

CLINE, HOWARD F. *The United States and Mexico*, Harvard University Press, 1961.

Mexico: Revolution to Evolution, 1940–1960, Oxford University Press, London, New York, and Toronto, 1962.

LEWIS, OSCAR *Five Families: Mexican Studies in the Culture of Poverty*, Basic Books, New York, 1959.

The Children of Sánchez: Autobiography of a Mexican Family, Random House, New York, 1961.

Tepoztlán: Village in Mexico, Holt, Rinehart and Winston, New York, 1962.

Pedro Martínez, Secker and Warburg, London, 1964.

MADARIAGA, SALVADOR DE *Latin America between the Eagle and the Bear*, Hollis and Carter, London, 1962.

Mexico. Yearly publication of the Mexican National Foreign Trade Bank, Mexico City.

OLIZAR, MARYNKA *A Guide to Mexican Markets*, privately published year by year in Mexico City.

QUEZADA, ABEL *The Best of Impossible Worlds*, Prentice-Hall, New Jersey, 1963.

ROEDER, RALPH *Juárez and His Mexico*, Viking Press, New York, 1947.

SCHMITT, KARL M. *Communism in Mexico*, University of Texas Press, 1965.

SCOTT, R. E. *Mexican Government in Transition*, University of Illinois Press, 1959.

TANNENBAUM, FRANK *The Mexican Agrarian Revolution*, Macmillan, New York, 1929.

Mexico: The Struggle for Peace and Bread, Knopf, New York, 1950.

TOYNBEE, ARNOLD *The Economy of the Western Hemisphere*, Oxford University Press, London, 1962.

TUCKER, WILLIAM P. *The Mexican Government Today*, University of Minnesota Press, 1957.

URQUIDI, VICTOR *Free Trade and Economic Integration in Latin America: Toward a Common Market*, University of California Press, Berkeley and Los Angeles, 1962.

VERNON, R. *The Dilemma of Mexico's Development*, Harvard University Press, 1963.

Public Policy and Private Enterprise in Mexico (ed. Vernon), Harvard University Press, 1964.

YATES, PAUL LAMARTINE *The Regional Development of Mexico*, Bank of Mexico Industrial Investigation Department, Mexico City, 1961.

LITERATURE

(*Mexican literature in English translation, and foreign literature dealing with Mexico.*)

AZUELA, MARIANO *The Bosses* and *The Flies*, published in one volume by the University of California Press, 1956.

The Trials of a Respectable Family and *The Underdogs*, published in one volume by Principia Press, Trinity University, San Antonio, Texas, 1963.

BECKETT, SAMUEL *Anthology of Mexican Poetry*, Thames and Hudson, London, 1958.

CASTELLANOS, ROSARIO *The Nine Guardians*, Faber and Faber, London, 1959.

FUENTES, CARLOS *Where the Air is Clear*, Ivan Obolensky, New York, 1960.

The Death of Artemio Cruz, Farrar Strauss, New York, 1964.

GREENE, GRAHAM *The Power and the Glory*, Heinemann, London, 1940.

GUZMÁN, MARTÍN LUÍS *The Eagle and the Serpent*, trans. Harriet de Onis, Dolphin Books, New York, 1965.

Memoirs of Pancho Villa, trans. Virginia H. Taylor, University of Texas Press, 1965.

HUXLEY, ALDOUS *Beyond the Mexique Bay*, Penguin Books, London, 1955.

LAWRENCE, D. H. *Mornings in Mexico*, Penguin Books, London, 1956.

The Plumed Serpent, Penguin Books, London, 1955.

LOWRY, MALCOLM *Under the Volcano,* Penguin Books, London, 1962.
PAZ, OCTAVIO *The Labyrinth of Solitude: Life and Thought in Mexico,* Grove Press, New York and Evergreen Books, London, 1961.
RAMOS, SAMUEL *Profile of Man and Culture in Mexico,* University of Texas Press, 1962.
RULFO, JUAN *Pedro Páramo,* Evergreen Books, New York, 1959.
TRAVEN, B. *The Treasure of the Sierra Madre,* Knopf, New York, 1935.
YAÑEZ, A. *The Edge of the Storm,* Texas University Press, 1963.

ART AND ARCHITECTURE

BAIRD, JOSEPH ARMSTRONG, JR. *The Churches of Mexico, 1530–1810,* University of California Press, 1962.
CHARLOT, JEAN *Mexican Art and the Academy of San Carlos,* University of California Press, 1962.
The Mexican Mural Renaissance, 1920–25, Yale University Press, 1963.
FABER, COLIN *Candela: The Shell Builder,* Reinhold, New York, and Architectural Press, London, 1963.
GROTH-KIMBALL, I. *Mayan Terracottas,* Zwemmer, London, 1960.
and FEUCHTWANGER, F. *The Art of Ancient Mexico,* Thames and Hudson, London, 1954.
JOYCE, T. A. *Maya and Mexican Art,* The Studio, London, 1926.
KUBLER, GEORGE *The Art and Architecture of Ancient America,* Penguin Books, London, 1962.
OROZCO, JOSÉ CLEMENTE *Autobiography,* University of Texas Press, 1962.
PLENN, VIRGINIA and JAIME *A Guide to Modern Mexican Murals,* Ediciones Tolteca, Mexico City, 1963.
SANFORD, TRENT, E. *The Story of Architecture in Mexico,* Norton, New York, 1947.
SHIPWAY, VERA COOK, and SHIPWAY, WARREN *Mexican Interiors,* Architectural Book Publishing Co., New York, 1962.
WESTHEIM, PAUL *The Sculpture of Ancient Mexico,* Doubleday, New York, 1963.
The Art of Ancient Mexico, Doubleday, New York, 1965.

Index